Character and Satire in Postwar Fiction

CONTINUUM LITERARY STUDIES SERIES

Forthcoming titles:
Beckett's Books by Matthew Feldman
English Fiction in the 1930s by Chris Hopkins
Fictions of Globalization by James Annesley
Joyce and Company by David Pierce
Masculinity in Fiction and Film by Brian Baker
Novels of the Contemporary Extreme edited by Alain-Phillipe Durand and Naomi Mandel
Re-writing London by Lawrence Phillips
Women's Fiction 1945–2000 by Deborah Philips

Character and Satire in Postwar Fiction

IAN GREGSON

Continuum
The Tower Building
11 York Road
London SE1 7NX

15 East 26th Street
New York
NY 10010

www.continuumbooks.com

British Library Cataloguing-in-Publication Data
A catalogue record for this book is available from the British Library.

ISBN: HB: 0-8264-8747-5
ISBN: 978-1-8470-6265-9

Library of Congress Cataloging-in-Publication Data
A catalog record for this book is available from the Library of Congress.

Typeset by RefineCatch Limited, Bungay, Suffolk
Printed by Lightning Source

Contents

For Dave Faggiani and Steve Ormrod

Acknowledgements

I'm especially grateful to my colleague Tom Corns who made important suggestions about this book, especially about the ordering of chapters. I'm grateful as well to Stephen Wall who did painstaking (and subsequently influential) work on the prose style of the Muriel Spark chapter, which first appeared in *Essays in Criticism* (where he is the editor).

Thanks as well to Linda Jones who did invaluable work on the manuscript.

Introduction

It has been poststructuralism which has most influenced recent theorizing about characterization. J. Hillis Miller, for example, argues that the realist novel has two, apparently contradictory, functions. On one hand, it promotes social cohesiveness because it reassures its readers about the existence of the unitary self. The examples of that self which it provides are so vivid that life imitates art and reproduces them so that 'England after 1836 begins to be filled with Dickensian characters'.[1] On the other, however, it interrogates the concept of character, calls it radically into question, through a process of 'autodeconstruction'. It does this in order to respond to the very doubts about the unitary self which its first function appears to dismiss. By allowing these doubts to be expressed aesthetically, and therefore in an arena which does not pose a social threat, it paradoxically reinforces the reassurance offered by its first function. In order to display this autodeconstruction in action, Hillis Miller argues that the realist novel is much less realist than it appears; he cites examples from George Eliot's novels to show how they interrogate realist assumptions about the self. He summarizes his argument by declaring that the novel is a

> perpetual tying and untying of the knot of selfhood for the purpose, in the psychic economy of the individual and of the community, of affirming the fiction of character by putting it fictionally in question and so short-circuiting a doubt which, left free to act in the real social world, might destroy both self and community. (98)

Leo Bersani and Thomas Docherty use poststructuralist methods to analyse subjectivity in novels. For Bersani it is desire which most threatens that unitary self which Hillis Miller sees as being protected by realism. Bersani is ambivalent about Freudian theory, but he draws upon psychoanalytic thought in order to explore the ways that desire subverts psychic coherence; he traces a literary development from Racine, through Flaubert, Stendhal, Henry James and D. H. Lawrence, and into avant-garde theatre of the 1970s in order to follow 'stages in the *deconstruction of the self* in modern literature'.[2] He is preoccupied with the impact of repression and sublimation – how they ensure the psychic continuities which constitute personality, but at the cost of 'a serious crippling of desire' (6). His politics are close to those of Gilles Deleuze and Felix Guattari, so much so that his arguments about psychoanalysis amount to a refinement of the thesis of their *Anti-Oedipus* and its 'militant intellectual campaign against the sublimating processes' (7). He finds their politics, and those of other 'anti-psychiatry' theorists such as Norman O. Brown, Herbert Marcuse and R. D. Laing, to be simplistic. Nevertheless he is in evident sympathy with their liberationist tendencies, and is as fascinated as they are by the ontological deconstructiveness of desire:

> a new emphasis on the *peripheries* of our desiring attention would not only diversify desire but would also keep it mobile. Peripheral seductions would no longer be discarded because they can't be related to a dominant interest – our 'centers' of desire – would have merely a provisional, peripheral appeal. *The* desiring self might even disappear as we learn to multiply our discontinuous and partial desiring selves. (7)

Thomas Docherty, in his *Reading (Absent) Character*,[3] has a less political agenda but is also preoccupied with the discontinuous self. He draws upon a reader reception model in order to evoke characterization as a process in which both author and reader are involved in the creation of character, and the meaning of character. Like Hillis Miller, Docherty deconstructs realism. He dislikes the realist emphasis on mimesis and prefers the experimental writing of the *nouveau roman*; his concluding chapter prescribes a turn away from the Protestant, Individualist and Cartesian models of realism towards a Catholic and communal model which he hopes will characterize postmodern writing, and he declares that 'the conceptual notion of Character is replaced in post-Modern fiction by the process of Characterization, the continual re-creation or re-positioning of character as a "becoming" rather than as an "essence" ' (268).

The unexamined assumption of Docherty's and, to a lesser extent, Bersani's model of characterization is that the focus should be upon the depiction of subjectivity. Reader reception theory is helpful to Docherty because it emphasizes reading as a process, so that the reader's activity rhymes with poststructuralist conceptions of the subject as fluid and performative, and in constant interaction with other subjects. The open-ended interactions between author, character and reader in this way become analogues for how meaning is produced unstably, provisionally and intersubjectively. Docherty extends this into a generalized reading of postmodern fiction, where 'characterization, on the theory of reading which is offered here, grants the reader the possibility of escape from a fixed selfhood into an existence as a series of subjectivities, always in first-personal (and hence direct) experience of the environment' (xvi).

However, this ignores the important postmodern writers who I discuss in this book, who repeatedly call subjectivity into question and often ignore or even satirically erase it. Leo Bersani seems to be referring to this when he expresses surprise at 'an extraordinary *indifference* to character' in certain eighteenth-century writers, but finds less surprising 'indifference or hostility to character in our own wilfully antipsychological literature' (59). The depths of subjectivity which preoccupy modernist fiction, and which are most conspicuously represented by stream of consciousness, are often replaced by mere surfaces in contexts related to postmodernist irony and parody. Fredric Jameson refers to these as 'pastiche', and relates them to what he calls a 'new depthlessness'; in particular he names four depth models which have been repudiated:

> (1) the dialectical one of essence and appearance (along with a whole range of concepts of ideology or false consciousness which tend to accompany it); (2) the Freudian model of latent and manifest, or of repression . . . (3) the existential model of authenticity and inauthenticity whose heroic or tragic thematics are closely related to that other great opposition between alienation and disalienation, itself equally a casualty of the poststructural or postmodern period; and (4) most recently, the great semiotic opposition between signifier and signified, which was itself rapidly unravelled and deconstructed during its brief heyday in the 1960's and 1970's. What replaces these various depth models is for the most part a conception of practices, discourses, and textual play . . . here too depth is replaced by surface, or by multiple surfaces.[4]

This depthlessness is connected to other losses: the withering away of Nature, the decline of a historical consciousness and the 'waning of affect' (10). Jameson's emphasis on multiple surfaces can be compared to Jean Baudrillard's emphasis on the postmodern dominance of simulation, on a culture so influenced by the technological media that any sense of the real is lost and replaced by the multiplying of signs and representations. I would argue that its impact on novelistic characterization has been to draw attention away from the subjective interior, and to flatten characters in a process of ontological reduction in which they are rendered static and mechanical.

Caricature has played a key part in this process. Much of what has been labelled as 'postmodernist' in postwar fiction can be more specifically defined by reference to this much older tradition which includes Hogarth and Gillray in the visual arts, and Dryden, Pope, Swift and Dickens in literature. Its dominant images depict the human as reduced to the status of an object, an animal or a machine, or the human body as dismembered to represent the fragmentation of the human spirit.

I am not denying the relevance of postmodernism as a cultural and historical context for postwar writers: what I want to do is to explore the significance of caricatural effects in fiction that express postmodern conceptions of the self. The most important overlap between postmodernism and caricature is in shared anti-humanist assumptions which lead to a subverting of realism and its assumptions. This partly accounts for why postmodernist authors have drawn upon caricature to mock realist conventions – 'fully rounded' characters, linear plotting – with confrontational comedy. For this also crucially involves questioning the humanist assumptions behind realism – how 'fully roundedness' takes for granted that human personality is complex, coherent, substantial and capable of endless development.

This overlap is relevant to how some 'magic realist' characterization is caricatural in its deliberate confusing of the human with animals and things and its deliberate refusal to bestow vividly 'human' uniqueness on its characters (so, for example, Garcia Marquez's *One Hundred Years of Solitude* contains seventeen characters dismissively called Aureliano). It is for this reason that Charles Dickens, one of the key authors in the caricatural tradition, could be described as magic realist *avant la lettre*. It is for this reason, too, that caricatural effects and surreal ones are sometimes indistinguishable from each other.

Fiction writers, then, in the process of evoking the sense of ontological diminishment and fracturing which characterize the postwar period, have drawn upon resources which predate that period but which form an historically sanctioned part of the range of representations of the self which fiction-writing makes available. My main point is that caricature is one of these resources but also an especially significant one because its widespread use is symptomatic of a satirical attitude to the self which is tellingly characteristic of contemporary culture.

It is broadly that satirical attitude to the self which is shared by all the authors in this book. The contexts out of which that attitude arises, however, differ markedly and I have focused upon defining those contexts in each of their cases in order to indicate why caricatural imagery has different meanings for different authors. All of the texts under discussion are orientated politically: all of them are preoccupied with relationships in which power is a dominant issue. This is why the puppet, the dummy and the doll are so significantly recurrent: all of the writers discussed here are drawn to thinking of the relationship between characters, and also, self-reflexively, between characters and author in terms of the attempt of one person or group to colonize other persons and groups and to make them speak their language. However, the identity of the puppets and the puppet masters is different for each author, and each chapter is dedicated to exploring that identity.

The multiplicity of these authorial contexts itself provides a clue to why caricature has been so important in the period. One of the most important features of the postmodern has been its deconstruction of the traditional monolith of Western and masculine cultural values, and its replacement by a cultural polyphony in which self-consciously gendered and racial perspectives have claimed their right to assert themselves. That polyphony has markedly increased awareness of how one cultural group can stamp a reductiveness on others which it perceives as beyond its own aggressively imposed pale.

Caricature can express that awareness because its resources define above all the dehumanizing of the demonized or reified other.

Caricatural imagery has therefore been significantly deployed by writers with racial and gender preoccupations. The novels of Ralph Ellison and Toni Morrison are preoccupied with the deconstruction of racial stereotypes; the caricatural elements in their work arise from the link between how slavery literally and horrifyingly treated its human materials, and how caricature metaphorically treats them. That is to say: caricature satirically shows human beings being transformed into objects, machines and animals, but slavery *actually* treated its victims in this way. The later work of Joyce Carol Oates has been similarly focused upon the reification of women, especially evident in her recent novel *Blonde*, where Marilyn Monroe is repeatedly referred to as a terribly vulnerable sex doll.

Oates's career is instructive because she started out with spiritual preoccupations and has increasingly turned to political ones. This means that some of her anger arises from a post-Christian disillusionment about the secular human condition, and in this it resembles the desperate aggression which has characterized the brilliant recent writing of Philip Roth, whose questioning of 'character' is connected to a central preoccupation in the caricatural tradition with whether or not human beings are fundamentally just glorified machines. So his occasional references in *Sabbath's Theatre* to stream of consciousness – 'the way J. Joyce pretended people thought' – are largely used to demonstrate that 'The mind is the perpetual motion machine. You're not ever free of anything.'[5]

In Oates's case, disillusionment has led to a movement from an emphasis on love to an emphasis on aggression and anger. This trajectory is symptomatic of the growth of the caricatural culture upon which this book is focused. The emphasis on love is a powerful component of the idiom of classic realism and its ideology of liberal humanism which were dominant in nineteenth-century fiction and produced so many of the great canonical works of that period. The waning of that idiom is itself a sign of the sense of ontological diminishment which leads to caricatural flatness. Where classic realism is premised upon sympathetic identification on the part of both author and reader towards a synecdochically diverse range of characters, caricature is driven by suspicion, rebellious anger and satirical contempt.

All of the authors discussed in this book question the liberal humanist emphasis on the individual; they focus instead upon institutions. They share a concern with the ontological impact of capitalism and deploy caricature to indict the commodifying and mechanizing of human beings. This is most explicit in the work of Joseph Heller, who obsessively depicts his characters as turned into things or broken into pieces. In *Catch-22* the characters of soldiers and prostitutes are linked by being compared to slaves: both are disposable commodities. Heller's deconstruction of 'character' works by dwelling not on presence and fullness of being, but on a felt absence, the sense of characteristics crucially lacking.

It is for similar reasons that Angela Carter and Salman Rushdie both self-reflexively present their characters as authorial puppets in order to reinforce the point that no one is an autonomous individual, that everyone is at the mercy of systemic forces. Because political context looms so large in magic-realist fiction, its characterization is coloured with preoccupations and images which are shared with political cartoonists. The heroine of Carter's 'The Tiger's Bride' reflects on her own commodification: because her father used her as a bargaining chip in a game of cards and so lost her to 'The Beast' – because, therefore, she has been 'bought and sold, passed from hand to hand'[6] – she has been reduced to a similar mechanical state as the Beast's maid who is not human but a 'marvellous machine' (60).

These caricatural methods put authorial anger fully on display and their effectiveness arises from confrontational crudity. The fairy tale element, as a form of *faux naiveté*, disrupts realism. A key impact of caricature, similarly, arises from the contrast between its often crude material and how it is mastered by a mature technique. So the metafictional voice of magic realism sardonically deploys childishly crude images, and this is highly appropriate because it repeatedly satirizes the oppression of innocent victims by tyrannical figures who are meretricious and cynical.

Systemic forces ensure that character is kept restricted in its scope, that it cannot acquire the nuanced ramifications and the powers of development which classic realism bestows on it. Such caricatural restrictedness marks the characters of Martin Amis who thereby become what John Updike has called posthuman automata. Amis's assumptions arise out of a Romantic humanism to which Charles Dickens also felt a continuing allegiance: both writers use caricature in order to satirize the thorough trashing that Romantic humanism has received at the hands of loveless capitalism. The flatness of Amis's characters evokes absence and loss – this makes that flatness all the starker, and it makes his comedy resonate because its origins in desperation are so apparent.

Amis has learned many of these techniques from Muriel Spark, whose caricatural vision, nonetheless, has very different origins, in a Catholic anti-humanism which leads her to satirize conventional ideas about human 'personality'. Her satire is directed not so much at specific targets but at human beings as a species, so where the traditional novel strives for dialogic and adulterated capaciousness, Spark's fictions strive for a deathly and poetic purity. Her novels are paradoxically orientated away from what is most meaningful and towards a spiritually perverse focus on the ultimately meaningless. From her Catholic perspective the merely human and worldly is inevitably flat and two-dimensional because the richest and most complex meanings lie elsewhere.

Spark is an unusual writer in the postmodern period in being driven by a theological perspective. However, that perspective makes an explicit entrance into her work only occasionally, and mostly obliquely. This means that the impact of her satirizing of the self is in the end surprisingly similar to that of her secular contemporaries, because their shared anti-humanism leads to the depicting of human beings who are starkly and laughably limited. No one could be a less-Christian writer than Will Self, but his novel *How the Dead Live* shares its premise with Spark's much earlier *The Hothouse by the East River*: in both the characters are dead and are living a severely attenuated and surreal existence in a metropolitan after-life.

Like her Catholic predecessor Graham Greene, Muriel Spark shows her characters trapped in structures of meaning which are entirely not of their own making. Their resultant transformation into puppets works both self-reflexively and ontologically. It also links Spark's work to that of her post-modernist contemporaries with whom she shares a caricatural sensibility because, like them, she is profoundly opposed to liberal humanist assumptions about the autonomous subject.

1 *Subverting Racist Caricature: Ralph Ellison and Toni Morrison*

In both Ralph Ellison's *Invisible Man*[1] (1952) and Toni Morrison's *Beloved*[2] (1988) there are references to a kind of 'piggy bank' which takes the form – not of a pig – but, as Ellison puts it, of 'a very black, red-lipped and wide-mouthed Negro' (319). In Ellison's version this piggy bank has a hand in which money can be placed and then posted through its mouth; in Morrison's the coins are placed directly in its mouth which is 'wide as a cup' (*Beloved*, 255). For both writers the link between this artefact and slavery is obvious, and in *Beloved* it has a pedestal inscribed with the words 'At Yo Service'.

The fascination with this grotesque caricature, which is shared by Ellison and Morrison, arises from their shared preoccupation with the contemporary African American burden of the memory of slavery, and therefore the reduction of their humanity to the status of a commodity. This is why, during the riot, the Invisible Man finds himself carrying a slave legacy – Tarp's leg chain (557) – as well as a briefcase that contains both the piggy bank and Tod Clifton's 'Sambo' doll (539–40): this is the 'baggage' of slavery made literal, the psychological weight of all the oppressed history of his race.

The caricatural elements in Ellison and Morrison all originate in their deconstruction of racist stereotypes, but I will be concerned, in particular, with the connection between how slavery literally and horrifyingly treated its human materials, and how caricature metaphorically treats them. That is to say: caricature satirically depicts human beings transformed into objects, machines and animals, but slavery *actually* treated its victims in this way. In *Beloved*, Sethe finds herself to be the subject of a classroom exercise (193) in which the white pupils have been instructed by Schoolteacher to divide her into her human and her animal characteristics (this shows how slavery could be justified by an official ideology which was a crude distortion of Darwinism). And Paul D finds himself turned into a 'rag doll' (126): here Morrison is indicating that male slaves, alongside their other oppressions, faced being feminized and so subjected to the same reifications that patriarchy imposes on women.

In Ellison's case the caricatural references are linked to an explicit aesthetic and philosophical outlook present in the comic image which, as John

S. Wright has noted, Ellison found in 'Henri Bergson's *Laughter* of human behaviour become mechanized, rigid, life-denying, robotic, and hence comically maladjusted'.[3] The key point for Ellison is that things are not inevitably like this: his work is political and satirical precisely because it contains the assumption that they could be totally different. In principle, he supported the official ideology of his country, he believed in individualism and liberal humanism; what he satirizes is how much the political reality falls short of the political ideal. The Invisible Man reflects, after one of his speeches, on how he has surprised himself by talking about becoming 'more human' and is reminded of his literature classes in college. His teacher, Mr. Woodridge, had declared – alluding to James Joyce – that

> The conscience of a race is the gift of its individuals who see, evaluate, record . . . We create the race by creating ourselves and then to our great astonishment we will have created something far more important: We will have created a culture. Why waste time creating a conscience for something that doesn't exist? For, you see, blood and skin do not think! (354)

Ellison would not question in general the assumptions about the self which underlie this passage. In this he differs from Toni Morrison who, in *Beloved*, and especially in *Jazz*[4] (1992), deconstructs notions of ontological wholeness and stability in identifiably postmodernist ways. Ellison's point is that the plenitude of self promoted by liberal humanism is monstrously unavailable to African Americans. It is not individuals of that race who are maladjusted in not attaining such plenitude, but American society in boasting its provision of it to all its citizens – while ensuring, in practice, its stark unattainability for vast numbers of them. Mr. Woodridge is complicit with this oppressive ideology because he insists that it is possible for individuals to create themselves in isolation from prevailing social conditions, and then for them to join with other self-created individuals to shape what those social conditions will be. The Invisible Man is sent out into the world thoroughly inculcated with this misleading ideology; he bumps repeatedly against its untruth as he gradually realizes how starkly the odds are set against his acquisition of a fulfilling identity. Mr. Woodridge's insistence that race is irrelevant turns out to be one version of a widespread deception which suggests that these are not systemic, political issues but merely questions of individual aspiration.

It is significant that the Invisible Man hears this ideology in a literature class because it indicates how liberal humanism is championed (though usually implicitly) by literary realism. This is partly a question of how realism draws upon consensual assumptions which imply a common human fate that is therefore readily understood by all: as Elizabeth Deeds Ermarth says, 'the uniformity at the base of human experience and the solidarity of human nature receive confirmation from realistic conventions'.[5] The liberal tolerance with which realism treats its characters allows them space to come alive and breathe so that their subjectivities are gradually and organically unfolded. Caricature is driven by the opposite impulses, by flagrant intolerance, by anti-humanist contempt and loathing which confrontationally flatten the characters.

The Invisible Man's literature teacher has led him to believe that society will treat him in the way that a realist novelist treats his characters: instead, he increasingly learns that society regards him as more akin to the piggy bank and the Sambo doll than a Henry James character. The caricatural elements of *Invisible Man* prove that the realist dependence on consensus, and its assumption of 'uniformity at the base of human experience', disqualify realism as a mode when the focus of a novel is on fundamental conflicts and divisions. It is precisely because there is a ruling ideology which suppresses those divisions – by imposing a belief in uniformity and solidarity – that outsiders and minorities who do not conform to that uniformity are treated with suspicious contempt and so caricatured. The point of the novel's title is that 'realist' modes of thought are so dependent on appeals to familiarity that they rigidly structure the world according to preconceived patterns and are therefore blind to what falls outside this reassuring circle: the protagonist is invisible because he is so alien to these familiar patterns that conventional vision erases him completely.

The appeal to readerly recognition which is made by realism affirms the shared humanity of the reader and the characters who can be the objects of 'identification' because they inhabit the same world. Ellison's writing stresses how such humanity is denied to African Americans precisely because the element of sharing and recognition is so thoroughly lacking. This failure of realism is crucial because it is synecdochic of how African Americans are seen more generally. When realism works most effectively it evokes a subtle and nuanced sense of individual subjectivities in articulate interaction with each other; these can then accumulate to celebrate a richly conjoined humanity.

Ellison's satire is directed against the failure of this ruling aesthetic – and the ruling sensibility it is complicit with – to comprehend what does not correspond to its prejudices. So where realism is characterized by this fullness and conjoining, Ellison's writing dwells on absences and disjunctiveness. In *Juneteenth*[6] (1999), the novel that was published after Ellison's death, there is a passage of call and response which contains a sequence of brilliant imagery that explains the history of African Americans in just these terms. Significantly, it is preceded by an italicized passage of the Reverend Bliss's thoughts as he mentally refuses to sermonize (when called upon to do so by the Reverend Hickman) and thereby recall the role he was groomed for as a child by Hickman. Recoiling, he thinks of himself then as a 'six-seven-year-old ventriloquist's dummy dressed in a white evening suit', a 'puppet with a memory like a piece of flypaper' (118). Ironically, Bliss, though a white child, was turned by Hickman, an African American, into something resembling the piggy bank and Sambo doll – into a mechanized toy.

The sermonizing dialogue that follows between Hickman and Bliss traces the history of African Americans from their African origin through their capture, transport and enslavement and into their later increasing self-definition as a race and a religious culture. It dwells on how those of a 'Mayflower' origin denied to those who came on slave ships the rights they had insisted on for themselves (120) and so thoroughly dehumanized them. Their ships were 'floating coffins' and those who survived them were treated like 'one great unhuman animal without any face' (121). They became a people defined by lack: 'eyeless, earless, noseless, throatless, teethless, tongue-less, handless, feetless, armless . . .' (125). They were left unable to express themselves, and it is especially appropriate that this should be described in that form of call and response which is characteristically African American:

. . . They cut out our tongues . . .
. . . They left us speechless . . .
. . . They cut out our tongues . . .
. . . Lord, they left us without words . . .
. . . Amen! They scattered our tongues in this land like seed . . .
. . . And left us without language . . . (122)

The patterns of imagery in this passage combine associations of absence with those of fragmentation. This also works caricaturally because it subverts realist assumptions about ontological wholeness and uniqueness. The whites 'chopped us up into little bitty pieces like a farmer when he cuts up a potato' (122) and 'took us like a great black giant that had been chopped up into little pieces and the pieces buried . . . our memory of Africa ground down into powder and blown on the winds of foggy forgetfulness . . .' (124).

For Hickman it is religion that can heal fragmentedness. Although their race was 'like the valley of dry bones' (125) they heard God's word and so 'sprang together and walked around. All clacking together and clicking into place' (127). Hickman propounds a sacred ontological wholeness and so subscribes to one of the philosophical strands underlying liberal humanism (which has historically been able to draw upon religious beliefs of this sort). Hickman's disapproval of the cinema which increasingly fascinates the young Bliss is premised upon this because it arises from his suspicion that cinema disrupts the sacred stability of self. He complains that 'folks are getting themselves mixed up with those shadows spread out against the wall, with people that are no more than some smoke drifting up from hell or pouring out of a bottle' and further complains that this makes them forget that they were made in 'God's *own* image' (222–23).

Ellison by contrast clearly enjoys such multiplying and problematizing of selves, as is shown by his fascination with the exemplary figure of Rinehart in

Invisible Man. He endorses cinema, also, because he sees it as linked to a comic view of life, with that moment 'when a joke was outrageously simple-minded and yet somehow true' (*Juneteenth*, 232). This is a key aesthetic belief for him and helps to explain his deployment of caricature. As Tony Hilfer says, *Invisible Man* is built around 'combinations of comic riff with allegorical suggestion' and 'for Ellison, at his most serious, American identity *is* a joke'.[7] From this point of view it is enough to disqualify Hickman's sermonizing against cinema that it can be dismissed as simply 'too serious' (231).

However, it is even further disqualified because it is immediately followed by another sermon which contradicts it and which carries more weight because it emerges out of Hickman's actual experience. For Hickman now declares that a man 'lives more lives than a cat' (223) – an idea that resembles the multiple lives and selves that are attributed, in Toni Morrison's *Jazz*, to Joe Trace, who says that before he met Violet he had already been 'changed into new seven times' (123). This explains the exemplary status of jazz for both Ellison and Morrison. Ellison associated Hickman with jazz, as is clear from the novel-in-progress 'Notes' which are appended to *Juneteenth.* There he refers to Hickman as an 'ex-jazzman' and declares that a jazzman and a religious leader both inspire 'emotions that move beyond the rational onto the mystical' (354).

Jazz is connected to cinema – as it is discussed in *Juneteenth* – and both are modernist forms which experimentally wrench their material into defamiliarizing shapes. When applied to questions of identity, jazz as an example suggests an improvizatory and performative outlook as opposed to the essentialist attitude implied by Hickman's insistence on ontological stability. This also explains its eponymous status in Morrison's novel, which is preoccupied with polyphonic style and racial and ontological hybridity.

For these reasons it is linked to another key idea in Ellison, his fascination with 'masking'. It is here that Ellison most explicitly differs from realist assumptions about the stable self, because he not only regards the self as inevitably fissured and plural, but celebrates that plurality. As he himself has said:

> For the ex-colonials, the declaration of an American identity meant the assumption of a mask, and it imposed not only the discipline of a national self-consciousness, it gave Americans an ironic awareness of the joke that always lies between appearances and reality, between the discontinuity of social tradition and that sense of the past which clings to the mind. And perhaps even an awareness of the joke that society is man's creation, not God's.[8]

That last point indicates the sense in Ellison's own mind that Hickman's Christian view of identity is starkly unhelpful and wrong when it comes to explaining what it means to be African American – and even what it means to be American in general. His emphasis again is on disjunctiveness and the incongruity which arises from it and which produces ironic humour. Because society is a human construct – not natural or spiritual – it requires cunning and trickery, and a political tinkering with the boundaries between appearance and reality: national identity is acquired, ironically, through deception. This is an exemplary activity, as Berndt Ostendorf has indicated:

> Role playing and the assumption of the other mask indicate a political credo, namely, an anti-imperialistic and anti-colonialistic willingness to begin to understand the other, though it be in stereotype or in unavoidable initial ignorance. We recall Ellison's evaluation of Faulkner: He began with the stereotype but then took pains to discover the humanity behind it.[9]

The crucial function of masking is in how it works to evade the dead hand of the stereotype. Where stereotyping imposes oppressively rigid boundaries, the mask of role-playing insists on plurality and possibility. The stereotype is static, like caricature: the mask is mobile and transformative, like jazz and cinema, which makes Bliss 'dizzy with the vastness of the action and the scale of the characters' (234). That Ellison associates cinema and masking is evident from the similar terms in which he talks about the two of them, so that Bliss, when he directs films, feels that 'a duplicity was being commissioned' but also that he himself is the dupe, because there is always 'the awareness of the joke implicit in being me' (266). Ellison connects all these activities with that of the novelist; Bliss as a film director is aware of 'this desire to identify with others, this need to extend myself and test my most far-fetched possibilities' (266).

The novelist for Ellison, then, should work like the film director and the jazzman to improvize variations on the self, and this is not just an aesthetic but a political imperative. The figure who exemplifies this most thoroughly is Rinehart, who appears near the end of *Invisible Man* but still personifies the novel's coruscating, hallucinatory quality. That he continued to haunt Ellison's imagination is evident from how *Juneteenth* continues to meditate on the 'rind' versus 'hart' binary (260, 300) and how Bliss to some extent reprises the earlier character – Rinehart, like Bliss, was a preacher when he was only a 'twelve-year-ole boy' (*Invisible Man*, 496). Rinehart's multiple masks thoroughly subvert any sense of a 'solid life' (*Juneteenth*, 266) and replace it with a 'vast seething, hot world of fluidity': 'Still, could he be all of them: Rine the runner and Rine the gambler and Rine the briber and Rine the lover and Rinehart the Reverend? Could he himself be both rind and hart?' (498)

Rinehart's multiple role-playing expresses an ironic awareness of the gap between racial appearance and reality: each role he adopts is a different black stereotype, but multiplying them calls into question the stereotypicality of each and so deconstructs racist caricature. The fixity of the stereotype is again subverted by fluidity, in this case the fluidity of the masking device. This does work as an anti-imperialistic, anti-colonialist ruse, as Ostendorf says, because it stresses the human ability to change and leave behind the fixed and reductive racist image. However, the mask seems to me ultimately unsatisfactory from a political point of view: as I argue in my discussion of Angela Carter, it is too obviously tied to the idea of deception to be a thoroughly convincing solution (even as a strategy) to problems of identity. It is less problematic in Ellison's case, though, because it is so obviously provisional and devised in the face of an identity oppressively fixed on African Americans from their slave history. It is not meant to provide a final answer to how African Americans should present themselves.

The trickster elusiveness of Rinehart recalls an African American myth that both Ellison and Morrison have drawn upon – the story of Brer Rabbit and the Tar Baby. The Invisible Man is reminded of this when he is working at Liberty Paints and his immediate boss engages him in a fight. This man, Mr. Brockway, has already been described as wearing overalls that make him look 'as though he had been dipped in pitch' (207). Significantly, though, it is after the protagonist has mentally applied a series of racist epithets to him – 'slavery-time, mammy-made, handkerchief-headed bastard' – that he notices that Brockway is covered in 'goo' and thinks 'Tar Baby' (227). The Invisible Man is repelled by Brockway because he is the worst-case stereotype which African Americans must struggle their hardest to escape – his fight with Brockway could even be seen to stand for this allegorically. What must worry him, though, is that he has touched Brockway at all because the myth embodies the fear of contamination: Brer Rabbit is deceived into touching the tar baby and ends up stuck to it.

This arouses the anxiety that Brockway's example will drag the protagonist down, as Craig H. Werner's interpretation of the myth indicates – for 'the tar baby could evoke materialism or the white stereotypes of blacks (it is black, stupid, lazy and smells bad)'. It could mean that the protagonist is made to conform to one of the 'Euro-American myths' which 'present Afro-American character in terms of simple stereotypes: the mammy, the black beast, and so forth'.[10] So, when Brockway's trickery traps him in an explosion which lands him in hospital, it is important that the Invisible Man is identified with Brer Rabbit (242) who wins out in the end against the tar baby by adopting devious tricksterism of his own, which will ensure his survival. By contrast, in Toni Morrison's *Tar Baby* (1981), the roles of Tar Baby and Brer Rabbit keep switching from one character to another, which indicates the human ability to evade stereotyping but also stresses the power of stereotyping to reassert itself unexpectedly. So, at the end of the novel, when Son runs 'Lickety-lickety-lickety-split',[11] it is ambiguous whether he is running towards or away from entrapment.

The Invisible Man, though, is remarkable for his lack of deviousness. The principal of his college is astonished by his naiveté: when Dr. Bledsoe questions him about his deepening predicament when chauffeuring an important white man called Mr. Norton, Bledsoe is amazed by his trusting passivity in constantly acceding to Norton's wishes and so allowing Norton to see too much into the actual lives of African Americans. Bledsoe simply assumes that an intelligent young man will know enough to use the necessary cunning: as he says, 'the dumbest black bastard in the cotton patch knows that the only way to please a white man is to tell him a lie!' (139). Bledsoe considers that this level of idealistic ingenuousness constitutes a danger to his own cause (which is only secondarily collective and mostly dedicated to his own self-interest). As a result he expels the protagonist and – with characteristic cunning of his own – dispatches him with seven letters addressed to important white men, which turn out to be letters of deviously insinuating disrecommendation (190–91).

The protagonist's ingenuousness leads him to become the serial victim of everybody else's designs, so that one repeated caricatural motif reduces him to a mere machine or plaything. Under the impression that a group of important whites is interested in his skills as a public speaker, he is tricked into joining in a blindfolded boxing match with several other young blacks designed for the watching pleasure of these 'big shots' (21ff). After he is expelled from his college he convinces himself that Bledsoe was right and that he must 'submit to punishment' (147). When he tries to see Mr. Emerson, the last of the addressees of Bledsoe's letters, he meets instead with Emerson's son who imposes on him all the burden of his narcissistic white liberal guilt (182ff) and then gets him a job at Liberty Paints where a ten per cent black taint is used paradoxically but symbolically to make white paint even whiter. This is meant to ensure, as it were, the racial purity of public monuments (199–200). When he finally learns enough alienation to recoil from the ruling white political system, he is taken up by a Leftist organization called the Brotherhood which turns out to want to use his oratory and his race for its own purposes: it is a sign that he is finally learning to be sceptical when he impatiently wonders, 'What was I, a man or a natural resource?' (303).

Even after this point, however, the Invisible Man is still so pliable that he wishes to copy Rinehart and lose himself in that trickster's multiple identities. He is lacking not just in deviousness but in almost every other quality as well: one of the most remarkable features of *Invisible Man* is how thoroughly it sustains the featurelessness of its central character. He is so much a *tabula rasa* that he allows the narrative to dwell with vivid intensity on the world through which he moves: one of the surreal effects of the novel is its evocation of the permeable and wavering boundary between the character and his world. This is linked to his invisibility but it also confirms that he is, as the war veteran in the Golden Day describes him to Mr. Norton, 'a walking personification of the negative' (94). That idea was important enough to Ellison for him to use it again and apply it to Bliss, in *Juneteenth*, who uses exactly the same phrase about himself (434). It signifies a very radical deconstruction of realist notions of 'well-rounded' characterization and liberal humanist faith in ontological wholeness and stability.

The one quality consistently attributed to the protagonist is his prowess as an orator. Given what happens to him, however, he appears to be more the victim of language than its master, more a parrot and a passive mouthpiece than someone capable of deploying language to stamp his authority and define his identity. Repeatedly, he is depicted as saying what his hearers want to hear. He is shocked when he realizes he has departed from the required script: this is as true of a speech he makes for the Brotherhood – which some consider 'incorrect' (349) – as it is when he delivers his prize speech to the white big shots (29ff). Like Bliss, the Invisible Man is treated like a 'ventriloquist's dummy' and a 'puppet' (*Juneteenth*, 118).

His most vivid fantasy of himself involves an 'eloquence' that glamourizes him to such an extent that he comes to resemble Ronald Colman. He imagines inventing alternative vocal roles for himself with 'one way of speaking in the North and another in the South' (164). However, the imagery that follows this fantasy implies the dangers that it poses him. First, he thinks the streets are full 'of hurrying people who walked as though they had been wound up and were directed by some unseen control': this implies that his fantasy of becoming 'charming' will turn him into a sort of wind-up toy for the use of those in power, who exercise that power invisibly. An insidious kind of slavery has replaced the actual kind: amongst these hurrying people he sees occasional 'Negroes who hurried along with leather pouches strapped to their wrists' who remind him of 'prisoners carrying their leg irons as they escaped from a chain gang' (164).

This threatens him with the diminution of his identity – on the following page he takes an elevator that rises so swiftly he feels 'as though an important part of myself had been left below in the lobby'. Ellison uses a similar image to suggest the danger posed by the Brotherhood when the protagonist is at the height of his commitment to it, and is therefore 'becoming someone else': just before he has put on the new suit that makes him feel this, he feels 'as though I stood simultaneously at opposite ends of a tunnel. I seemed to view myself from the distance of the campus while yet sitting there on a bench in the old arena' (335). It is significant that this happens as he is waiting to give that speech on behalf of the Brotherhood which is most fully transcribed in the novel, for the eerie image of the split self hints that it is through his self-consciously rhetorical language that the protagonist is fragmenting himself, alienating one part of himself from the other.

However, the passage that focuses most tellingly on the issue of language and identity is the one in the hospital after the protagonist has been caught up in the explosion at Liberty Paints. Here the protagonist is asked a series of capitalized questions that are meant to discover who he is. When he is asked his name he discovers that he has forgotten it, but this moment is made all the more bafflingly vivid because it reminds readers that he remains nameless throughout. So the novel's absent centre echoes with redoubled hollowness.

The issue of identity is the central concern of *Invisible Man*, which takes the form of the Bildungsroman in order to subvert it by questioning the whole concept of 'psychological development'. Almost half-way through the novel, at the point in a conventional Bildungsroman when a growing sense of the hero's mature self would be emerging, the Invisible Man decides to stop doing what is expected of him and do what he likes – which turns out to be eating yams. He decides he *is* what he eats because the cuisine of his early youth most closely defines his identity. He declares, 'I yam what I am!' (266). This is Bildungsroman impatiently mocked by the confrontational crudeness of a bad pun combined with a reference to Popeye; the earnestly complex, painstaking and discreet tracing of an individual's growth of soul is reduced to a cartoon.

What the protagonist has in fact crucially learned at this point is that the apparent complexity of the world run by powerful middle-aged men is a sham. Underneath its superficial sophistication there are crude drives towards attaining and retaining power at all costs; the protagonist has achieved development of sorts when he understands Bledsoe in these terms and entertains himself by envisaging the college principal as a secret eater of 'hog bowels' (265). The idea of hidden appetites, of the grotesque body concealed under clothing, is a key one in the caricatural tradition. It arouses characteristic horror in Swift, and in the etchings of James Gillray there are repeated depictions of dinner-table scenes where eating is often treated as a metaphor for territorial greed – so, in 'Dumourier Dining at St. James's' of 1793, a French general, who had led an invasion of Holland, holds a knife and fork and is being welcomed by the British political establishment with a surreal feast of 'ecclesiastical pudding, roast Pitt and stewed crown, liberally garnished with frogs'.[12]

In identifying himself and Bledsoe with the characteristic food of his race the Invisible Man is satirically colluding with that traditional form of racist stereotyping that metonymically reduces a race to its most notorious eating habits. Gillray is referring to this in the frog garnish served up to Dumourier; and in this period the French derided the English as 'rosbifs'. In proclaiming 'I yam what I am' the Invisible Man is doing something similar to what African Americans have done more recently in calling each other 'nigger': he is pre-empting the racist stereotype by adopting it for his own ends. By accusing Bledsoe of the same eating habits he is exposing the principal's hypocrisy in distancing himself from his own people. In preferring yam life to sham life, despite its being 'wild and childish' (265) he is preferring simple childlike truth to adult factitiousness.

The equation of 'I am' and 'yam' is another sign of how thoroughly the Invisible Man's character is reduced, how close he comes to personifying the negative. Each time he appears to develop, his development is curtailed and he is pared back again. In the hospital the questions he is asked – who is he? what is his name? what was his mother's name? (239–41) – suggest that his identity is receding to its point of origin. That is a frightening passage because it shows that he is being psychically manipulated; he is subjected to a non-surgical lobotomy which will produce a complete 'change of personality' (236). The shifts in linguistic register which characterize his doctors' speech hint at medical/psychoanalytical officialese being used to cover up crudely racist motives as they move from references to Gestalt to taunting references to African American 'rhythm', when in fact his 'dancing' (237) is really a response to the electric current they are passing through his brain.

The assumptions here are that he is simply a malfunctioning machine that they must get 'started again' (232) with another, medical, machine. So when he is asked his mother's name he is so confused that he seems to confirm these assumptions: 'Who was it that screamed? Mother? But the scream came from the machine. A machine my mother?' (240). Throughout the novel it is the repeated mechanistic imagery which most caricatures the protagonist by dehumanizing him. Early on, the veteran in the Golden Day prefigures this by declaring that the Invisible Man represses his emotions so thoroughly that he also represses his humanity, which turns him into a 'mechanical man' (94), an 'automaton', 'a thing and not a man; a child, or even less – a black amorphous thing' (95). It is this which connects him to those key images in the novel, the piggy bank and the Sambo doll: the former is a 'Negro' yet it has a lever on its back that flips coins from its hand into its mouth; the latter has head and feet which are made to dance the Boogie-Woogie by 'some mysterious mechanism' (431) and is linked to those rootless 'Negroes . . . who shoot up from the South into the busy city like wild jacks-in-the-box broken loose from [their] springs' (439).

The brain manipulations carried out by the doctors are only a more literal version of the way almost all the characters in the novel try to adapt and use the protagonist for their own ends. The sense, too, that his brain is exposed and made available to radical alteration is a more literal version of the alarming vulnerability that characterizes him throughout in the absence of other defining qualities. He becomes a passive receptacle for the prejudices, fantasies and designs of the other characters. Even when he learns the need for cunning and, modelling himself on Rinehart, decides to seduce the wife of one of the leaders of the Brotherhood into giving him information, he finds the tables turned on him so that it is him, not her, who is being seduced. For this woman – Sybil – treats him as an object of her sexual fantasies concocted around the figures of Joe Louis and Paul Robeson (516) in which he is 'Brother Taboo-with-whom-all-things-are-possible' (517). She resembles another woman with Brotherhood affiliations who is aroused by the fear he inspires in her, aroused by what she sees as his primitiveness, the 'tom-toms beating in [his] voice' (413). When Sybil calls him 'Anonymous brute 'n boo'ful buck' (528) she is close to the nub of why the namelessness of the protagonist is part of the relentlessly caricatural style of *Invisible Man*: he is anonymous and invisible because he is the blank page onto which reductive stereotypes are projected.

However, in response to Sybil's fantasies, the protagonist wonders: 'Had life suddenly become a crazy Thurber cartoon?' (517) and this hints at how the caricatural outlook of the novel is not confined to its treatment of the protagonist but to that of almost all of its characters and the world in which they live. Sybil herself is not only a stereotypically sexually rapacious middle-aged woman but, more importantly, wants to caricature herself as part of the sexual role-play – wants, for these purposes, to think of herself as a 'nymphomaniac' (519). Her sexual fantasies are inextricable from assumptions about power; their transgressiveness involves the image of a rich white woman feeling an uncontrollable desire to be overpowered by a subservient black man, where the urge itself is so powerful that it can overturn conventional power relationships.

Such sexual role-play can be seen as involving the adoption of masks – anonymous brute, nymphomaniac – and therefore as part of the novel's treatment of the theme of masking in its relationship to issues of power. It is because characterization in the novel is so bound up with these themes that it is so constantly marked by caricatural effects of exaggeration and self-conscious crudity: the characters so relentlessly embody a political position that they inevitably resemble personifications more than persons. It is an indication of Ellison's sophistication as a writer, however, that he adds a telling self-reflexive element to this. For these characters self-consciously simplify themselves, knowingly turn themselves into a fiction by adopting a mask for their own political ends. Sybil's version is the most harmless and Ellison makes her fantasy seem, for the most part, comically endearing – his treatment of the scene is conspicuously innocent of misogyny.

Much more unsettling is the mask adopted by Dr. Bledsoe. His deception resembles that of Dickens's Uriah Heep: he presents a display of humility that in fact allows him to accrue and maintain his power. As he turns from furiously reprimanding the protagonist to approaching his white superior, Mr. Norton, he stops and composes 'his angry face like a sculptor, making it a bland mask' (102). The fragmentation of self that is inflicted against his will on the protagonist (as shown by the elevator image) is deliberately contrived for himself by Bledsoe, so that part of him seems to rise up 'leaving his other part smiling in the chair' (118). He caricatures himself so as not to frighten powerful whites, he models himself on the Sambo doll so that he makes it seem – even when he is wearing a smart suit – that 'Somehow, his trousers inevitably bagged at the knees and the coat slouched in the shoulders' (114). He is subservient to powerful whites, but autocratic to his African American students: 'He was our coal-black daddy of whom we were afraid' (116).

The protagonist himself adopts a mask when he becomes a member of the

Brotherhood which gives him a 'new identity' in the form of a new name supplied him in the self-consciously secret form of a slip of paper inside an envelope (309). He welcomes this because he feels it will save him from 'disintegration' (353): he is deeply troubled throughout by ontological instability and the Brotherhood seems to promise him a safe haven with a benevolent dictatorship that tells him who he is and at the same time tells him exactly what to do to be that person. Other people keep trying to define him with dismissive epithets, so that in the space of three pages he is identified with 'field niggers' up from the South (328) and then with 'young New York Negroes' (330). By contrast the Brotherhood offers him a sense of self that will be as fulfilling as that of Frederick Douglass, who had taken this name in his role as an orator and thus 'became himself, defined himself' (381).

Ironically, though, it is precisely in the direction of disintegration that his membership of the Brotherhood leads him. What its members do is similar to what Bledsoe does because they must adopt a mask which simplifies them for political ends. When the protagonist first meets Brother Jack, his immediate boss in the organization, he notices 'that somehow he was acting a part; that something about him wasn't exactly real' (288) and this prefigures what also happens to the protagonist. The issue of language and identity, which is surreally explored in the hospital scene, arises again here as the protagonist feels an increasing gap between who he thinks himself to be and how the person with his new name is perceived. As he looks back on his recent experiences he thinks that they 'seemed not to happen to me but to someone who actually bore my new name . . . and yet I am what they think I am . . .' (379).

It is through its caricatural style that the novel exposes the Brotherhood's ideology as a distortive simplification. Its grand narrative, its 'all-embracing idea', which gives the protagonist 'a vital role' and the world 'a new shape' in which 'everything could be controlled by our science', is satirized as being achieved through a tunnel vision which conveniently tidies up 'loose ends' (382). When Ellison represents this with Jack's glass eye he is drawing upon the resources of the political cartoon. As Jack reprimands the protagonist and furiously tells him he must accept 'discipline', his glass eye erupts out of his face and he drops it into a glass of water (474). This stands simultaneously for the fissuring of self that the Brotherhood inflicts on its members (the protagonist perceives it as a form of 'disembowelling') and the selective monolith which is its view of the world: 'So that is the meaning of discipline, I thought, sacrifice . . . yes, and blindness' (475). The glass eye forms part of an image cluster centred on blindness that recurs throughout the novel and which forms a symmetrical and interlocking pattern with an even more important (and eponymous) image cluster centred on invisibility. This is at its most intense when the protagonist makes his early speech on behalf of the Brotherhood: the imagery of blindness here is joined by that of light and dark and culminates in his stumbling 'as in a game of blindman's buff' (347).

It is when the protagonist encounters Rinehart that he feels he has 'just discovered Jack's missing eye' (499). The Brotherhood's science resembles a 'machine' (505); its mechanistic monolith lacks any sense of the chancy multiplicity personified by Rinehart and embodied by the cinematic inter-cuttings and montages and jazzy polyphony of *Invisible Man* as a whole. Rinehart is endlessly plural but threatens also to dissolve into nothing, to be all 'rine' and no 'hart': *Invisible Man*, too, is poised between a celebration of plurality and a descent into nihilism. It opposes not only the simplifications of the Brotherhood and the opposite black nationalist simplifications of Ras the Exhorter, but all grand narratives, and worries that history is a 'gambler': 'What if history was not a reasonable citizen, but a madman full of paranoid guile?' (441).

This takes *Invisible Man* close to the absurdism of *Catch-22*, whose publication it preceded by five years. Like Heller's novel, its caricatural techniques are so pervasive that it constructs a whole world which is edged with grotesque caricatural madness. Shocked by the waste of the talented and beautiful young Tod Clifton, the protagonist declares in his funeral oration that when he was killed, 'The blood ran like blood in a comic-book killing, on a comic-book street in a comic-book town on a comic-book day in a comic-book world' (458).

* * *

Ralph Ellison's finest achievement lies in his exploration of the implications of African American invisibility. By contrast, Toni Morrison's project is to make African Americans visible: it has involved re-telling American history in order to emphasize that African Americans have been a constant and highly significant presence inside that history. So while Ellison draws upon caricature in order to weigh the impact on African Americans of a highly partial and distorted white establishment vision, amounting to near blindness, Morrison struggles self-consciously against caricature. It is in the process of this explicit resistance that Morrison refers to caricatural imagery in order to evoke the African American struggle to be regarded as fully human.

What must also be stressed, however, is how much Morrison draws – in novels like *Song of Solomon* (1977) and *Tar Baby* – upon realist techniques to aid her in this same struggle. She appropriates realism, but deploys it in contexts which subvert its liberal humanist premises. Because she is dealing with the lives of African Americans, her subject matter is radically at odds with that of the white tradition and therefore does not arouse the consensual response upon which realism conventionally depends. Because her subject matter subversively denies the assumption (as Elizabeth Deeds Ermarth puts it) of 'the uniformity at the base of human experience and the solidarity of human nature' (65), it interrogates realism itself: the lives being described are self-consciously *not* uniform with those which white readers, or even their ancestors, have lived. Morrison's accounts of these histories reveal, not solidarity, but disorientating disparity. It is not surprising, then, that critics have underestimated how much Morrison operates in a realist idiom because her defamiliarized realism can easily blend into the postmodernist and magic-realist idioms for which she is more famous.

Both those latter terms have their uses when discussing Morrison in her non-realist modes, but they need to be joined by another much older term – allegory – if her non-realist modes are to be fully accounted for. This term is indispensable when accounting for the overall impact of her trilogy of works (*Beloved*, *Jazz* and *Paradise*) which, as Missy Dehn Kubitschek has pointed out, correspond to 'the three works of Dante's *The Divine Comedy*: *Inferno*, *Purgatorio*, and *Paradiso*'.[13] Michele Hannoosh's account of the meaning of allegory is revealing here, as it also is when applied to Joseph Heller (as I do in my next chapter). Drawing upon Walter Benjamin's account of the caricatural art of Jean Grandville, she says that

> allegory both speaks and reveals the fragmentation behind the alleged order and causal evolution of history . . . Grandville's allegorical art, like Baudelaire's, expresses the fragmentation, commodification, and dehumanization of experience in capitalist culture, and thus demystifies it.[14]

Morrison's trilogy derives much of its power from how it draws upon these allegorical effects in tracing the increasing self-determination of African Americans. It follows their history from slavery through to a period close to the present, in *Paradise*, when they can even be regarded as in some ways too narcissistically preoccupied with their self-determination, and to have imposed racial and other kinds of stereotyping on members of their own race.

However far they have travelled, though, the structure of the trilogy stresses that the trauma of slavery is still felt by African Americans and still inflicts cultural damage on them, some of which – like the narcissism and black racism diagnosed in *Paradise* – is self-inflicted. One of the most powerful aspects of Morrison's writing is her avoidance of any sentimental belief in the nobility of suffering – she reveals how thoroughly it diminishes its victims, and even leads to their inflicting of further damage on themselves. This is the key narrative premise of *Beloved*, in which slavery leads a woman to kill her own child. Its major achievement is its evocation of the systemic destructiveness in slavery that drove the woman, Sethe, to this destructive act.

Beloved is a very different novel to *Catch-22* – Heller's mode of absurdist farce is very alien to Morrison – but both novels draw upon the allegory of Dante's *Inferno* because both novels are about a form of hell. Slaves, even more than soldiers, are thoroughly dehumanized because they are reduced to the status of commodities. Like Heller's soldiers, therefore, Morrison's slaves are necessarily caricatures (though Morrison has none of Heller's ironic enjoyment of this fact). When Morrison adopts the perspective of the hunters of slave runaways she shows how far they are from regarding their quarry as human: 'Unlike a snake or a bear, a dead nigger could not be skinned for profit and was not worth his own dead weight in coin' (148). The point here – that the slaves are equated with animals – is confirmed by Morrison's own account, in her major critical work *Playing in the Dark*, of the word 'nigger' as it is used by Hemingway in *To Have and Have Not*: 'The term occupies a territory between man and animal and thus withholds specificity even while marking it.'[15]

The central characters of *Beloved* struggle against the caricatural generalizing inflicted on them by slavery and yearn for human 'specificity'. The constant obstacle they face is that they are systematically drained and depleted, so that – like Heller's soldiers and Ellison's Invisible Man – they are constantly defined, not by the presence of human qualities, but by the lack of them. Away from Sweet Home and its unusually liberal owner they are 'trespassers among the human race', they are 'Watchdogs without teeth; steer bulls without horns; gelded workhorses whose neigh and whinny could not be translated into a language responsible humans spoke' (125). Because they are denied a proper identity they are denied anything like a full presence in language. Therefore, like the Dead family in *Song of Solomon* and Joe Trace in *Jazz*, their names indicate less who they are than what they lack. Stamp Paid, once called Joshua, has changed his name because he considers that he has paid the debt, as it were, of himself, by allowing his owner's son to have sex with his wife; the alternative was to kill him, which would also amount to suicide: 'With that gift he decided he didn't owe anybody anything.' (185) So his name indicates that he has a price instead of an identity; similarly Paul D, when he has run away and been recaptured, learns the 'dollar value of his weight, his strength, his heart, his brain, his penis, and his future' (226).

This is why slaves can be accurately equated with the piggy bank that haunts both Ellison and Morrison – equated with 'a blackboy's mouth full of money' (255). Commodification leads to reification and fragmentation. What a novel above all can indicate is how slaves are deprived of that which constitutes, generically, the novel's central subject and which it usually analyses in minute detail: the emotional life. The novel also traditionally focuses (unlike lyric poetry) on the emotional life seen against the background of economic circumstances: *Beloved* reveals that these particularly extreme economic circumstances are so dominant that they marginalize emotions altogether. This amounts to a very extreme challenge to the genre's liberal humanist assumptions by exposing how a society supposedly based on liberal humanist ideals grew historically out of a society which was so illiberal, and so inhumane, that it erased the humanity of millions of its inhabitants.

The slaves in *Beloved* can never fully acquire the status of novelistic 'characters' because slavery generalizes and at the same time depletes them so that it deprives them of the required ontological uniqueness and wholeness. Slaves are so threatened by the possibility that their partners and children can, at any point, be taken away from them that they cannot allow themselves to love: 'you protected yourself and loved small' because 'a big love . . . would split you wide open' (162). Because Sethe has never been able to see her children develop she has sadness in the core of her being, in 'the desolated center where the self that was no self made its home' (140). Paul D, similarly, has hardened himself to such an extent that he has a 'tobacco tin buried in his chest where a red heart used to be. Its lid rusted shut.' (72–73)

In the realist novel an author might draw upon a caricatural image like that last one in order to define a personal inadequacy in an individual who would thus be contrasted with those characters, usually more central, who are sensitive and capable of love and are therefore celebrated by liberal humanist values. Here, by contrast, the origins of Paul D's inhuman hardness of heart are located very deliberately not in him as an individual but as a general condition imposed by an appallingly inhuman system. *Beloved* deconstructs the concept of 'love', and shows how forces much larger than the individual can control even that part of the human sensibility which liberal humanism regards as most definitively 'human', and as most bestowing meaning on human lives.

Beloved herself personifies murdered love. As a ghost who returns to haunt the mother who murdered her, and then enters the narrative almost realistically resembling an adolescent girl, she functions similarly to some of the hybrid characters in magic realist fiction. However, her meaning can be much better appreciated if she is thought of as allegorical and with a name that refers to the desperate need to love and *be* loved in an historical context that dictates systemic lovelessness. It is significant therefore that the reason Sethe gives her that name is because she fails to hear any of the Reverend Pike's funeral sermon except the first two words: 'Dearly Beloved, which is what you are to me and I don't have to be sorry about getting only one word' (185). 'Beloved' is a fragment of speech and the ghost she becomes is 'a greedy ghost and needed a lot of love, which was only natural, considering' (209); she is threatened by the possibility of progressive bodily disintegration (133), thinks in a fragmentary stream of consciousness (210–17) and personifies broken love.

Jazz centres, like *Beloved*, on an act of murder motivated by too much love, and also explores the connection between love and violence which arises when the love is haunted by a profound sense of loss. It even mentions the possibility that the murdered girl might return as 'a young ghost with bad skin' (223). These links with its predecessor in the trilogy indicate its purgatorial quality, and that it is still dealing with the ontological legacy of slavery. Its transitional status is confirmed by how it dwells on the shift from the generation of Joe Trace and his wife Violet – who participated in the Great Migration from the rural South to the urban North, and whose memories of slavery were still vivid – to the generation of Dorcas and Felice, young women defined by their urban sensibilities and their taste for jazz. By naming the latter in its title, the novel stresses the point that the 1920s initiated the possibility of a specifically African American form of expression.

Jazz is exemplary because of its hybridity and its improvizatory polyphony. These qualities are crucial for Morrison, as they are for Ellison, because they construct identity as fluid, dialogic and performative, and not fixed to any distortive essentialism of the sort suggested to Ellison by Ras's black nationalism. Jazz is hybrid as African Americans are hybrid. To try to ignore the hybridity and refer your identity, as Ras does, to a pure African origin, is to collude with a racist outlook that leads to stereotyping.

In Morrison's *Jazz* two characters – Golden Gray and Joe Trace – are guilty of a simplistic state of mind analogous to Ras's primitivism. Golden Gray's racism causes him traumatic problems of identity when he discovers his mixed-race origins; it leads to similar ontological mutilations to those inflicted by slavery. As Angela Burton says:

> In abjection, the collapse of Gray's racist 'blindness' enables him to 'see' that living without a father has been like an amputation, and that this loss – the denial of his father – is what it has cost him to live in white ideology. The trope of disfigurement and amputation is a metaphor Morrison uses to illustrate the idea that the price of white ideology is inversely related to the loss of the (black *or* white) self, psychically or physically. In her fiction it becomes a measure of the cost black Americans pay to live in societies governed by white ideology.[16]

Joe Trace similarly amputates himself by obsessively thinking that the route to discovering his identity lies in retracing his steps back to the woman called Wild who he thinks is his mother. It is significant that the novel leaves it unclear whether or not she is in fact his mother because *Jazz* wants to stress above all that identity questions cannot be solved simply by equating them to questions of origin. Joe's name is also significant because it is based on a childhood misunderstanding: he was told that his parents 'disappeared without a trace' and so thought that 'the "trace" they disappeared without' was him (124). Summing up his identity totally in terms of his parental origin reduces him to the status of a mere vestige. His longing to retrace himself back to Wild, who lives without clothes in a cave and is unable to speak, arises from a misguided emphasis on a natural origin, and denies the importance of his social experience. Most damagingly, it defines him entirely in terms of absence and loss; a key strand in the narrative shows Joe moving from having Wild 'always on his mind' (176) to his obsessive and finally destructive love for Dorcas which can be seen, from this perspective, to arise from a desperate attempt to fill an ontological void.

Morrison sums up such damaging distortiveness in a paragraph whose terms are explicitly allegorical. Here Joe is described, in his third attempt to find Wild, searching a hillside for a tree 'whose roots grew backward as though, having gone obediently into earth and found it barren, retreating to the trunk for what was needed' (182). Joe is searching for his 'roots' but finds roots that mock the perverseness of his own obsessive retrospectiveness: given the wider context of Morrison's concerns with race, there is an echo in this passage of the genealogical quest embodied in Alex Haley's *Roots.* Morrison's point is that identity will be misunderstood when it is simplistically retraced. The rest of the paragraph confirms this allegorically by referring to the landscape below the tree where there is a river called 'Treason', which can only be approached by terrain that threatens 'treachery' with its porous ground: 'A step could swallow your foot or your whole self'.

That landscape resembles the allegorical places in John Bunyon's *Pilgrim's Progress* and threatens to turn Joe Trace into a personification of the self misled and lost through obsessive preoccupation with 'roots'. Like Golden Gray he is threatened by an amputation and a simplification that amounts to a form of self-caricature. Morrison's larger allegorical point, however, is that African Americans need to pass through a purgatorial transition to arrive at a more thorough self-determination. So the novel ends happily and proleptically by implying that Joe and Violet Trace have come to resemble 'real' characters who can be discussed as such in an epilogue with Morrison herself intruding into the narrative: 'Busy, they were, busy being original, complicated, changeable – human, I guess you'd say' (220).

The hopeful ending suggests that the trend will continue in *Paradise*[17] (1997), but this is frustrated as the title is revealed to be ironic; indicating Morrison's anxiety that African Americans have moved from slavery – the opposite of self-determination – to a marked tendency, amongst some of their race, to what might be called being over self-determined. In depicting an all-black community Morrison directs her satire against African Americans who impose their own stereotypes by insisting on conformity to their own prejudices. This leads to discrimination directed against those who are too light-skinned, and those – like the women of the 'convent' – who are regarded as alien because of their gender and bohemian way of life.

In Jill Matus's account of this theme, the link with Joe Trace's mistaken preoccupation with 'roots' becomes clear. She points out that while Morrison's earlier novels dwell on the importance of memory in order to come to terms with a traumatic history, *Paradise* 'explores the excesses of commemoration as a symptom of enduring trauma'.[18] Joe Trace's efforts as an individual could have only a limited effect – but in a community like Paradise, whose identity is constituted out of the fetishizing of commemoration, this self-regarding obsession leads collectively and even institutionally to a rigid stereotypical vision.

The preoccupation with the 'nine large intact families' (188) who founded Paradise is invented by Morrison to satirize the creation of an aristocratic lineage which mirrors the same preoccupation amongst white Americans with a Mayflower ancestry – it leads to an equally hierarchical vision. In response to their 'horror of whites' (189) these families evolved, in reaction, a hierarchy that valued people according to how black they are. All of the original nine families were 'eight-rock, a deep deep level in the coal mines' (193) and so Paradise is dominated by 'a new separation: light-skinned against black' (194). It is a similar rigidly stereotypical vision that leads to their deep suspicion of those 'convent' inhabitants whose outlandishness in terms of gender and bohemianism can lead to their being stigmatized – as unconventional women have traditionally been stigmatized – as 'witches' (276).

The prestige bestowed on 'eight-rock' purity drives a caricatural dismissiveness of anyone beyond its boundaries; it results in the massacre of the convent inhabitants with which the novel begins and ends. The narcissistic 'eight-rock' self-regard is satirized most tellingly by the image of twins which dominates the book. Matus quotes the Reverend Misner musing that it was as though the citizens of Paradise wanted 'duplicates' rather than children (*Paradise*, 161). She suggests that 'Morrison's critical emphasis on duplication here is also expressed in the novel's unusually large cast of twins: Deacon and Steward; Coffee and Tea; Brood and Apollo; Merle and Pearl' (Matus, 161–62).

The most telling way of talking about twins in *Paradise*, however, is to contrast them with the dominant image of amputation in *Beloved* and, to a lesser extent, in *Jazz*. Amputees and twins are caricatures for opposite diminutions of the self: respectively for how slavery halves the self, and for how the black racism of Paradise doubles and then multiplies the self by imposing tyrannical sameness. Both are ultimately diminishing because both reduce the specificity of individuals and deplete ontological possibilities. Twins are especially significant for understanding the ontological shudder that caricature arouses: like visual caricature, they trouble the viewer with a start of recognition which is made problematic because it is unexpected. Henri Bergson says that the presence of complete similarity leads to the suspicion of 'some mechanism at work':

> Analyse the impression you get from two faces that are too much alike, and you will find that you are thinking of two copies cast in the same mould, or two impressions of the same seal, or two reproductions of the same negative, – in a word, of some manufacturing process or other.[19]

The sense of what is fully human – which is conceived as organic and unique – is troubled by this introduction of the mechanistic, which implies something inhumanly generalized, rigid and repetitive. This is linked, as Gombrich and Kris point out, to the mocking of the caricatural victim when their sense of uniqueness is unsettled by duplication of their physical appearance:

> To copy a person, to mimic his behaviour, means to annihilate his individuality. The very word 'in-dividual' means inseparable. If we succeed in singling out and imitating a man's expression or way of walking, we have destroyed this individuality.[20]

So in *Paradise* the multiplying of twins satirizes an 'eight-rock' insistence on spreading its own likeness everywhere, thereby imposing a racist stereotype hardly better than the one that has traditionally oppressed African Americans. The mistake they make is the one that Ellison says that he wanted Hickman to warn Bliss against:

> Hickman has tried to teach Bliss not to turn himself into a figure based upon the materialization of himself, i.e., into someone whose identity is based on color alone. He has tried to teach him to see himself and those close to him in terms of their inner spirit, their human quality, their quiet understated heroism. (*Juneteenth*, 'Notes', 355)

The 'eight-rocks' spread the materialization of themselves everywhere across their community, and twins represent their narrow and separatist self-regard. This resembles the image of incest used by Gabriel Garcia Marquez, in *One Hundred Years of Solitude*, to satirize a similarly overheated self-preoccupation in the isolated citizens of Macondo. Such a materialization of self leads to a stereotyping and flatly diminishing vision of both the self and of others; and this leads, in turn, to hatred and violence.

2 *Joseph Heller's Allegories of Money*

Joseph Heller's most distinctive achievement is in his caricaturing of institutions. When his career as a whole is considered, he is seen to tackle the most important institutions in turn so that he has now tackled all of the most prominent ones. *Catch-22*[1] (1961) satirizes the military-industrial complex, *Something Happened*[2] (1974): corporate business and the family, *Good as Gold*[3] (1979): the family again and Washington government, *God Knows*[4] (1984): religion, *Picture This*[5] (1988): art and philosophy, *Closing Time*[6] (1994): the metropolis, but also reprising and parodying much of his earlier career and those of some of his precursors and contemporaries (and therefore, to some extent, caricaturing the institution of literature).

His most consistent theme can consequently be seen to be the impact of institutions on what is conventionally taken to be 'the individual' – how thoroughly the supposed autonomy of that individual is compromised by far larger political and cultural forces. The implication throughout Heller's career is that institutions are responsible for turning what might have been individuals into two-dimensional characters, in fact into caricatures. Heller's historical works of the 1980s, *God Knows* and *Picture This*, insist that the shaping force of institutional thinking is an inescapable fact in human experience – that no individuals have ever existed outside or before institutions. What is especially clear from *Picture This*, however, is how much Heller considers that the rise of capitalism is responsible for the ills which his novels indict:

> whenever there is more money to be made from money than from anything else, the energies of the state are likely to be devoted increasingly to the production of money, for which there is no community need, to the exclusion of those commodities that are required for health, physical well-being and contemplation . . . There will be many who flourish in this environment of finance, and a great many more who can go straight to hell. (56)

The institutions that Heller anatomizes in his non-historical works can all be regarded as being most crucially shaped by the devotion to the production of money. The consequent impact of commodification on every area of human life underlies Heller's most brilliant writing, and lies behind his obsessive habit of inventing characters who are turned into things or broken into pieces.

The relationship between this critique of capitalism and the technique of caricature is best understood by reference to Walter Benjamin's discussion of Jean Grandville's treatment of the theme of commodification. He shows how, 'under Grandville's pencil, a way of designating goods which came into use around this time in the luxury industry, transformed the whole of Nature into specialities' and how, therefore, the work of this nineteenth-century French caricaturist reveals how commodification

> stands in opposition to the organic. It prostitutes the living body to the inorganic world. In relation to the living it represents the right of the corpse. Fetishism, which succumbs to the sex-appeal of the inorganic, is its vital nerve; and the cult of the commodity recruits this to its service.[7]

Michele Hannoosh very usefully expands these arguments in her book *Baudelaire and Caricature* by dwelling on the importance of allegory both in Baudelaire's theories of caricature and in the work of Grandville himself:

> allegory both speaks and reveals the fragmentation behind the alleged order and causal evolution of history; it represents and exposes the brutal separation of humanity from the world of nature; it embodies and uncovers the chaos behind the logic of the universe, the arbitrary nature of the systems humanity has constructed. Grandville's allegorical art, like Baudelaire's, expresses the fragmentation, commodification, and dehumanization of experience in capitalist culture.[8]

Heller also deploys allegorical effects linked to caricature, as I shall discuss later. He, too, is preoccupied with the unnaturalness of capitalism when he says that 'money follows different laws from the rest of nature, flows swiftly not where it is most needed but where it will increase fastest, and is without loyalty or nationality' (*Picture This*, 63). Jess Ritter points out one impact of this on Heller's fiction when he says that 'the Yossarian-Milo relationship concretely illustrates Norman O. Brown's thesis that capitalism is a sublimation of the death instinct, that money converts the world to matter (feces). Before a world of commodities to be accumulated, Eros withdraws.'[9]

Milo is a cartoon capitalist because exchange value in his dealings becomes everything: whatever use the commodities might have is erased in the labyrinth of buying and selling. As he says to Yossarian:

> I distributed my plum tomatoes in markets all over Pianosa under an assumed name so that Colonel Cathcart and Colonel Korn can buy them up from me under their assumed names at four cents apiece and sell them

> back to me the next day for the syndicate at five cents apiece. They make a profit of one cent apiece, I make a profit of three and a half cents apiece, and everybody comes out ahead. (*Catch-22*, 295)

The assumed names and the reference to the 'syndicate' are significant because they hint at how the obsessive emphasis on exchange erases individual humanity at the same time as use value. Milo's activities synecdochically satirize what capitalism does to individuals; this culture, and the army as its typical institution in *Catch-22*, produce what Judith Ruderman calls the 'deficit of character exhibited by many of the key figures in the book'. She sees this in its 'rhetoric of negatives, combined with caricature as a method of characterization'.[10] Heller uses the latter to deconstruct 'character' as it is conventionally understood. The characters in *Catch-22*, with the important exception of Yossarian, are all precisely *not* what characters in realist novels, with their liberal humanist assumptions, are supposed to be. They are not 'fully rounded', not charged with complex and vivid life – nor do they learn or develop. They are flat, they compulsively repeat themselves, they are all touched proleptically, one way or another, by death. Their humanity is repeatedly called into question by the way they are compared to animals or machines.

Milo himself is not invested with realist 'motives': he is driven by a reductive compulsion. Though he is supposedly the mastermind of the profitable exchanges he endlessly describes, he is effectively their helpless servant because he is unable to stop himself from facilitating them. The network of exchanges is so complex that it has a life-denying life of its own, with its own engine, and Milo is so bound up in their network that he could not extricate himself if he tried. That this is part of a self-perpetuating cycle is made explicit in Chapter 39 when Yossarian realizes that

> Every victim was a culprit, every culprit a victim, and somebody had to stand up sometime to try to break the lousy chain of inherited habit that was imperilling them all. In parts of Africa little boys were still stolen away by adult slave traders and sold for money to men who disembowelled them and ate them. (512)

This reference to slavery is connected to the frequent references to prostitution in the novel because both slaves and prostitutes are literally commodities. In this chapter it leads to Yossarian's search for the younger sister of Nately's prostitute girlfriend, a search in which Milo at first seems willing to join – until he learns about the traffic in illegal tobacco which is rife in Rome, and is compelled to participate in its smuggling. Though Yossarian pleads with him to continue searching for the twelve-year-old girl, Milo can only keep repeating the phrase 'Illegal tobacco', and is gripped by a 'blind fixation' (519).

Commodification turns people into things or machines, and the novel's caricatural imagery reflects this. The 'soldier in white' is the most extreme example, 'encased from head to toe in plaster and gauze' (16), reduced to the 'frayed black hole over his mouth', and 'filed next to the Texan' (17). That last verb conflates the effects of war with those of bureaucracy, an association characteristic of an army whose senior officers are preoccupied with formal correctness and due process and largely oblivious to the actual deadliness of what they are engaged in. It is Yossarian who keeps insisting on that deadliness, and with a childlike simplicity that resembles the tactical naiveté of the cartoonist deploying a defamiliarizing obviousness: 'strangers he didn't know shot at him with cannons every time he flew up into the air to drop bombs on them' (26). It is Yossarian, too, who asks the obvious questions about the soldier in white. While the Texan talks to him and the nurses maintain him, Yossarian questions whether he is really a person, and not the 'stuffed and sterilised mummy' (216) that he resembles: 'How the hell do you know he's even in there?' (217). When Yossarian goes on to declare that the soldier in white might actually be Mudd, who is otherwise known only as the dead man in Yossarian's tent, the link between the two reinforces the idea of being reduced to a thing. Just as the soldier in white is reduced to plaster and gauze, Mudd is reduced to the equipment he left behind before his first mission, when he was killed.

The name Mudd suggests that Heller's deconstruction of 'character' also has non-political meanings to do with the essential materiality of the human; these lead to Heller's reputation as an 'absurd' writer. He is preoccupied with the human condition after religion, and his work confrontationally lacks any spiritual dimension. This is most explicitly tackled in *God Knows*, in which the first-person narrator is King David and where the joke largely depends on the incongruity of such a crucial figure in Judaeo-Christian history being characterized in carnivalesquely secular terms – as a scheming soldier and politician, a vain and jealous author, and above all as a formerly virile and opportunistic (though now much less potent) lover. David and God are no longer on speaking terms and God's presence is symptomatically attenuated in comparison with the vivid worldliness of early Jewish society. The possibility that God is dead is raised several times and David himself complains about the spiritually reduced circumstances. He feels a kind of nostalgia for a time when God was closer and more sympathetic, but, given David's earliness in the tradition, this nostalgia is itself expressive of more deep-seated doubt – is it a characteristic of 'God' always to seem to loom less large than He did? David is impatient that the consolation that he is most allowed is sexual: in his old age even the beautiful Abishag the Shunammite, who is supposed to warm his bed, is cold comfort. As he says in the last sentences of the novel: 'Abishag my angel has risen from her chair and approaches without noise, wearing only a vivid scarf . . . I want my God back; and they send me a girl' (353).

The same frustrated spirituality is at times also close to the surface of *Catch-22*, whose most disturbing moments deal with the finality, and the physical messiness, of death. Heller draws vivid attention to the fact that dead soldiers are simply waste. The name Mudd, and that dead man's reduction to his belongings, both say this, as does the repeated scene, perhaps the key scene in the whole book, where Yossarian tries to comfort the dying Snowden. Just as the dead man in Yossarian's tent is mud, so Snowden is snow that either melts or is swept away, and is 'cold' – the word he says over and over to Yossarian as he dies. So, too, both are referred to in puns: 'His name is Mudd' and 'Where are the Snowdens of yesteryear?' (49). Here the slight linguistic frisson, with its self-conscious cleverness, suggests that the language itself is only cruelly self-regarding; it also dismisses any 'fully roundedness' that Mudd and Snowden may have had.

Apparent cruelty is one of the most conspicuous features of caricatural art, the origins of which lie in the horror and fear aroused by the sense that humans are merely corporeal. It is at its most conspicuous in Swift, in the revulsion evident in his description of enlarged human bodies, and in his invention of the Yahoos, in *Gulliver's Travels*. But it goes back at least as far as Hans Holbein's *Dance of Death* series of 1523–26, in which the figure of Death haunts all sections of society.[11] It is part of the anti-humanist impulse in caricature, but in Heller's case it is related also to satire of an official ideology which accepts a superficially religious outlook unthinkingly. Colonel Cathcart is under the impression that atheism is against the law (247) and when he asks the chaplain to lead prayers before each bombing mission he wants him also to erase any mention of death and even God in those prayers. Cathcart's version of religion is in fact entirely secular and only a way of endorsing ruling ideology by religious show.

The felt loss of a spiritual dimension leads to the felt loss, also, of the rich subjective life imagined by the realist novel. Except for Yossarian, the characters in *Catch-22* are all surface. The most extreme example is the soldier in white who is horrifyingly 'back' in Chapter 34 (460ff), but who is obviously a different person. Yossarian concedes that he has 'lost a few inches and added some weight' but insists, with everybody else, that he is 'the same one' (461). This is enough symptomatically to erase individuality but it is carried even further when Dunbar yells 'There's no one inside!' – yells that he is 'hollow inside, like a chocolate soldier'. This is connected to the description of Colonel Cathcart as 'his own sarcophagus' (240), combining associations of hollowness and death. Both are part of what might be called the 'unknown soldier' motif in *Catch-22*, which works oppositely to such monuments normally so-called, which memorialize the war dead. In this novel the motif embodies obliviousness and forgetfulness, and how war hurries the individuals caught up in it towards anonymity.

These ideas dominate the scene where Yossarian is forced to act out the death of a soldier for the benefit of that soldier's family, who arrived too late to witness the real thing. The premise of Yossarian's impersonation is exactly the anonymity evoked by the sarcophagus and plaster. As the doctor says, 'To a scientist, all dying boys are equal' (234). The dead man's parents are surreally willing to accept Yossarian as their son, and the dead man's brother is surreally willing to accept that his brother was called Yossarian. His mother's insistence on calling him Giuseppe is made, by a comic reversal, to seem like senile forgetfulness. The dialogue is handled with such deadpan economy that by the end of the scene it seems to create a Yossarian/Giuseppe hybrid:

> 'Giuseppe,' he began.
> 'Yossarian,' corrected the son.
> 'Yossarian,' said the father.
> 'Giuseppe,' corrected Yossarian.
> 'Soon you're going to die.' (238)

Taken as a whole, Heller's canon suggests that the draining away of the spiritual dimension was inevitable, but he does satirize the pretence that this has not happened, and the confrontational soullessness of his characters is part of that satire. What is much more the focus of his satirical anger, however, is the rapaciousness of the values which hold sway in the absence of spirituality, values which make one person literally exchangeable for another, where 'Yossarian' and 'Giuseppe' can simply swap places. This is also apparent in the letter that Doc Daneeka's wife receives from Colonel Cathcart:

> Dear Mrs., Mr., Miss, or Mr. and Mrs. Daneeka: Words cannot express the deep personal grief I experienced when your husband, son, father or brother was killed, wounded or reported missing in action. (436)

This parody of the register of official forms again mocks the blithely bureaucratic attitude of senior officers. The incongruity between this and the actual horror of war emphasizes how cheaply lives are being held because the register involves the listing of alternatives as though individual differences are irrelevant. The fact that Doc Daneeka is actually still alive enforces the point still further that individual lives are disregarded except for their exchange value: the letter's 'deep personal grief' satirizes the opposite responses – superficiality, impersonality and indifference.

Soldiers, like prostitutes and slaves, are as disposable as things or machines. Heller's deconstruction of 'character' works by dwelling not on presence and fullness of being, but on a felt absence, the sense of characteristics crucially lacking. This is why his characters are so often reduced, by simile or metaphor, to objects. Giuseppe's parents 'seemed made of iron and old, dark clothing' (235). Orr is 'as oblivious to fatigue as the stump of a tree, and almost as taciturn' (397). When Yossarian punches him, it is said to be 'like sinking his fists into a limp sack of inflated rubber' (192). Other characters are compared to animals so that the boundaries of the human are constantly called into question. Doc Daneeka is 'birdlike' (31) but he also has the features of a 'well-groomed rat' (32). The twitching veins behind Hungry Joe's eyes are like 'severed sections of snake' (70).

Because the subject of *Catch-22* is war, its deconstruction of character is literal: it dismantles expectations about, and constructions of, well-rounded complex life by placing characters on (and over) the threshold of death. Hungry Joe looks one morning like 'an eaten shell of a human building rocking perilously on the brink of collapse' (72). Although this is one character at a particular moment, it has more general significance. Like almost all the novel's imagery, it substitutes for those moments in realist novels in which character is defined in action, in interaction with other characters and in dialogue. These effects in *Catch-22* are so calculatedly non-realist that they say little that is specific about individual characters. The imagery that does the work of characterization appears to be used in a 'telling' (or diagetic) way, but what it tells is often more important for the themes of the novel as a whole than it is for the individuals to whom it is applied. There are so many characters in the novel that most of them are difficult to keep track of, which this itself contributes to the depersonalizing I have been describing. The imagery is also significantly unhelpful in distinguishing between the characters: in fact it contributes to the sense that they are all bewilderingly similar because of their depersonalizingly similar circumstances. Hungry Joe is like a collapsing hollow building, but this links him very closely to the 'sarcophagus' called Colonel Cathcart and the 'mummy' who is at least two soldiers encased in plaster and gauze.

Caricature, here, makes the human mingle problematically with the non-human so that they threaten to become interchangeable with each other. Death can make this happen literally. Snowden is the only character who has a significant interior, which is the 'eternal, immutable secret concealed inside his quilted, armor-plate flak suit'. These are the terms in which traditionally the soul might have been described, but it is actually Snowden's wounded intestines which are meant, and this 'secret' is then described 'spilling . . . all over the floor' (438). This memory recurs to Yossarian after the description of another piece of the human horrifyingly mingled with the non-human – Kid Sampson's legs, which have washed up on the shore. Heller is careful to refer to their skinniness, which suggests individuality, but also careful to locate them on the 'wet sand' and then apply his characteristically dehumanizing vision to them, to say they are rotting 'like a purple twisted wishbone'. He goes on to say that 'Now that bad weather had come, almost no one ever sneaked away alone any more to peek through bushes like a pervert at the moldering stumps' (437). This invokes exactly the same area as Norman O. Brown in his diagnosis of a deathly displacement of eroticism.

A more systematic aspect of characterization in *Catch-22* fixes its soldiers in rigidly repetitive patterns which make them resemble faulty machines. This can be more thoroughly understood by contrast with the organicist assumptions behind realist characterization where the stress is on 'natural' development and gradual unfolding. By contrast, the characters in *Catch-22* are self-reflexively constructed – their fictiveness is fully in evidence – and this also suggests how much the system makes them what they are. The emphasis on how often the characters do and say and think the same things over and over makes them mechanisms rather than organisms. Heller's point here is part again of the caricatural tradition, in this case that part which satirizes what Swift calls 'the mechanical operation of the spirit', where human behaviour is reduced to mindless, pointless and usually compulsive repetition. Its impact in a novel is especially marked because the novel's traditions lead its readers to expect linear progression.

Catch-22 reinforces this by its habit of stylistic circularity which includes, as David Seed has pointed out, the devices of 'inverted . . . or self-cancelling propositions' and 'echolalia',[12] which are connected to the leading idea of the whole book. 'The characters are trapped and the rhetorical expression of this entrapment is found in the circle, and specifically in Catch-22' (57). Heller crucially deploys this as his instrument of institutional caricature in this novel, for it enacts an authoritarian wielding of power which is divorced from any considerations of rationality, fairness or humanity. The crude starkness of Catch-22, as it is finally revealed, is its most telling point: 'Catch-22 says they have a right to do anything we can't stop them from doing' (514). Earlier in the book, Catch-22 has a kind of bogus sophistication; here its totally transparent part in the brutal operation of power makes the point that those without power are its reified and mechanistic puppets.

Circularity of this kind is important because it defines more precisely the nature of repetition in the novel. Repetition might imply substance, coherence, fullness: when however it is joined by self-cancellation it suggests the opposite. In this respect it resembles the déjà vu experienced by the chaplain, who hopes it might provide a clue to spiritual meaning. When Yossarian nods perfunctorily in response to the chaplain's question as to whether he has also experienced it, the chaplain hopes that the two of them together will 'rip away at last the voluminous black folds shrouding the eternal mysteries of existence' (341). But here as elsewhere spirituality is satirically undercut when Yossarian explains that déjà vu is 'just a momentary infinitesimal lag in the operation of two coactive sensory nerve centers that commonly functioned simultaneously' (341). Rhetorically this works like the passage where Snowden's interior is first treated as though spiritual and then revealed to be merely material. What the chaplain hoped was spirit turns out to be only mechanism.

In fact it turns out, symptomatically, to be a *faulty* mechanism, which is important because it is when mechanisms malfunction that the mechanistic is revealed as such. War as a subject works extremely well for Heller because it provides the perfect context for deconstructing the 'human' by portraying human beings as broken machines. His other novels are more problematic and mostly less successful (with the exception, to some extent, of *Something Happened*) partly because they pose him more difficulty in insisting on his characters as caricaturally compulsive mechanisms. This is because constructs in peacetime hold together much more consistently, so that the machinery of capitalism can often function so persuasively that it seems natural – not machinery at all.

Heller's insistence on systemic craziness is entirely persuasive in *Catch-22* because the madness of war is much easier to depict than the madness of the system in peacetime. What is crucial, however, is how much the former is used to represent the latter, so Heller has said

> I regard this essentially as a peacetime book. What distresses me very much is that the ethic often dictated by a wartime emergency has a certain justification, but when this thing is carried *over* into areas of peace . . . this wartime emergency ideology transplanted to peacetime, leads not only to absurd situations, but to very tragic situations.[13]

Catch-22 reveals how the political system displays itself more clearly *in extremis*, how war brings its mechanisms to the surface. This also provides justification for Heller's confrontationally simplistic method in the novel, which makes his army an enterprise and a bureaucracy whose business is to promote death. What in peacetime is a military-industrial *complex* can therefore be pinned down with deliberate *un*-complexity in the co-operation between Milo and the senior officers. That local alliance is treated as a cartoon synecdoche for the alliance of capital and the military, and then satirically and geographically expanded to incorporate the colonial conquests of Western capitalism, for Milo is not only 'the Vice-Shah of Oran' but also

> the Caliph of Baghdad, the Imam of Damascus, and the Sheik of Araby. Milo was the corn god, the rain god and the rice god in backward regions where such crude gods were still worshipped by ignorant and superstitious people, and deep inside the jungles of Africa, he intimated with becoming modesty, large graven images of his mustached face could be found overlooking primitive stone altars red with human blood. (302)

Milo is here mock-heroically compared to the Kurtz of Conrad's *Heart of Darkness*, but in a context that alludes to both the literal and metaphorical elements in Marx's theory of the fetish. The fetishizing of commodities can lead to Milo being deified so that his status as a god satirizes the human sacrifices that are made in the name of money, the scapegoats it requires. This brilliant passage also draws upon the traditional satirical theme of the 'world upside down' which echoes throughout *Catch-22*; that which is supposed to promote fertility promotes only death. This theme is connected to the novel's 'rhetoric of negatives' (Ruderman, 37) as when Major Major's father, who was a farmer specializing in alfalfa, is paid by the government for not producing it: 'The more alfalfa he did not grow, the more money the government gave him, and he spent every penny he didn't earn on new land to increase the amount of alfalfa he did not produce' (110). These two passages share a metaphorical concern with fertility which they both link to Biblical language. There are 'graven images' of Milo – enough in itself to insist that he is a false god – and Major Major's father counsels everyone 'As ye sow, so shall ye reap' (110). This enforces the novel's anti-spirituality, but more specifically it emphasizes the world's upside-downness, the sowing and reaping of nothingness, the worshipping of false gods.

Perhaps the most important satirical reversal of this kind in the novel is its reversal of sanity and madness. It imagines an institution that depends upon the madness of those who maintain it, which why Catch-22 is its dominant rule. Only madness can exempt a pilot from flying combat missions: to be exempted, however, he must ask to be exempted, and to ask is a sign of sane awareness of his danger, and therefore disqualifies him from exemption (62–63). This particular circularity works to perpetuate the institution, and means that madness is inscribed in that perpetuation. Crazy people are its normal citizens and sane people are its pariahs: the repetition of the word 'crazy', therefore, is another of the novel's key effects. It defamiliarizes sanity and madness: this is where Yossarian is particularly distinctive because he is complex enough to be involved in paradox. It is his sanity which makes him seem 'crazy': as Dr Stubbs says, 'That crazy bastard may be the only sane one left' (144). This is also the premise of Yossarian's scene with the psychotherapist Major Sanderson, who tells him that he is 'immature' because he has been 'unable to adjust to the idea of war' (384). Here Heller is writing in opposition to that sort of Bildungsroman that follows a callow character in the process of making a mature and necessary adjustment to the way of the world, as in for example Jane Austen's *Emma.* His point is that, since the way of the world is crazy, adjustment to it must be avoided at all costs, and Yossarian is exemplary in continuing to be antagonistic to and depressed by it.

It is for similar reasons that Heller has constructed, in *Catch-22*, a sort of anti-plot, which is another of its self-consciously faulty mechanisms. As David Seed says, the 'possibility that all events fit together is something which the reader only suspects and it is a combination of suspicion and uncertainty which gives the novel so much of its power. To overnaturalise or oversystematise its time-sequences would undermine this power' (44). Partly, this is a parody of the complex time-sequences invented by Conrad and Faulkner in modernist novels which enact epistemological confusion: there, the reader's attempt to piece together events in the right order anxiously evokes the difficulty of discovering patterns of meaning. That device is alluded to in *Catch-22* but crucially exaggerated because the reader's attempt to impose order is confrontationally frustrated. 'By fracturing the continuity of his narrative Heller forces the reader to examine the nature of its connections.' (Seed, 46)

How completely Heller is in charge of this, though, is open to question. The earliest reviewers of the book are now made to seem obtuse by all of Heller's major champions, but most of them thought the book a mess, and it is easy to see what they meant. The problem with criticism of postmodern writing is that it can easily make weaknesses seem like subversively avant-garde strengths. The structural messiness of *Catch-22* does fortunately reinforce its major themes and is never irrelevant enough to be seriously damaging, and maybe there is always some luck involved in the production of masterpieces. Heller should obviously be given the benefit of the doubt and to do otherwise runs the risk of speculative writing about authorial intention. On the other hand, the extent to which what might elsewhere be faults work as strengths in *Catch-22* might help to explain why there is such a gulf in quality between Heller's best two books and the rest of his canon. His other great book, *Something Happened*, is also *sui generis* in working like a short story expanded to enormous length. More of this later, but what is clear is that Heller's particular talents are unusual in a novelist. He seems actually to lack some of the skills which lesser novelists have in abundance – those required to organize abundant and discrete narrative components into persuasive and elaborately interconnected patterns, and to imagine complex psychological substance in a wide range of characters.

On the other hand he has more unusual skills, related to caricature and to some extent allegory, which have enabled him to write two of the greatest postwar novels. The fractured plot of *Catch-22* disables any possibility of character 'development': instead the characters and their actions are 'framed' as in the individual frames of a comic strip. Where the traditional novel and even most modernist novels are concerned with movement and change, there is a curious stasis in *Catch-22*, as though an animated cartoon were slowed down into its component stills. Instead of change and development there is repetition and aggregation. Again and again, though with slight variations, Doc Daneeka says 'You think you've got troubles . . . What about me?' (41, but see also 45, 55, 69, 222, 224). He is frozen in time like the characters in a Beckett play: 'What about me? My precious medical skills are rusting away here on this lousy island while other doctors are cleaning up. Do you think I enjoy sitting here day after day refusing to help you?' (222). His negativity is a widespread feature of the novel, and so is his self-enclosedness, but those qualities are especially conspicuous in a doctor.

Stasis and repetition dominate the characters of both Heller and Beckett, but that is partly because of their common ancestry in Dante. In *Picture This* Heller says that there will be many who flourish in a culture driven by money, but others 'who can go straight to hell' (56). In *Catch-22* the characters resemble the damned of Dante's *Inferno* in being condemned to endless frozenness or circularity. Like them, too, they are trapped in a living death, and systematically dehumanized by being compared to animals or things through what might be called vestigial allegory. The book's occasional habit of significant, but reductive, naming – Mudd, Snowden, Korn, Black, Aarfy, Scheisskopf – contributes to the allegorical atmosphere, suggesting that these are personifications rather than characters.

Sometimes the allegorical ideas are more sophisticated, as when Clevinger is described as looking 'like one of those people hanging around modern museums with both eyes together on one side of a face' (91). The cultural allusion is appropriate because Clevinger is an academic, but Cubist portraiture is more specifically relevant because it evokes the modern reassessment of human identity. It is very much of a piece with Heller's own art in its shift away from a three-dimensional humanity towards the grotesquely two-dimensional. Its link with allegory is made explicit when Clevinger's appearance is said to be generated by his 'predilection for staring fixedly at one side of a question and never seeing the other side at all' (91). This crude equation of physical appearance and character is one which realism knows to be untrue, and anyway this particular physical appearance is impossible. The allegorical point is made as a deliberate affront to realist expectations in order to satirize another narrowly institutional kind of thought which turns Clevinger into someone with 'lots of intelligence and no brains' (91).

A similarly allegorical effect is produced by the description of Milo, although this works by contrast with the monolithic single-mindedness portrayed in Clevinger. Milo's nose was 'always pointing away from where the rest of him was looking' and his moustache was 'unfortunate because the separated halves never matched. They were like Milo's disunited eyes, which never looked at the same thing at the same time. Milo could see more things than most people, but he could see none of them too distinctly' (86). Milo personifies capitalism, so parts of him pull away from the rest: his appearance embodies the contradictions and incoherencies of a system founded upon exchange value, a system in which, as Thomas Blues says, 'human life has no value except as commodity, as manipulable object'.[14]

Capitalism is itself a faulty mechanism and this sanctions Heller's deployment of allegory, which is self-evidently a mechanistic construct. Paul de Man's discussion of the theorizing of symbol and allegory by Romantic poets is useful for explaining this aspect of the idiom. He shows that the 'valorization of symbol at the expense of allegory' happens simultaneously to the rise of 'an aesthetics that refuses to distinguish between experience and the representation of this experience'.[15] The symbol is endowed with 'organic substantiality' (193). Moreover, 'the material perception and the symbolical imagination are continuous, as the part is continuous with the whole' whereas 'the allegorical form appears purely mechanical' (191).

The allegorical idiom, by contrast with the symbolic one, displays the fact that it is a construct. Clevinger's physical appearance is flatly fictive: Cubism is a style of painting that draws attention to its frame and its flat surface.

Moreover, the relationship between the faces and the characters of Clevinger and Milo is purely mechanical, and made mechanistically explicit. Effects of this sort, which mingle allegory and caricature, are present throughout *Catch-22*: Heller's comedy often arises from the cracks that open between representation and that which it represents.

These references to allegorical idiom prepare the way for the *Inferno*-like horrors of Chapter 39 which have reminded critics of Dante.[16] What these critics do not sufficiently stress is how much for Heller the modern inferno arises from capitalism, something which is more explicit in his 'sequel' to *Catch-22*, his 1994 novel *Closing Time*. Chapter 10 of that novel begins:

> At a rolltop desk many levels below, Mr. George C. Tilyou, the Coney Island entrepreneur, who'd been dead almost eighty years, counted his money and felt himself sitting on top of the world. His total never decreased. (122)

Heller's preoccupation with satirical reversal is again evident here. Tilyou's site is subterranean but he feels 'on top of the world'. What is most regarded, traditionally, as mutable is here eternal – he has 'disproved the experts' and succeeded 'in taking it all with him', his worldly goods have survived into the afterlife: 'His cash was indestructible and would always have value' (123). Tilyou knows that 'Without money life could be hell' (125) and the allusions to hell accumulate to suggest that that is the only genuine hell there is. The rest is literature. Barbara Gelb in her interview with Heller about *Closing Time* asks about

> your subterranean basement beneath the Port Authority Bus Terminal in Manhattan that obviously represents Hades, and . . . the terminal itself – with its hordes of homeless, its runaways, its depraved, and its Police Department holding pen – which represents a kind of limbo, if not hell.[17]

But Heller insists 'It's symbolic, yes, but it's also very real and present. The terminal *is* a hell on earth' (18). The inscription on the tycoon's tombstone, 'MANY HOPES LIE BURIED HERE' (123) alludes to Dante's line about abandoning hope but reverses it, for Tilyou's financial hope still survives in his subterranean kingdom. Similarly, in Chapter 18, which is called 'Dante', the now sixty-eight-year-old Yossarian avoids the beggars in the terminal: 'He had not thought American free-market capitalism had undone so many of its disciples' (276). So what is diagnosed in *The Waste Land* – by comparison with Dante's hordes of the damned – as a living spiritual death, is here traced by Heller to an economic source.

Closing Time is a depressing failure and all the more depressing because it contains some brilliant moments. Its narrative messiness serves no purpose at all, and, unlike the messiness of *Catch-22*, is not mitigated by a central thematic purpose. This novel's main usefulness is in the information it provides about Heller – it is partially autobiographical and contains a character called Joey Heller – and the gloss it provides on *Catch-22*, as some of the characters from that novel reappear and reflect on parts of its narrative. The points I have been making are confirmed when Sammy Singer and Yossarian remember how Milo bombed his own squadron, and Yossarian reflects that 'That's another one of the contradictions of capitalism' (420). It also confirms that this is the allegorical meaning of Milo's 'disunited' facial features.

Closing Time is self-consciously literary, with its allusions to Kurt Vonnegut, in particular, as the writer of *Slaughterhouse 5*, but also to Thomas Mann and to a location – as from *The Divine Comedy* – where writers live on after death (Hemingway, Faulkner, O'Neill, Joyce, James, Conrad, Dickens, etc.). All of this, combined with other metafictional elements, like the author's presence in his own text, is too much the common material of novels of the past twenty years, and all by now a bit stale. The best idea in *Closing Time* is that the chaplain (the one from *Catch-22*) now urinates tritium, or heavy water (66). This is very much something of Heller's own and briefly hints at how caricatural images of the *Catch-22* sort might be used in a peacetime context. It does suggest how a false wartime mentality can be imposed during peace, and also how much it is linked to the demands of capitalism, as when the powers-that-be try to exploit him as a resource. So when tritium goes up 'another two points' on the stock exchange, the chaplain is 'up in value and completely safe' (209).

The problem with such ideas is how difficult they are to develop and integrate into the patterns of development which novels usually invent. They so much resemble something delivered in a single frame like a caricatural portrait that they unavoidably carry with them a high degree of isolation and stasis. Heller solved this problem in *Catch-22* by multiplying their number and providing a unity of time and action which endowed them with their own dynamic, as well as an impressive level of thematic coherence. The setting of *Closing Time* in a late-twentieth-century New York by contrast evokes bewildering plurality – the very opposite of the obsessiveness of Pianosa where caricatural single-mindedness can thrive.

The chaplain urinating tritium suggests a number of resonant possibilities. It is clearly connected to the satire of commodification which also motivates much of the caricature in *Catch-22*. Even better, it is part of the central theme of *Closing Time*, that of impending apocalypse, which is developed by many of the cultural allusions in the novel – for example to *Dr. Strangelove* and to Wagner's *Gotterdammerung* – and to Milo's arms dealing. That seems entirely appropriate for Milo in the 1990s, but Chapter 6, in which he tries to sell his new bomber to the military, is so fatuous that it makes the reader lose faith in the whole novel at this early point. The chapter begins:

'You can't hear it and you can't see it. It will go faster than sound and slower than sound.'
'Is that why you say your plane is sub-supersonic?'
'Yes, Major Bowes.'
'When would you want it to go slower than sound?'
'When it's landing, and perhaps when it's taking off.' (71)

This is followed by a description of the circular chamber in which the meeting takes place, and then a colonel asks if the bomber will go faster than light:

'It will go almost as fast.'
'We can rev it up to go even faster than light.'
'There would be some increase in fuel consumption.' (71)

Such mere silliness reveals the risks that Heller has taken throughout his career (except in *Something Happened*). There are passages in *Good as Gold* that are tainted with this, though none that fail as abjectly. What this failure reveals is the nature of his success in *Catch-22* in scenes like the one where Colonel Cathcart tries to get the chaplain to lead prayers before bombing missions (244–49). This scene works brilliantly because its deviation from realism is so deftly and economically managed, and timed to increase with gradual relentlessness. It is carefully premised on a realist assessment of Cathcart's obsession with self-publicizing, his rigidly hierarchical mentality, unthinking authoritarianism and total incomprehension of genuine religious feeling. The caricatural input works by hyperbole that has its clear beginnings in these elements of realism, and works in the comic gap between the two. Hence his utter astonishment when the chaplain tells him that enlisted men pray to the same God as officers:

'And He *listens*?'
'I think so, sir.'
'Well, I'll be damned.' (248)

By contrast, Milo's sales pitch in *Closing Time* seems like mere fantasy, and also lacks that crucial sense of a defining context which helps us to understand and comically almost-believe Cathcart's indignant obtuseness.

It is also that lack of a defining context that makes the chaplain's surreal predicament less effective than such a brilliant idea warrants. In Heller's most successful novels that defining context is provided by a synecdochic (but caricatured) institution. *Catch-22* and *Something Happened* are held together in the end very rigorously by this method, *Good As Gold* not quite as rigorously, or successfully. *Closing Time* gesticulates in this direction and its hellish bus terminal is very promising material for this purpose in evoking an urban underworld. Its equation of the bus terminal's inhabitants with Dante's damned is also sanctioned by the vision of the city in Baudelaire and Eliot, and fits tellingly with Heller's caricatural method, since, as Baudelaire pointed out

> the city is . . . the space of the comic and caricatural – the monstrous, grotesque, terrifying, sinister, farcical, and fantastic. Like the comic, the Baudelairean city is satanic, demonic, infernal, the product and mark of a Fall. (Hannoosh, 300)

Also promising material is *Closing Time*'s reprise of the Catch-22 motif itself. When the chaplain first tries to find out what his problem is he is frustrated by a 'catch' in the Freedom of Information Act which says that government agencies are obliged 'to release all information they had to anyone who made application for it, except information they had that they did not want to release' (64–65). Then he is arrested. 'They read him his rights and said he did not have them' (65). Later in the novel, the Vice President says, 'I can't appoint a chief justice until I'm the President, and he can't swear me in until I appoint him. Isn't that a Catch-22?' (193). Heller's most famous invention satirizes the duplicity of the powerful; *Closing Time* shows how his catchphrase has entered the language but changed nothing, even though it has become part of the vocabulary even of those in power.

Ideas of this sort are highlighted in *Catch-22* by the centripetal tendency of its use of the presiding institution of the military, which also acquires much wider significance. When this technique works best it resembles that of the mature Dickens in novels like *Bleak House* and *Little Dorrit*, where caricatural versions of presiding institutions like the law and the prison service are used as a focus for a much wider satire of Victorian society: Dickens's 'Circumlocution Office' seems in particular to anticipate Catch-22. Dickens manages to organize huge stretches of diverse narrative material by referring them all back to the influence of these institutions, which thereby manage to be the source, paradoxically, of both social chaos and textual coherence. Heller achieves the same when he is writing at his best and seems explicitly aware of this in *Good As Gold*, where he actually invokes Dickens by name (378). In that novel the contradictoriness and self-serving, self-perpetuating small-mindedness of Washington government is given a deliberately Dickensian colour, as in the parade of capitalized titles in Chapter 6 (192–93): Governor, Deputy, Chief, Consul, Chancellor, Solicitor-General, Major, Coach, which reads like an explicit reminiscence of Chapter 21 of *Little Dorrit*: Bishop, Treasury, Horse Guards, Admiralty, Bar. Similarly, in *Closing Time* the lawyer Noodles Cook is given a Dickensian name and treated with Dickensian dismissiveness: he is 'a sneak and a snake' and 'could always be trusted to lie' (178).

One crucial difference, however, between Dickens and Heller is Heller's failure to take the power of these institutions seriously enough. This makes them too marginal in *Good As Gold* and *Closing Time* to exert sufficiently consistent influence to impose coherence on the narrative action. Institutional power is treated with such thorough contempt that those who wield it seem too entirely crass to be dangerous. It is then that the caricatural method becomes counter-productive. Much of the time after *Something Happened* Heller seems too preoccupied with being funny to make his comedy work to make meaningful points. There is also, though, a more fundamental reason why these problems arise in his work: although there is a Dickensian preoccupation in his novels with institutional power, Heller is actually much more sentimental than Dickens in his attachment to a form of individualism. Dickens insists that his institutions are inescapable in their influence on his characters' fates: there is no hiding-place in which to live a sequestered life entirely away from them. Heller seems to believe something similar *some* of the time but at other times he suggests that institutional power can be thoroughly escaped. That is most significantly and damagingly the message of the ending of *Catch-22*, although as David Seed points out this is the culmination of a belief present throughout: constantly in the novel, he says, 'Yossarian has been yearning to get to a sanctuary (Majorca, Switzerland and Sweden are mentioned), a symbolic point outside the cycle of corruption and death' (32). Actually, though, this yearning and its fulfilment, as Yossarian rows away towards an idea of 'Sweden' at the end, contradict what would otherwise be the most powerful message of *Catch-22*, which is that social institutions simply cannot be escaped in this way.

Robert Merrill asserts that, 'When he deserts, Yossarian finally does something that will affect the system: he ceases to serve it' (Merrill, 51). But this is disproved by one of the novel's most potent concepts, the 'unknown soldier' motif – the 'soldier in white' – which says that one soldier is simply exchangeable for another. Yossarian's desertion will have no impact whatsoever. Moreover, such sentimentalism made a version of *Catch-22* facilely attractive to 1960s America through its association with a sort of hippie 'drop-out' mentality, with which the novel as a whole is deeply at odds. Our next encounter with Yossarian, in *Closing Time*, as a sixty-eight-year-old, proves the point that rowing to Sweden is metaphorically as well as literally impossible, that there is no 'sanctuary' outside institutions. Having detailed Milo's horrifying implication in the 'contradictions of capitalism', Yossarian says 'That fucking Milo. I cursed him a lot. Now I work with him' (421).

* * *

By contrast with the belief in a sanctuary outside institutional structures, *Something Happened* presents those structures as inescapable: its relentless dwelling on their impact is the most important reason why the novel is so single-minded and thoroughly coherent. This is especially conspicuous given the tendency to narrative chaos elsewhere in his work. *Something Happened* is literally single-minded, moreover, being entirely dominated by its first-person narrator Bob Slocum, who is characterized by his obsessiveness and partialness of vision. As Heller said in his interview with George Plimpton:

> Bob Slocum tends to consider people in terms of one dimension, to think of people . . . as having a single aspect, a single use. When they present more than that dimension, he has difficulty in coping with them. Slocum is not interested in how people look, or how rooms are decorated, or what flowers are around.[18]

This accounts for the relationship between realist and caricatural effects in the novel. It is under the realist pressure of Slocum's significantly obtuse vision that his world is reduced and simplified in a series of specific and stark ways. The end product of this is a form of minimalism paradoxically extended to 569 pages. Kurt Vonnegut has characterized this most vividly:

> Slocum's sentences are so alike in shape and texture, from the beginning to the end of the book, that I imagined a man who was making an enormous statue out of sheet metal. He was shaping it with millions of identical taps from a ball-peen hammer. Each dent was a fact, a depressingly ordinary fact.[19]

Something Happened seems to be preoccupied with exploring Slocum's psyche in detail, and doing it with the most direct methods available, doing it with 'telling' or diagesis. Yet it leaves a paradoxical enigma, like a short story delivered solely through 'showing' or mimesis. This, too, is linked to a sense of something, or a number of things, crucially missing in Slocum himself, a sense of loss of affect, in particular, most chillingly in evidence in the matter-of-factness with which he treats his son's death. This is especially disturbing given that his son appears to be the only person he has genuinely cared about. The possibility that Slocum is mentally ill is intermittently present throughout and might explain the sense of something in him eerily not there.

This is where Yossarian and Slocum are most obviously opposites. Yossarian and his presiding institution define each other by contrast – the one sane, the other crazy. Slocum's subtle madness is seamlessly joined to that of his institution, and synecdochically represents it: it is all the more disquieting because it makes his madness invisible by hiding it in plain sight. The institutions in question – the army and corporate business – ought to be entirely different from each other, but are in fact shockingly similar. The army in *Catch-22* is satirized as a bureaucracy blithely ignorant of the horrors it is involved in: the business in *Something Happened* creates an atmosphere of fear and hatred which would be more appropriate in war.

It is here that caricature comes into its own because fear and hatred are the emotions which most often motivate it, especially in contexts where power relationships are involved. The frictions between Colonel Korn and Colonel Cathcart prefigure those in the office relationships in *Something Happened*: 'Colonel Cathcart was greatly indebted to Colonel Korn and did not like him at all. The two were very close' (241). The anxiety in both cases is that power structures create relationships characterized by closeness bordering on intimacy while at the same time ensuring that those relationships are spiked with hostility. *Catch-22* and *Something Happened* need to be understood together in order to recognize Heller's point about the uncanny resemblance of their power structures.

The clearest way of seeing this is to explore how those structures are reflected in their caricatural impact on their personnel. The pyramid of fear which Heller describes in the second chapter of *Something Happened* is implicit in *Catch-22*. It generalizes fear, but also mechanizes it. The latter point is important because the generalizing of fear might make it metaphysical and tragic like *angst*, and that has the tendency to ennoble the human by evoking existential courage in the face of the void. By contrast, the mechanizing of fear is anti-humanist and blackly comic:

> In the office in which I work there are five people of whom I am afraid. Each of these five people is afraid of four people (excluding overlaps), for a total of twenty, and each of these twenty people . . . (13)

This rhetoric of repetition continues (repeating 'each' and 'of' followed by a number) for the first paragraph, which carefully regulates its three sentences to lengthen so as to include an increasing number of people. This stresses how the office as an institution builds fear into its structure and ensures that fear is an automatic response.

So the employees of *Something Happened* – as much, shockingly, as the soldiers of *Catch-22* – are the puppets of an institutional structure. By contrast with existential *angst*, the fear they experience allows no scope for choice. They are machines and prone to breaking down. This has happened to two people in Slocum's department, one of whom 'hasn't been fixed too well . . . and will probably break down again soon' (22). The point is confirmed by Slocum's habit of thinking of people mechanistically, of turning them into statistics – the number who die of natural causes or of car crashes – and then of generalizing: 'The men all flirt. The women all respond, except for a few who are very religious or very dull . . .' (22).

The mechanistic as a caricatural concept is especially telling when applied to sexual behaviour because it is there that people most want to think of themselves as individual and spontaneous. Heller carefully insinuates the idea that sexual norms – including even those that relate to extra-marital sex – are being dictated by the company. 'This fiscal period,' Slocum says, 'I am flirting with Jane' (23). The satirized bureaucracy in *Catch-22* makes death happen to a set pattern and schedule – so that the soldier in white is 'filed' next to the Texan (17), and 'chalky people with aged blue lips' are 'dying on time'. In *Something Happened* a similar bureaucracy imposes an implicit manual of sexual behaviour, in which breasts are the 'starting place' (23) and Slocum has Jane 'scheduled' for just before the approaching convention. Slocum appears to have no choice therefore because the sex is made to seem like something that happens to him, whether he likes it or not, so that he says 'I seem to be doing most of my sleeping these days with girls who are slim and pretty and mostly young' (25).

Or so he claims. There is quiet humour here which is akin to the much more obvious kind when Colonel Cathcart refuses to waste his time and energy making love to beautiful women unless there is 'something in it for him' (*Catch-22*, 269). The free indirect speech in which this is delivered obviously mocks Cathcart. By contrast, Heller's deployment of the conventions of first person narration in Slocum's sentence questions how much his passivity in this context is actually a kind of 'bad faith' in which he pretends not to have choices available to him which could in fact – if he made them – change the whole tenor of his life. This is related to the central motif of the novel, whose title implies the question of how much we have things happen to us, and how much we make them happen. It is certainly the former that Slocum always insists on; he asks, of his wife and himself, in elegizing their lost youth: 'What happened to us? Something did. I was a boy once, and she was a girl, and we were both new' (119). Similarly, he is convinced that 'Something bad is going to happen' to his son (230–31). This attitude erases any sense of human agency from the events of human lives.

Heller questions whether human beings are shaped in advance by institutional structures, or have freedom to operate within them – whether they might have possibilities of choice which they refuse, thereby confirming the power of those institutions. This is much more subtle and persuasive than the attempt to imagine a kind of 'sanctuary' outside them because it insists that the change would have to come from within. The ambiguities that inevitably arise from first-person narration by a dubious character like Slocum work brilliantly to enact the complexities that arise in the relationship between institutions and their personnel – for those ambiguities everywhere question whether things are happening to the characters, or whether those characters make them happen. This amounts to an interrogation of individualism, and its limits, as opposed to the sentimental assumptions about it which damage his work elsewhere.

It is that interrogativeness which endows the caricatural imagery and language of *Something Happened* with a complexity which belies their usually simplistic tendency. In focusing on a character involved in corporate business and the routines of his middle-class life (where nothing much seems to happen), Heller has chosen the territory of stereotype and cliché. Reviewing the novel, Kurt Vonnegut referred to its 'rewriting of this written-to-death situation' (1). The novel's point therefore is both that Slocum is an individual – which defamiliarizes the stale material – but also that individuals like him really can be thoroughly absorbed by the corporate demands imposed on them. This is part of what Vonnegut calls its 'utter hopelessness', a pessimism so complete 'that it can be called a daring experiment' (2).

The unreliability of first-person narration by characters treated with authorial scepticism suggests that Slocum may have the power, in fact, to make things happen. The novel's point, however, is that he does not use that power. The control that is consequently exercised over him by his work also ensures that his psyche, and therefore also his private life, are structured in an alienating way. So the family, which might be a form of sanctuary outside institutional structures, and so be the site where individualism can be exercised, becomes instead just another institution. This makes it shockingly – again – not different enough from the army and corporate business. It becomes yet another structure, even a hierarchy, which combines closeness and hostility. Slocum has a wife, a daughter and two sons: it is these latter two who are crucially the only ones not to understand power structures. One of them, Derek, cannot understand because he is retarded. The other, called 'my little boy' throughout, cannot understand because of his innocently generous nature which distinguishes him from everybody else in the book. His consequent incomprehension of competition causes him endless problems and infuriates others – as, for example, when he refuses to run competitively (238ff, 314ff). Given the relentlessness of the power structures which the book indicts, he is made shockingly vulnerable by what is essentially his goodness. This means that he baffles other people, so that when he offers his cookie to another boy that boy assumes he is playing some kind of complex power game (310). The novel's pessimism is confirmed above all by its being this poignantly loveable character who is killed.

Slocum's 'little boy' has a representative significance also as a pre-institutional self, before the shades of the prison-house – to put it in Wordsworthian terms – encroach on him. Slocum certainly identifies with his son in this way and invokes the idea that every adult still contains inside them the child that they were: 'hiding inside of me somewhere, I know (I feel him inside me. I feel it beyond all doubt) is a timid little boy just like my son who wants to be his best friend and wishes he could come outside and play' (231). This boy, however, is now 'irretrievable' (307) and Slocum's son is shown to be starting the process that will make this happen:

> My boy likes to laugh and would be laughing and kidding jauntily all the time if there were not so many of us in the atmosphere surrounding him to inhibit and subjugate him. I have this constant fear something is going to happen to him. (342)

Something Happened is in a sense an extended elegy for the loss of this genuine self that should have grown into a fully mature and genuine adult, on a Romantic model of organic growth. Slocum, instead of going through this process, has been psychically crippled and so resembles not the son who dies, but the retarded son who survives. This is why he imagines the adult Derek as 'a thickset, clumsy, balding, dark-haired retarded adult male with an incriminating resemblance to a secret me I know I have inside me and want nobody else ever to discover' (391).

Derek is a living caricature; he is a 'simulacrum'. But then so too is his father. Even though his psyche is presented in such exhaustive detail, this evokes not a rich inner life, but an echoing hollowness; not an exploration of realist 'motive', but mere compulsiveness; not a complex organism but a faulty mechanism. Slocum is compelled to phone up Ben Zack, who works in the office where he worked as a young man, and ask about his first love, Virginia, who gassed herself to death. He does so under false pretences, claiming for example to be 'a former eastern inter-collegiate boxing champion from Duke University' (489). His compulsion gets intertwined with what seems Heller's authorial compulsion to test the boundaries of humour – to write comedy and then push it further and further until it becomes sickeningly not-comedy. At the start of Heller's career he has Yossarian point out that his combat situation 'wasn't funny at all. And if that wasn't funny, there were lots of things that weren't even funnier' (26). In *Closing Time*, he has his characters repeatedly say 'I don't find it funny' (145, but see also 162, 171, 267, 530). What Slocum does may start as a sort of practical joke, but its compulsiveness pushes it close to madness: 'It did not feel like a joke. It felt like a wilful, destructive crime, a despicable act of obscene perversion. It felt thrilling and debasing' (489).

Compulsion like this constitutes the mechanizing of desire and makes the self not itself; it leads to Slocum's equation with Derek, and his habit of mimicry, of 'acquiring the characteristics of other people' (72) which Judith Ruderman relates to his 'compulsion to repeat' (Ruderman, 54) and which Slocum traces to his identity problems: 'I don't know who or what I really am' (74). This is why he considers his morbid compulsion [to be] 'a double agent' (493), someone foreign inside him. It turns him into someone, or even something, else: 'fungus', 'asbestos', 'rock' (492).

Not to be in possession of your own desire is a profound alienation; the caricatural imagery of *Something Happened* insists that this alienation is imposed by the institutional structures which shape the pattern of Slocum's life. These are the beginnings of the preoccupation with the intertwining of sexuality and power which characterize his novels after *Something Happened.* Slocum feels that he is not empowered by his sexuality but made vulnerable by it; he says that he never felt it as an instrument of domination, that he has always felt 'need, not power' (365). This is why he says 'Our dicks are so pathetic' (364) which initiates an important pattern in Heller's work where the penis is treated as a metonymy for male powerlessness. Later in this novel, Slocum says, 'How would top management feel about someone in middle management who'd been punched in the jaw and felt sexually impotent? Not good, I think' (422). *Good As Gold* takes Lyndon Johnson's remark 'I've got his pecker in my pocket' as its epigraph, equates a 'successful career' with the serial pocketing of peckers (196) and takes Gold's ability to commit adultery successfully as a prerequisite for his rise in the Washington establishment. *Closing Time* calls the Vice President 'The Little Prick' (11) and equates a cop's gun and badge with his cock and balls (405).

The dick, the pecker and the prick are cartoon penises. As metonymies of caricatural maleness they indicate the extent to which (masculine) desire and identity are politically constructed. Heller's sensibility is too relentlessly masculine, too preoccupied with sexual conquest, for example, and too bounded by straight masculine values (as in the tedious homophobia of *God Knows* where David seems obsessed with disproving any gayness in his love for Jonathan). He is brilliant, however, in his evocation of what happened to males of his generation in their interactions with institutional structures, how their identities got mechanized and reified. Slocum is the most extreme example of this. Other people are so flat to him, so reduced to a 'single use' (Plimpton, 3) that in his dreams they are thoroughly dehumanized. They are made of 'varnished glass wax'; they are ghouls, midgets and carcasses. He himself is frozen and transformed into 'an illustrated flow chart' (401), a simulacrum of himself that represents his business use for his company and his fictive use for Heller.

3 *Philip Roth's Vulgar, Aggressive Clowning*

Philip Roth's writing at its best is charged with the energy of confrontation and aggression, and bristles with hatred and fear. This makes him a satirist of a flagrant and caricatural kind; but it is necessary also to acknowledge his talents for realism and highly elaborated narrative in order to place the satirical element in its accurate context. The co-existence of these apparently contradictory elements is explained, partly at least, by Roth's impatience with stereotypical thinking: this leads him to use caricatural techniques against caricatural narrow-mindedness. Paradoxically, therefore, it could be said that it is Roth's preoccupation with the 'real' which makes him deploy non-realism; but it is also clear that he is drawn to confrontation and aggression for their own sakes. These conflicting motives are in evidence when he describes himself as a young man reading *The Wings of the Dove*:

> I would find myself as transfixed by James's linguistic tact and moral scrupulosity as I had ever been by the coarseness, recklessness, and vulgar, aggressive clowning with which I was so taken during those afternoons and evenings at 'my' booth at the corner candy store. As I now see it, one of my continuing problems as a writer has been to find the means to be true to these seemingly inimical realms of experience that I am strongly attached to by temperament and training – the aggressive, the crude, and the obscene, at one extreme, and something a good deal more subtle and, in every sense, refined, at the other.[1]

Roth's writing is most successful when it fluctuates between these two 'realms' rather than when it settles in either one of them too firmly. *When She Was Good* (1967) and *Our Gang* (1971) are his least successful novels because they are so single-minded in their modes – the former realist and the latter satirical. *Our Gang* is a cartoon version of Richard Nixon's government; it is the more interesting of the two because of its links to subtler cartoon effects insinuated throughout most of Roth's fiction. Its author's own remarks on it also reveal his awareness of the relevance to him of the tradition I discuss throughout this book:

> the same techniques of distortion apparent in the work of Herblock, Jules Feiffer, and David Levine – or, to invoke the names of giants, in the satirical drawings of Hogarth and Daumier – are operating in prose satire. Distortion is a dye dropped onto the specimen to make vivid traits and qualities otherwise only faintly visible to the naked eye. (*Reading Myself*, 49)

Roth's realism and satire share a desire to uncover the truth of postwar American social and political history. This is brilliantly reflected in his three novels of the 1990s (*Sabbath's Theatre* (1995), *American Pastoral* (1997) and *I Married A Communist* (1998)),[2] which will be my main focus. It is muted, however, in his metafiction of the mid-1970s to mid-1980s, novels such as *My Life As A Man* (1971), *The Professor of Desire* (1977), and *The Counterlife* (1986). For this reason, these are comparatively unpersuasive: Roth's talents, though extensive, are not best suited to the multiplying of these self-reflexive labyrinths.

The striking effectiveness of Roth's most recent novels may be partly attributable to his absorption of the lessons of metafiction and their incorporation into his more personally congenial modes of story-telling. *Sabbath's Theatre* takes puppetry as its controlling metaphor and connects it to the habit of its hero, Sabbath, of dramatizing himself in a series of stereotypical roles. This raises the metafictional question of the relationship between this self-dramatizing and Roth's working of this character, and the other characters, as authorial puppets. More suggestively than in his obsessively metafictional novels, however, this questioning of 'character' is linked to a central preoccupation in the caricatural tradition with whether or not human beings are fundamentally just glorified machines. So the novel's occasional references to stream of consciousness – 'the way J. Joyce pretended people thought' (198) – are largely used to demonstrate that 'The mind is the perpetual motion machine. You're not ever free of anything' (297).

The depiction of the communist Johnny O'Day in *I Married A Communist* similarly merges metafiction and caricature – this time in order to satirize the impact that his 'zealotry' (223) has had on his appearance and personality. Here the machine metaphor is joined by an animal metaphor – perhaps even more important in the caricatural tradition. O'Day is 'constructed like a heron' but his physique is 'a filament of steel, enviably narrow' and mirrors his ideology which is 'tool-like and contoured like the edgewise silhouette of the heron's fuselage' (228), so that he becomes a hybrid of bird and machine. So he is doubly inhuman; this is reinforced even further by the metafictional idea that 'His story has been made up beforehand. He has no choice about anything' (228). The combination of these two sentences reveals how much the stylistic preoccupations I have been outlining arise from existentialist assumptions that Roth shares with most of his American generation. In his case this is most pressingly an expectation – ultimately frustrated as I will show – that people should be authors of themselves and so manfully resist conventional tendencies that lead to life becoming a predictable and stereotypical narrative. Roth's concern here is gendered, often explicitly so, and may also be racially located as a preoccupation with *menschlikeit* which, as Tony Hilfer has pointed out, is a consistent preoccupation of Jewish American literature. A '*mensch* is neither a creature reduced to its material needs nor a divinity able to alter a world to its heart's desire'.[3] However, it is consistent with Roth's determinedly anti-stereotypical thinking that he should above all question what might most limit him – Jewishness and maleness. The restless interrogation of these themes is one of the key motives of his work.

It is a sign of Roth's determination to subvert expectations in the process of this interrogation that in *The Ghost Writer*[4] (1979) it is a young woman who embodies *menschlikeit* far more thoroughly than any of the men. She is Anne Frank who may or may not have grown up into Amy Bellette who rejects the Frank identity because it involves being, not a person, but a personification: 'I was the incarnation of the millions of unlived years robbed from the murdered Jews. It was too late to be alive now. I was a saint.' (108) To reject this identity is to refuse to be, like Johnny O'Day, a story made up beforehand: it is to choose complex life as opposed to the deathliness of representation. There is an implied rebuke in this to E. I. Lonoff, the ageing Jewish writer who is visited by the young Nathan Zuckerman – the fictive persona Roth adopts here and then repeatedly ever afterwards. Lonoff is a potential role model for Zuckerman and is certainly exemplary in his dedication to his art, except that his dedication is so thorough it seems to have terminally desiccated him. There is mutual attraction and even love between Lonoff and Bellette but Lonoff is too ascetic to act upon it.

The style which Roth chooses for the Lonoff part of *The Ghost Writer* is designed self-reflexively to make its own point. This is Roth in Jamesian mode, a point confirmed by its explicit and lengthy allusion to James's story 'The Middle Years', which itself concerns a terminally fastidious novelist and a young doctor who eschews a fortune because of his infatuation with the novelist's work. Roth's treatment of Lonoff is characterized by Jamesian linguistic tact and moral scrupulosity which are appropriate for respecting, while at the same time being anxious about, Lonoff's self-denial, which has helped him to write highly regarded books but is also self-regarding. The scenic form which Roth deploys here shows that Lonoff thinks of himself as a sort of martyr to his art who has erased all kinds of turbulence from his life in order endlessly to refine his sensibility and perfect his sentences. It reveals how his self-denial leads his wife to think of herself as merely one of his inescapable duties, and leads him to arouse Amy Bellette's passion but refuse to satisfy it.

The mimetic realism of Roth's style in the Lonoff passages allows him the tact and subtlety to define all the moral ambiguities which arise from this situation. What the next Zuckerman novels make clearer, however, is that

Roth is leaving this manner behind and making the breakthrough into irresponsibility. In *Zuckerman Unbound* (1981), Zuckerman 'felt stultified writing "proper responsible" novels and living behind his "drearily virtuous face" '(221); in *The Anatomy Lesson* [5] (1983) he has torn himself loose 'from the moral propriety of his early books' (315). For Zuckerman this involves the writing of *Carnovsky*, for Roth the writing of *Portnoy's Complaint* (1967) which is still his most famous novel. In *The Ghost Writer* the element of vulgar, aggressive clowning is muted, though the irreverent treatment of the Anne Frank story hints at it obliquely. Roth is aggressively determined to make it exemplary that Amy Bellette refuses to make psychological capital out of that story: his aggression explains why some of his early readers could consider him anti-semitic.

There is certainly a satirical component in Roth's metafictional treatment of Anne Frank. The Jewish girl in Amsterdam really existed but her ambiguous presence in *The Ghost Writer* indicates how much she has been fictionalized by her appropriation for political ends. On a small scale, Lonoff performs a similar act of appropriation: he thinks that Amy Bellette impersonates Anne Frank in order to 'bewitch him'. His narcissism leads him to believe it would require a figure of such power to unsettle his moral scruples – the unreality and futility of Lonoff's fastidious detachment turns life into literature with finicky self-consciousness.

He is not as different, therefore, as he may first appear from Felix Abravanel, the other senior Jewish writer and possible role model for Zuckerman in *The Ghost Writer*. What principally differentiates them is that Abravanel is charged with caricatural energy and leads a glamorous life. But both – disturbingly, given that they are writers – are rigidly self-enclosed. Abravanel's charm is 'like a moat so oceanic that you could not even see the great turreted and buttressed thing it had been dug to protect' and he reminds Zuckerman 'of a radio tower with its tiny red light burning high up' (42).

The juxtaposition of this mode with the realist discretion and scenic form of the Lonoff passages defines the two modes by contrast. The caricaturing of Abravanel may seem crude, but it works particularly well in combination with that other method by introducing a shift in narrative rhythm – a distinct quickening of pace – and a shift from oblique implication to energetic directness. The Abravanel imagery evokes him as almost aggressively withdrawn: where Lonoff lives in seclusion, Abravanel carries his seclusion around with him. The anxious defensiveness of both writers may well have racial origins and covers them with the appearance of thorough assimilation. Lonoff is the butt of jokes for having married a New England aristocrat and for living in the '*goyish* wilderness of birds and trees' (4). Abravanel's equivalent of this is his *goyish* style, and it is similarly incongruous. His head is a radio tower because as a writer he both receives and transmits, but as a Jewish writer of his generation he is deeply undermined by insecurity: the radio tower is 'at the edge of a precipice' (43). This leads him to wear 'a five-hundred dollar shantung suit', but the overall impression is still one of a defensive but transparent facade so that he seems like 'somebody's stand-in' because of his obvious contradictoriness: 'fully Semiticized little transistor on top, terrific clothes down below' (43).

Roth's caricature appears simple and even simplistic, but it can be very complex in its effects – not least because he is so self-conscious about it as both a device and a pitfall. He uses the word repeatedly (as my quotations will prove) so that he might be said to invent a kind of meta-caricature, a form of caricature that reflects upon itself. He has been, throughout his writing career, a theorist about fiction-writing as well as a practitioner – most obviously in his essays collected in *Reading Myself and Others* but also inside his novels – his metafictional narratives involve him in discoursing about the relationship between the fictive and the real.

The other source of Roth's meta-caricature is his awareness of racial stereotype as a source of caricature as pitfall. This must have been part of his own experience from early in his life, but it is continually present as an issue in his fiction, most pressingly because Roth has himself been accused of perpetuating such stereotypes. In his essay 'Writing About Jews' he describes how one of his earliest stories, 'Defender of the Faith' (which appeared in *The New Yorker* in April 1959) was attacked for confirming an 'anti-Semitic stereotype' in its portrayal of Sheldon Grossbart, who tries to persuade his immediate superior, Nathan Marx, to do him favours by pleading their shared racial background. In fact the story shows how Jews are led to this kind of mutual aid by their collective suffering of persecution, and, as Roth says,

> If people of bad intention or weak judgment have converted certain facts of Jewish life into a stereotype of The Jew, that does not mean that such facts are no longer important in our lives, or that they are taboo for the writer of fiction. Literary investigation may even be a way to redeem the facts, to give them the weight and value that they should have in the world, rather than the disproportionate significance they obviously have for some misguided or vicious people. (*Reading Myself*, 158)

Roth's point about redeeming the facts is crucial because it indicates how his fiction defamiliarizes stereotypes: instead of pretending that there is no truth in the caricature, Roth reveals the extent of its truthfulness and the background that explains it. Given the incomprehension with which the Jewish soldiers are regarded by the army, it is unsurprising that Grossbart should turn to a fellow Jew to use what power he has to compensate for that incomprehension, and then to push it beyond mere compensation.

'Defender of the Faith' is in Roth's realist mode which is used, as in the depiction of Lonoff in *The Ghost Writer*, to suggest moral ambiguities. Roth has got himself into hotter water when he has treated racial issues in his more irreverent mode, and been repeatedly reminded – as Shuki reminds

Zuckerman in *The Counterlife* – that 'the Jews aren't there for [his] amusement or for the entertainment of [his] readers'.[6] He has also been upbraided for ignoring the gravity of the situation. Zuckerman is cautioned by Shuki, who is a history academic, that 'every word I write about Jews is potentially a weapon against us, a bomb in the arsenal of our enemies, and that, largely thanks to me, in fact, everyone is now prepared to listen to all kinds of zany, burlesque views of Jews that don't begin to reflect the reality by which we are threatened' (161).

Irving Howe is the most conspicuous of Roth's detractors with this sort of complaint against him. His attack so wounded Roth that he appears in *The Anatomy Lesson* under the guise of Milton Appel, who accuses Zuckerman of producing 'tendentious junk' and insists that 'No Jews like Zuckerman's had ever existed other than as caricature' (344). Later in the novel Zuckerman claims to be the editor of a pornographic magazine called *Lickety Split* and that his name is Milton Appel. Here the comedy arises out of gratuitousness, out of the sheer irrelevance of this as an attack on Howe – except perhaps as a rude gesture aimed at Howe's humourlessness. The charge of 'tendentiousness' is one that Howe specifically makes in his essay 'Roth Reconsidered' where he says that it is this which mars much of Roth's fiction; he sees it resulting from a first-person narrator like Neil Klugman or Alex Portnoy being allowed to swarm 'all over the turf of his imaginary world'.[7] He also sees it as a result of a failure in 'literary tact' arising from Roth's habit of 'exposing' rather than 'revealing' a character (77). Howe's terms indicate his own (apparently unexamined) literary assumptions: he expects narrative fiction to conform to the tenets of Jamesian realism. He would clearly be happier with the mode of the Lonoff depiction than that which 'exposes' Abravanel, and evidently therefore sees caricature as inevitably a pitfall and never a legitimate device. To have Zuckerman impersonating a pornographer called Appel is to stress that narrative fiction is *fictive*, and to enforce the point with confrontational tactlessness.

What Howe ignores is that all narrative fiction is tendentious – it is only that some kinds of fiction display their tendentiousness more than others. Roth has become less and less interested in 'tact' as he has become more and more political. This is partly a role that has been forced on him because the success of his fiction, especially *Portnoy's Complaint*, has turned him into a public figure, and being a famous Jew makes him political whether he likes it or not, makes 'Philip Roth' a story made up beforehand, which is why Roth invents Zuckerman. So Milton Appel, during the Arab-Israeli conflict of 1973, turns to Zuckerman to write in support of the Jewish state (352).

One less predictable use which Roth has made of his fame is his promotion of writers, like Milan Kundera, from eastern Europe; this also may have influenced his writing towards exploring the impact of the state on individuals. Even here, though, Roth portrays himself, as Zuckerman, being pursued by a public version of himself as stereotypical Jew. In *The*

Prague Orgy[8] (1985) he is accused – because he wants to smuggle out of Czechoslovakia some stories written in Yiddish – of being a 'shallow, sentimental American idiot Jew who thinks there is virtue in suffering' (551). It is crucially characteristic of Roth, however, that he does not simply dismiss this charge but takes it seriously enough to ponder its actual psychological significance: 'Is this a passionate struggle for those marvellous stories or a renewal of the struggle toward self-caricature? Still the son, still the child, in strenuous pursuit of the father's loving response?' (557). The stereotype would have no power if it were not a version, simplified for political ends, of the truth: Zuckerman cannot understand himself thoroughly unless he can work out to what extent he is tangled up in this response to Jewish suffering, as Nathan Marx is tangled up in his ambiguous responses to Sheldon Grossbart's pleas for favour.

Zuckerman's direct questioning of his own motives, and his self-reflexive concern with characterization, are breaches of the realist 'tact' favoured by Irving Howe. However, it is only by acknowledging the propaganda power of racial caricature that Roth is able to redeem the facts behind the stereotypes. His repeated, often blackly comic, references to those stereotypes give him the freedom to weigh the impact of Jewish suffering on the psychology of individual Jews. Roth's readers know how knowing he is about Jewish platitudes, and how unsentimental he is, and it is this which makes so shocking and memorable his account of Zuckerman's mother inexplicably writing the word 'Holocaust' when asked to write her name. She has only been known previously to write out recipes and thank-you notes and knitting instructions: now a brain tumour has erased all the words she has – other than one she has never been known to say aloud.

The emergence, under these circumstances, of the word 'Holocaust' hints that the word and its associations have led a buried life under the surface of Mrs Zuckerman's domestic routine. Its substitution for her name suggests how much the identification of individual Jews with collective Jewish suffering affects their sense of identity. Another major Rothian preoccupation is at work here, one with a direct link to his exploration of the boundary between the caricatural and the 'real' – the notion of reductiveness. Zuckerman's mother is frighteningly reduced by her brain tumour to something alien to her and far more monolithic than her previous self. This is also what happens in racial stereotyping, as Roth points out when he describes a cartoon he had seen in the British newspapers when he was living in London during the Lebanon war. This featured Menachem Begin as a 'big-nosed Jew' standing on top of a heap of Arab corpses: 'Purportedly a caricature of Menachem Begin, then prime minister of Israel, the drawing was, in fact, a perfectly realistic, unequivocal depiction of a kike as classically represented in the Nazi press.'[9]

It is such knowingness that leads Roth to use caricature to deconstruct caricatural simplification – how individuals get caricatured, but also how they caricature themselves. The object of his satire is as much stereotypical behaviour as it is stereotypical labelling; he has aroused hostility from Jews because he has implied that they sometimes deserve to be stereotyped because (like everybody else) they often think and act in narrowly predictable and unthinking ways. In his early stories the Jews live in 'Woodenten' because their attitudes are wooden; in 'The Conversion of the Jews' the rabbi is called 'Binder' because his teaching imposes unthinking restrictions. His response is inadequate when he is challenged by a thirteen-year-old boy called Oscar Freedman who wants to know how the Jews can be 'The Chosen People' when the Declaration of Independence insists all men are equal.[10] At the climax of the story Oscar threatens to throw himself off the synagogue roof unless Binder admits that if God can do Anything he could create a child without intercourse.

This preoccupation has led to some of Roth's funniest writing. So in *I Married A Communist* – forty years after these early stories – Murray Ringold defines a 'taxonomy of Jews':

> the I – love – everyone – deeply Jews, the I – was – never – so – moved Jews, the Momma – and – Poppa – were – saints Jews, the I – do – it – all – for – my – gifted – children Jews, the I'm – sitting – here – listening – to – Itzhak – Perlman – and – I'm – crying Jews, the entertaining Jew of perpetual punning, the serial Jewish joker. (164)

The key points are that the author of this Jewish taxonomy is himself Jewish, and that it is identified by one Jewish character for the amusement of another. Caricature as a political weapon is interrogated when it is deployed or parodied by its victims, and it can even be turned back on its racist perpetrators and used against them. In *The Counterlife* Roth seizes gleefully upon the image of Menachem Begin precisely because he looks so much like a cartoon Jew: Roth asks rhetorically who could be better 'to make it perfectly clear to everyone that what matters now isn't what goyim think but what Jews do' (61). What is crucial here is that the meaning of the caricature is radically changed when it is opened up from within and lived from the inside. This is the most significant effect produced by the narrative device of *Portnoy's Complaint* (1967) where the central character declares himself to be living his life 'in the middle of a Jewish joke',[11] declares that he is the son in the Jewish joke – '*only it ain't no joke!*' (37).

Portnoy's Complaint presents itself as an extended joke and contains numerous jokes within it, but it is also the narrative of an analysand speaking to his analyst, Dr Spielvogel. It parodies these forms: both are oral discourses and therefore opposed to the textual strategies of the realist novel, opposed to its emphasis on the balanced and rational distribution of authorial sympathies and the tactful and gradual revelation of character. Their oral forms give a much more spontaneous and improvizatory quality to *Portnoy's*

Complaint whose tendency to exaggeration and fantasy is appropriate to this orality, which might be compared to the oral origins of magic realism. Both jokes and the 'talking cure' tend towards a kind of 'exposure' which is inimical to subtlety and tact of the kind favoured by Irving Howe. The joke aspect may imply a formulaic structure and reductive simplification, and both these elements are drawn upon. To this extent it may seem at odds with the complexities of psychotherapy, but this is part of the point of Roth's collision of these two kinds of talk which works analogously to his characteristic collision of caricature and realism. However, the idea of the joke is also related to the stand-up practice of Jewish comedians of the 1950s and after, comedians such as Lenny Bruce and Mort Sahl who expanded its boundaries to include material which radically diversified its potential in the direction of social and psychological observation. They also combined this with kinds of fantastical elaboration available to them by virtue of their own version of oral form.

Nonetheless, 'it ain't no joke' to find yourself actually living inside the joke. Roth, like Heller, characteristically tests the edges of humour with a self-reflexiveness that draws attention to the interpenetration of comedy and seriousness. *Portnoy's Complaint* takes the joking about Jewish mothers seriously enough to psychoanalyse it with explicit references to Freud and the Oedipus complex. It turns out, however, that this discourse is as reductive as the joking kind. When Portnoy finds himself attracted to a young woman in Israel he is aware of her resemblance to his mother, convinced therefore that she is a 'mother-substitute' (266) but then protests:

> Oh please, it can't be as simplistic as that! Not *me*! Or with a case like mine, is it actually that you can't be simplistic *enough*! Because she wore red hair and freckles, this makes her, according to my unconscious one-track mind, my mother? Just because she and the lady of my past are offspring of the same pale Polish strain of Jews? This then is the culmination of the Oedipal drama, Doctor? More farce, my friend! Too much to swallow, I'm afraid! *Oedipus Rex* is a famous tragedy, schmuck, not another joke! (266)

Psychoanalysis and joking are conflated in this passage to make a telling point about Roth as a caricaturist – that crude reductiveness about human psychology can turn out to be all too accurate. Portnoy would be travestied, not by simplification, but by Jamesian elaboration. This point is similar to that in Milan Kundera's *The Unbearable Lightness of Being*. For Kundera life turns out to be unbearably lacking in existential substance and weight: for Roth, for similarly anti-humanist reasons, it is shockingly lacking in complexity. The simplistic diagnosis is all too true.

So *Portnoy's Complaint* is focused on reductiveness. Stylistically it is conspicuously lacking in those lengthy expository scenes, with careful notation of setting and strategic use of dialogue, which allow for the cumulative evocation of 'well-rounded' characters. What scenes it has are mostly short while others are summarized and explicitly interpreted, and characters are treated almost dismissively or half-parodied through free indirect speech. When we are introduced to Portnoy's father, for example, it is his constipation which is mentioned first. This is justified (or excused) in narrative terms because it is Alex's first impression of his father, but it is inevitably reductive, especially by contrast with the magical powers he associates with his mother, her apparent ability to transform herself into his teachers, and to be ubiquitous. This establishes a pattern in which men – but particularly Alex Portnoy – are powerless as a consequence of female power: 'Poppa', he says, 'why do we have such guilty deference to women?' (88). This is why Portnoy's 'repressions' mark him 'like a road map from head to toe' (124).

It is this which prevents Portnoy from properly attaining manhood, let alone 'menschlikeit': he suffers from an arrested development which keeps him in the 'endless childhood' (271) of a mother's boy. Because Portnoy is narrating the story this also arrests the development of the novel's characters: his perspective, because it is crudely limited by his boyish obsessiveness, flattens himself and everybody else. He tells his therapist that a Jewish man whose parents are alive is a fifteen-year-old boy: 'excuse me, I meant ten! I meant five! I meant zero!' (111) The exclamatory rhetoric cuts him back until he is a 'helpless *infant*' and imprisons him again as the 'smothered son in the Jewish joke' but, again, this is no laughing matter – it '*hoits*' (111). His development is arrested partly because the smothering mother arrests his sexual development, she is 'castrating' (118) because she makes the son feel guilty every time he acts independently of her. This imposes such a sensitive conscience on him that his own sexuality makes him feel guilty, and therefore he feels that to become fully masculine he must learn 'to be bad – and to enjoy it! That is what makes men of us boys, Mother' (124). The alternative is to be obedient, which leads – again with confrontational reductiveness – to Fire Island or restaurant gayness (125–26).

The struggle to acquire heterosexual masculinity therefore centres on transgressive appetite. The self-consciously reductive metonymy of this masculinity is the penis or 'schlong' which, when owned by his father has 'magisterial length and girth' (42). Alex's penis, by contrast, is a 'little thing' and his mother's dismissiveness about it is a symptomatic humiliation, which leads him to want the status of a 'bad boy' with his 'prick firing salvos at the light bulb' (201). So he can be fully characterized by a 'complaint': the punning title refers both to the oral form, the extended complaining, but also to a pathology that combines powerful moral feelings with even more powerful sexual drives. This reduces characterization to diagnosis and invents a cartoon Freudianism: 'all the unconscious can do anyway, so Freud tells us, is *want. And* want! *And* WANT!' (103).

The repetition of that word, with changing typographic emphases, is characteristic of the significant repetitions that occur throughout. It invokes a subtler Freudianism, a compulsion to repeat, but more importantly it is linked to a comic emphasis on the mechanizing of human feeling and behaviour. Portnoy's application to himself of a (simplified) Freudian theory of 'want' focuses on how want is perpetuated in him by simultaneous responses of arousal and dissatisfaction. Each of his women is desirable but also limited and this leads endlessly onwards: 'You see, I just can't stop!' (104) What Roth's feminist critics take insufficiently into account is how much such moments in his work amount to a complaint about masculine sexuality. This mechanizing of desire does lead to women being reduced to 'apertures and openings' (104), to a mechanism in which objects are sexualized, as when an empty milk bottle addresses him as 'Big Boy' and begs him to give it all he's got (19). It also leads to women being reified, as when he ends up 'fucking some dank, odiferous combination of sopping Italian pubic hair, greasy American buttock, and absolutely rank bedsheet' (138).

The other key motive for mechanical imagery in *Portnoy's Complaint* is ruefulness about Jewish family life. This is significant because, as I have said, the novel does trace a cause-and-effect relationship between Portnoy's adult sexuality and his upbringing. Here the satire is especially angry. It is directed against the replacement of thought by unthinking platitudes: when a fifteen-year-old neighbour of the Portnoys commits suicide, the women wail 'With those golden hands!' and 'With that talent!' (97). Portnoy, remembering this, cries in exasperation:

> Can they actually be equipped with all the machinery, a brain, a spinal cord, and the four apertures for the ears and eyes – equipment, Mrs. Nimkin, nearly as impressive as colour TV – and still go through life without a single clue about the feelings and yearnings of anyone other than themselves? (97)

The boy's mother, Mrs Nimkin, is loudly indicted for 'SELFISHNESS AND STUPIDITY' because she has indoctrinated her son (as other Jewish mothers, it is implied, do routinely) with feelings for her that are too powerful to live with. Severe damage can be inflicted by a domestic regimen that imposes values through an unthinking repetition: this too is a form of arrested development that makes change and flexible insight impossible. This is why realist depiction is inappropriate – because it assumes that human behaviour is substantial and rich and above all capable of mature development. By contrast such people caricature themselves by freezing their attitudes into stasis and repetition. So Alex's mother obsessively cleans her Venetian blinds and every day at dusk 'begins pumping up the worry machine' (148) until she is frantic about her husband's lateness. So the language they use also becomes mechanical: some phrases and words are endlessly repeated – 'the hands of a born pianist', 'doctor', 'residency', 'his own office' (99) – while others like 'cancer' and 'sex' (65) are endlessly erased.

* * *

The mechanical cycle in which Portnoy is trapped, the repetition of wanting, suggests that desire caricatures those who are driven by it. He is half horrified that it is this which leads him to take 'The Monkey' as his girlfriend because he sees her as a transparent personification of mere desire and blames her hypocritically for the earliness of the sexual favours that she bestowed on him. This, again, satirizes masculine sexuality and how it can shift contempt for itself onto the object of its desires. Portnoy is convinced that the Monkey looks so much like 'a moll' that his association with her exposes all his lowest desires for all to see and reveals his professional eminence as Commissioner of Human Opportunity as a facade: 'Bull*shit.* Commissioner of Cunt, that's who you are!' (204)

His professional prestige contrasts with his father's status as an insurance agent and therefore as 'oppressed' and 'powerless' (40). The only source of masculine power his father has is his sexuality: 'between his legs . . . he was constructed like a man of consequence' (42). That is all he owns because in every other respect he is owned by the company. This is paralleled by Alex's powerlessness in the hands of his mother, a powerlessness which leads to the special emphasis on his secretive and transgressive sexuality: 'Doctor, do you understand what I was up against? My wang was all I really had that I could call my own.' (33) Gender, like race, is a key source of caricature in Roth. The penis plays the same role as a reductive metonymy for masculinity as the nose (145, 147, 149) plays for Jewishness.

It is the two themes of race and gender that most lead Roth to consider the impact of social and political pressures on individuals. *Portnoy's Complaint* is at its most political when it laments the social powerlessness of Alex's father, which reduces his potency in comparison with Uncle Hymie (51) and constipates him by placing his intestines 'in the hands of the firm of Worry, Fear & Frustration' (26). He falls short of 'menschlikeit' because he is too much 'a creature reduced to its material needs' (Hilfer, 74). When Roth takes up this theme more fully in the 1990s, it leads him to write his best novels as he explores the pressures that make it so difficult for individuals to become authors of themselves, and tend to turn their lives into stories made up beforehand.

When it first appears, this theme is comic and even frivolous and takes the form of revealing the impact of fame on identity: as the film star Caesara O'Shea says, 'fame is a very crude thing' (*Zuckerman*, 194). She describes how her male fans sleep with her image and are terribly disappointed when they finally realize that 'your you isn't the world's you'. Famous people do not own themselves: Zuckerman's 'nuts . . . are now in the public domain' (223). Famous people become stereotypes for the convenience of the media: an 'establishment roughneck' (192) or 'a tough journalist with a tender heart' (193). A public image is a postmodern ontological simplification.

In *Zuckerman Unbound*, however, Roth is sceptical about literature, and about the gulf between what happens to experience inside texts and what that experience really is. In particular this novel worries about the secludedness of novelists, the sense that they are severed from the real by the business of writing. Zuckerman remembers a story about Flaubert emerging from his writing and seeing his cousin looking after her children and remarking '*Ils sont dans le vrai*' (226). The accusations made against Zuckerman reflect an anxiety about distance from 'le vrai': an old man in the Public Library accuses him of leaving things out of *Carnovsky* in order to take revenge on his parents (139); he accuses himself of being a 'cutthroat caricaturist' (170); in *The Anatomy Lesson* Zuckerman thinks his sister-in-law steers clear of him in order not to become 'a caricature in a book'. However, it is Alvin Pepler in *Zuckerman Unbound* who is his most effective reality principle and sounds a note that will be crucially repeated in later novels. Pepler says that Zuckerman has invented a bland version of Newark that ignores its social reality: '*Moron*! Newark is a nigger with a knife! Newark is a whore with the syph! Newark is junkies shitting in your hallway and everything burned to the ground!' (243)

It is this preoccupation with the fictiveness of fiction that leads Roth to the metafictional novels of the late 1970s and 1980s. Eventually, however, it leads, more successfully, to the social realism of *American Pastoral* and *I Married A Communist*. This is entirely different from the Jamesian style of psychological realism that influences his early work. His dissatisfaction with that is signalled in *The Anatomy Lesson* when he refers to the self as an 'enclosure' that 'you keep trying to break out of' (442) and when he has Zuckerman say that all he has got to go on is his 'inner life' and he can't take any more of it: 'Subjectivity's the subject, and I've had it' (436). The central character of *American Pastoral* appears to have had, for much of his life, no subjectivity at all, and is entirely baffled by the subjectivity of others: 'How to penetrate to the interior of people was some skill or capacity he did not possess' (409). In inventing the character of Swede, Roth seems to have been driven by a wish to invent someone fundamentally different from the writer-personae who multiply in his fictions (Zuckerman, Kepesh, Tarpanol, etc.), to invent someone beyond the doubts that loom so large to writers, someone like the doctors, pornographers and chauffeurs who, according to Zuckerman, are 'all confidence' (*Zuckerman*, 488). Swede appears to be so lacking in doubt that he has made himself into a monolith: 'This caricature was *it*, arrived at spontaneously after a lifetime' (36). The novel centres on the process which shatters Swede's confidence, so that he acquires – shockingly against his will – a subjectivity at odds with himself. Where before his 'discontents were barely known' to him, he awakes 'in middle-age to the horror of self-reflection' (85).

It is important, however, that what first seems to draw Roth to the character of Swede is how much he embodies, as it were, the *outer* life. To this extent he is similar to Ira Ringold in *I Married A Communist*, except that this friend of the adolescent Zuckerman is far more politically knowing than Swede. Although Ringold is a communist, Roth stresses his Americanness: his life is 'intimately circumscribed' by 'American history' and 'American geography'. Zuckerman says he has never known anyone 'so immersed in his moment or so defined by it' (189) and for him Ira Ringold comes to personify America. This is linked for the young Zuckerman as a writer to his own 'native-son passions' which lead to his attraction to the novels of Thomas Wolfe and John Dos Passos (189), and explains much of what is going on in Roth's novels of the 1990s and after – how much he has been concerned with the social and political realities of postwar America. Such concerns take him closer to Wolfe and Dos Passos and away from Henry James.

In *American Pastoral* he accordingly adopts a mode of social realism which comes as a vivid surprise after the metafictional tangles of the Rothian 1980s, not least because it implies a shift in aesthetic philosophy. Roth's use of metafiction over such a long period indicates a postmodern scepticism about the ability of fiction, and even language, to reflect the 'real'. By contrast, since 1990 he has written novels that directly confront social and economic facts and seem confident of their ability to locate themselves 'dans le vrai'. *American Pastoral* adopts a documentary style at times, especially when it deals with the glove industry in which Swede has spent his working life: this involves an enjoyment of economic facts for their own sake and of the detail of factory work:

> The cutter would spit into the dry inking material in which he rubbed the brush for the stencil that numbered the pieces he cut from each trunk. Having cut a pair of gloves, he would touch his finger to his tongue so as to wet the numbered pieces, to stick them together before they were rubber-banded for the sewing forelady and the sewers. (126)

Something like this mode is in evidence throughout Roth's career – he has always had a remarkable facility for notating the details of rooms, personal possessions, physical appearance. The difference here is in the thematic prominence given to this material: the emphasis it acquires has political motives.

To acquire this significance fully, however, it has to be connected to the character of Swede. The point of Swede is that it is the externals of his life, like his prowess as a sports star and his marriage to a beauty queen, which define his identity rather than subjectivity which Zuckerman thinks, at first, has been erased in him in the process of achieving his 'perfection': 'There had to be a substratum, but its composition was unimaginable' (20). The documentary style therefore helps to reveal Swede as a man of action rather than thought, and to imply in him a specifically American kind of innocence.

American Pastoral establishes Swede's 'perfection' as its premise and associates that perfection with this mode of documentary realism. In doing so it draws upon the assumptions of that mode, which are that human beings can be rationally understood as products of their social conditions: their actions, and the motives of those actions, are thoroughly comprehensible when placed in that context. However, having established this premise, Roth spends the rest of the novel exploding it by introducing a grotesque incomprehensibility which makes a nonsense of decent reasonableness because

> [Swede's] daughter was an insane murderer hiding on the floor of a room in Newark, his wife had a lover who dry-humped her over the sink in their family kitchen, his ex-mistress had knowingly brought disaster upon his house, and he was trying to propitiate his father with on-the-one-hand-this and on-the-other-hand-that. (358)

The narrative argument of *American Pastoral* is best understood by reference to 'Writing American Fiction', which Roth wrote over thirty years before that novel, and published in *Commentary*, the Jewish American periodical. In this essay, dated 1961, Roth describes the bizarre public response to the murder of two teenage girls: the newspapers publish a cartoon-like drawing of them; a columnist reports daily from their house; television interviews their friends; a bum claims to be the murderer; *his* mother is photographed with the girls' mother; the bum becomes a sort of celebrity; the newspaper launches a contest to guess how they died; donations are sent to the mother, including a whole new kitchen – and so on. Roth's point is that American reality has become so bizarre that writers have a basic problem in making it believable:

> It stupefies, it sickens, it infuriates, and finally it is even a kind of embarrassment to one's meager imagination. The actuality is continually outdoing our talents, and the culture tosses up figures almost daily that are the envy of any novelist. (*Reading Myself*, 120)

Much of the motive for Roth's grotesque satire lies in the sense that only a wildly non-realist mode can deal with a reality as grotesquely aberrant as this. In *American Pastoral*, however, his strategy is radically different because he wants to establish a sense of stable normality in order to register the extent of the grotesque deviation from that normality. To that end he starts out by establishing Swede as a kind of *tabula rasa*. Though Jewish, Swede has such an 'unconscious oneness with America' that the Jew in him seems erased alongside any irrationality or temptations or mischief (20). It is on this blank page that the grotesqueness writes itself and he becomes 'history's plaything' (87). So Roth establishes realism as a mode in order to make his deviation from it more significant: the rationality on which realism is based is invaded by its opposite, a kind of madness which he sees as specifically American, 'the indigenous American berserk' (86). Swede searches his past endlessly to explain why his only child Merry turns into an insane terrorist, but nothing he comes up with can rationally explain it. In particular he remembers an 'anomalous moment' (92) when he was thirty-six and she was eleven and he kissed her, and then the next day, over-reacting, became too physically distant – but this is clearly his own irrational guilt rather than an explanation. Similarly, the attack that Swede's brother Jerry makes on him is based on simplistic assumptions about cause and effect when he blames him for making Merry 'the angriest kid in America' (279). Swede is right to insist that this 'bizarre horror' has nothing to do with how they lived as a family, that it is as 'disconnected as everything else – it's all a part of the same mess!' (281).

The sense that everything is 'disconnected' is the source of another aesthetic problem for novelists who, in constructing their texts, must find connections everywhere and in everybody. Roth's point in making Swede and his wife such paragons, who nonetheless produce a bizarre horror, is extreme disconnectedness, a level of randomness so wide-ranging it becomes a structural principle; social and economic factors are widely disconnected from what arises out of them. The painstaking evocation of those facts reveals how little they explain, how divergent the effect from any discernible cause.

American Pastoral transcends mere disconnectedness, however, by incorporating the pre-novelistic idioms of pastoral and allegory which confer a comprehending structure on its materials. The novel's title links it to classic American texts by authors like Thoreau, Whitman, Hawthorne and Melville, and to associations of America as a new Eden. Roth makes this less pretentious, however, by relating it most vividly to Johnny Appleseed who, as a character from a children's story, is especially appropriate in representing a childhood innocence so shockingly lost by Swede's daughter. This helps to expand the meaning of that individual experience into a more collective elegy for lost American potential, while keeping the specific allusions attractively homely and convincing as part of an interaction between father and daughter. Johnny Appleseed has neither race nor creed and so embodies the hope of American unity:

> Johnny Appleseed was just a happy American. Big. Ruddy. Happy. No brains probably, but didn't need 'em – a great walker was all Johnny Appleseed needed to be. All physical joy. Had a big stride and a bag of seeds and a huge, spontaneous affection for the landscape, and everywhere he went he scattered the seeds. (316)

Johnny Appleseed personifies a pre-social fertility and innocence and the pastoral mode he introduces is the opposite of the documentary realism applied to Newark and the glove industry. What the two modes share, however, is that both are activated in the narrative by their association with Swede, who resembles Johnny Appleseed in his animal vitality and in being 'handsome as hell, big, carnal, ruddy', and in throwing seed from a grocery bag across the land that he now owns in an action that parallels the 'unrestricted virility' he takes with him into the bedroom where he finds his young wife (318). Nothing in the social conditions, however complex, can explain the horror of what happens to Swede: this makes its own political point in flatly opposing any kind of economic determinism. Swede's association with Johnny Appleseed takes him outside the realist mode while his association with the glove industry and his ordinary family life routinely place him inside it. Where the realist mode leads to disconnection, a sense of baffled disruption of cause and effect, the introduction of the allegorical mode with its tripartite structure – 'Paradise Remembered', 'The Fall', 'Paradise Lost' – implies a more mythic way of comprehending the narrative.

Here, as elsewhere, Roth's collision of distinct modes opens up areas of significance that would otherwise be unavailable: the two modes interrogate each other so that their philosophical assumptions are defamiliarized. In this case, however, the collision shows the deepening of Roth's pessimism. From the start of his career, Roth has labelled himself as a pessimist; in 'Writing American Fiction' he laments what he sees as an increasing tendency towards the celebratory in his older contemporaries. What he says here again seems to have special relevance, curiously, to *American Pastoral* (considering that the novel post-dates the essay by thirty years):

> If the world is as crooked and unreal as it feels to me it is becoming, day by day, if one feels less and less power in the face of this unreality; if the inevitable end is destruction, if not of all life, then of much that is valuable and civilized in life – then why in God's name is the writer pleased? (*Reading Myself*, 131)

This pessimism is in evidence in Roth's earliest writing but obscured and tempered by his comic energy. In *Portnoy's Complaint* the mingling of Bildungsroman and caricature still leaves some room for the young hero to grow and define himself. Increasingly, however, Roth's heroes have less and less power in the face of unreality: David Kepesh, most extremely, is turned into a six-foot tall breast.[12] So Roth's existential assumptions, his tendency to believe in self-authorship, are increasingly eroded: his narratives increasingly reveal such aspirations being frustrated. Both of the stylistic modes in *American Pastoral* invoke the idea of large forces working to overwhelm individuals and their life choices, forces that encroach on the freedom of Swede and his family. Their impact on Swede is evoked partly by caricatural imagery, and this is significant because it indicates that these large forces dehumanize him. The pressures he suffers drive him into overworking: at work he is faced by suppliers' errors, by unions, by buyers' complaints, etc.; at home he is faced by his stuttering daughter and his interfering father. But it never occurs to him

> that this relentlessly impersonal use of himself might one day wear him down. He did not think like that any more than the ground under his feet thought like that. He seemed never to understand or, even in a moment of fatigue, to admit that his limitations were not entirely loathsome and that he was not himself a one-hundred-and-seventy-year-old stone house, its weight borne imperturbably by beams carved of oak – that he was something more transitory and mysterious. (202)

Here again Swede is the exact opposite of Roth's writer personae who endlessly examine their selves. By contrast with them he has difficulty even acknowledging his own humanity. The caricatural element in this passage resembles that in much of *Catch-22* in its indictment of commodification: Swede caricatures his humanity by turning himself into an instrument of work and then relentlessly using himself. This eventually crushes his Johnny Appleseed side and leads to the exhaustion of being which Swede later learns to diagnose – a development of sorts, however lamentable the object of his diagnosis. Later in the book Swede realizes 'how people seemed to run out of their own being' (329) which again suggests how the human gets reified. Being is now equated with fuel which can simply be exhausted.

This is what happens because the 'counterpastoral' (86) asserts itself, a kind of collective madness that turns Swede into 'history's plaything' (87) and drains him of any individual volition. So eventually Swede enters 'a coffin carved out of time from which he would never be extricated' (337). Where Johnny Appleseed personifies human vitality, the counterpastoral leads to a living death in which time itself diminishes and hardens into a terminally restrictive box.

* * *

American Pastoral is a brilliant novel. The one thing that mars it is its gender attitudes; there is a level of rancour directed at some of its female characters which is disturbingly disproportionate so that it seems to blame women for the destruction of pastoral, as *The Waste Land* also does by making its female characters so dominant and so associated with counterpastoral sterility. The novel gives the impression that leftist 1960s terrorism is the preserve of women. It not only has Swede's daughter Merry committing a terrorist outrage – but the friend, Rita Cohen, who liaises for her with Swede, is also female, and the only famous leftist mentioned is Angela Davis. In the portrayal of all three – though less in the case of Merry – there is a tendency to caricature as pitfall. Davis is beautiful but her hair makes her like 'a porcupine' (160) and constitutes a warning that crossing her will be painful. Most troubling of all, in a lengthy and detailed scene Rita Cohen tries to tempt Swede into having sex with her, in order, apparently, to gain a political advantage. Here there is an overflowing of misogynistic resentment as she exposes her labia to him and describes her genitalia as a 'swamp' (146).

This is a pity because elsewhere in his work Roth's deconstruction of gender stereotypes is one of the most challenging aspects of his work. It is especially relevant for my purposes because it frequently involves an interrogation of body politics in which identity questions are linked to the caricatural imagery of body fragmentation, and of body parts as caricatural metonymies.

One especially recurrent concern in Roth's work is with masculinity as inevitably transgressive. In *Portnoy's Complaint* he says that the struggle to be 'bad' is 'what makes men of us boys' (124). Thirty-two years later, in *I Married A Communist*, he theorizes the idea further: the authority exerted by Zuckerman's old teacher Murray Ringold leads the younger man to define masculinity as involving confrontational rebellion. *Portnoy's Complaint* shows that becoming a man involves the male distancing himself from the power of the mother: Roth's fiction is especially revealing about why this may involve animosity against the phallic female, and this causes him to slip, too often for comfort, into misogyny. However, *I Married A Communist* indicates that this transgressiveness can make a key social and political impact. The role model here is Tom Paine, who was 'savagely single-minded and unsociable, an epic, folkloric belligerent' (25).

That description could equally well apply to the hero of *Sabbath's Theatre* who is so obsessively transgressive that he has no interest in anything that is not transgression (126). The point about Sabbath is that he can be so thoroughly summed up in this way; he is entirely unencumbered – his mistress dies, he leaves his wife, he detaches himself from his friends. The extent to which he even has a self in the usual sense is in question because he is 'reduced the way a sauce is reduced' (126) and 'self-haunted while barely what you would call a self' (198). So Roth – very usefully for my purposes – describes Sabbath as 'a caricature of himself and entirely himself' (198). Roth is aware that creating a character so radically reduced can paradoxically make him larger than life.

The simplification of Sabbath allows him to be used, some of the time, as a satirical device, in particular when he is deployed strategically against feminism. Sabbath had been put on trial in the 1950s for performing – when he was a street puppeteer – an indecent sexual act in public, and has lost an academic post, much more recently, as the result of a sexual harassment charge. This makes him the personified culmination of earlier references in Roth's work to the spectacle of masculinity on trial. In *Portnoy's Complaint* there is an hallucinatory scene where Alex's mother is shouting at his father and this makes Alex himself feel guilty, so that it seems to him that he and his father are both on trial, or it is unclear which of them it is – 'the wrongdoer . . . is one of the two members of the family who owns a penis' (87). In *Deception* (1990) Roth is put on trial for the sexism in his books,[13] asked to explain why he hates women, why Mrs Portnoy is portrayed as hysterical, Lucy Nelson as psychopathic, Maureen Tarponol as a liar and a cheat (114) – but all of this turns out to be sexual by-play invented by his girlfriend to mutually arouse them.

The recurrence of this theme, however comically treated, does suggest feelings of paranoia and persecution in the author. It figures yet again in Roth's recent book *The Human Stain*[14] (2000), in which the protagonist, Coleman Silk, who is an academic specializing in Classics, is accused of racism and systematically hounded by the appalling poststructuralist feminist, Delphine Roux. The animosity that Roth evidently feels towards feminists, moreover, leads him at times to crude writing. Marcia, the feminist academic in *American Pastoral* is a caricature in all the bad senses, being the simplistic object of the author's anger. She is 'a slob, dressed even in college like somebody's grandmother' (340) and she is 'all talk – always had been: senseless, ostentatious talk . . . quarrelsome words expressing little more than Marcia's intellectual vanity' (343).

However, it is largely because Roth has positioned himself so conspicuously as an anti-feminist, and has therefore explored gender questions in his work, that *Sabbath's Theatre*, in particular, ends up saying such fascinating things about masculinity. This makes Roth in a sense a very unexpected beneficiary of feminist thought. It is a constitutive characteristic of masculinity generally to consider itself not as a gender but as a norm and to consider its values as not gendered but universal. Roth's encounters with feminism have sharpened his gender awareness – more so because of their hostility – and made him invent narratives that explore what it means to be a man. The starting-point for this is the view that, as Sabbath says, feminists tell 'terrible lies about men' and turn ordinary masculine desires into 'sinister villainy' (236), 'caricaturing us, insulting us, abhorring in us what is nothing more than the delightful Dionysian underlayer of life' (237). The anger this arouses is responsible for some of the most troubling but also some of the most powerful moments in recent Roth. *American Pastoral* ends with Marcia in a paroxysm of shockingly cynical laughter as she enjoys the spectacle of social collapse, 'enjoying enormously the assailability, the frailty, the enfeeblement of supposedly robust things' (423).

This is reactionary authorial scapegoating, but the level of hatred and fear it indicates is very telling. Something similarly intense is happening when Sabbath returns to his marital home only to witness his wife engaging in sex with another woman. The revulsion this arouses in him is immediately generalized: 'the odors that exist only within women wafted out of them and through the opening of the window, where they enveloped the flag-draped Sabbath in the violent misery of everything lost' (440). This passage transcends simple misogyny, however, because it suggests how much the sense of what it is to be masculine is based on the conviction of female alienness, and how much that arises from fear of the power of the phallic mother. Sabbath's sense of loss here is made to echo similar feelings in early childhood of being expelled from the mother, so that he 'felt as though he had been expelled from an enormous cunt whose insides he'd been roaming freely all his life' (440). So Sabbath experiences a kind of 'abjection' which could be theorized in Kristevan terms: he is expelled and shunned by a generalized notion of the feminine whose power is accordingly, and with horror and revulsion, registered.

The consequence of such an expulsion is profound ontological disorientation, and a sense of loss which gets inscribed into personal identity. It is a source, again, of horror and awe that the two women in this scene enact, through their sexual activities, something like the endlessly elusive meaning of this loss:

> A piece or fragment of something was missing, and they were speaking fluently together, purportedly about the missing piece, in a language consisting entirely of gasps and moans and exhalations and shrieks, a musical miscellany of explosive shrieks. (440)

The power that this attributes to women of being able to speak a pre-linguistic language that might restore a pre-linguistic wholeness leads to these two female characters discovering together the missing piece, 'that little piece that made the whole picture complete' (441). Roth's misogyny never leads to his being dismissive about women: it is based on a profoundly masculine anxiety about their power. Roth is closest to diagnosing the origin of that anxiety in this disturbing and ferociously imagined scene because it enacts how Sabbath's masculinity exiles him from a wholeness that it is possible for women to (re-)discover. The wholeness that is described in the scene is so close to that theorized by Julia Kristeva, especially her concept of the chora,[15] that it is hard to believe that Roth is not alluding to Kristeva's post-Lacanian feminist arguments.

His focus, nonetheless, is on the unavailability of this wholeness to Sabbath who, as a man, is left in Freudian and Lacanian pieces. This is by implication what happens to those whose identity is defined by masculine desire, and Roth was explicitly aware of this as early as *Portnoy's Complaint*: there his hero's inability to unite his sensuality with his tenderness leads to his being 'fragmented' (186). This is another key idea in Roth's work; fragmentation and reductiveness, which I have discussed, need to be considered together as sources of his caricatural thought. Both oppose realist and humanist assumptions about the ontological wholeness of the self.

The controlling metaphor of puppetry in *Sabbath's Theatre* underlies the novel's caricatural thought. For the reductiveness of puppets is emphasized by the link between metafiction and caricature, which the novel makes because its controlling metaphor raises the question of the extent to which novelistic characters are merely authorial puppets with their stories made up beforehand. When puppets mimic humans, then, their lack of volition is made to ask how much volition humans in fact have, how much humans are merely mechanical: 'The mind is the perpetual motion machine' (297). So Sabbath felt that when sex with his wife became mechanical his presence was unnecessary and he 'could have been one of those antique marionettes with a long wooden dick' (132). Near the end of the novel, Sabbath connects the suicide he is contemplating with being a puppeteer because both signify a form of self-erasure: 'disappear behind the screen, insert the hand, and instead of performing as yourself, take the finale as the puppet' (443).

It is also a form of reductiveness that only the hands and the voice are required for working a puppet. However, the desperate, nearly terminal celebratoriness of *Sabbath's Theatre* associates this reductiveness with a form of transcendence. Sabbath declares: 'Contentment is being hands and a voice – looking to be more, students, is madness' (245). Paradoxically, it is reductiveness that means that 'Puppets can fly, levitate, twirl' (244). Similarly, the novel's repeated allusions to *King Lear* invoke a humanity reduced as far as it can be, so that the nature of that humanity is more starkly revealed. Roth's satire in this novel is even more flagrantly confrontational and carnivalesque than usual; he is savage about political correctness because he wants to insist on the stark, and dominating, facts of human physiology. This is why *Sabbath's Theatre* is so obsessive about genitalia – why, in particular, it reiterates the word 'cunt'.

As a consequence, *Sabbath's Theatre* can be seen as the culmination of Roth's meta-caricatural thinking. It describes a humanity which has been so thoroughly reduced from its previous claims for itself that it needs a thorough reappraisal of its circumstances. It presents its hero as explicitly and representatively reduced, and deploys body parts as metonymies to indicate fragmentation. Throughout Roth's career, as I have mentioned, noses and penises are deployed in this way, but in *Sabbath's Theatre* they acquire more philosophical significance. In this context the hands and the voice are preceded by the fingers that were Sabbath's first minimal puppets. He gave each finger a voice; he drew a woman's stocking over one hand; he placed a tennis ball over one or more fingers and gave it 'a head with a brain' and supplied it with 'schemes, manias, phobias'; he put the middle finger of his left hand on trial for obscenity and then placed it in a meat grinder for punishment (122).

All of this leads back to desire: 'In the fingers uncovered, or even suggestively clad, there is always a reference to the penis' (122). Reductiveness and fragmentation are related to the relentless carnality that underlies human experience. This preoccupation was there in Roth as early as *The Anatomy*

Lesson where he dwells on the pun on 'corpus' that insists that even literary texts are a form of flesh. This is confirmed in the crucial narrative moment when Zuckerman thinks he sees a stain from his mother's milk in a book of hers called *Your Baby's Care* – and, closing his eyes, puts his tongue to the page (342). It is when he is exploring this carnality that Roth can most imagine men and women having a common fate; in *Sabbath's Theatre* the hero has a mistress, Drenka, who is at least his equal in transgressiveness. Earlier in his career – in creating the body part that looms largest in his work, the 155-pound breast that David Kepesh becomes – Roth had already implied something of this common fate:

> Surely if anybody has ever been turned totally into a 'sexual object' both to himself and to others, it is David Alan Kepesh. Isn't this all-encompassing sexualization exactly what he struggles with . . . The battle to be, not simply that shape and those dimensions, but simultaneously to be something *other*, constitutes the entire action of the book. (*Reading Myself*, 73)

There is a similar struggle against simplification in *Sabbath's Theatre* but the later novel is more pessimistic and less comic. Nonetheless, it is very powerful in its determination to continue to struggle, and not to be terminally overthrown, and to live on despite the reduced circumstances. Sabbath's refusal in the end to kill himself is one of the mentally healthiest moments in postwar literature.

4 *Joyce Carol Oates's Political Anger*

Joyce Carol Oates's canon is notoriously large and generically various, and her reputation has suffered because of a consequent bewilderment about how precisely to locate her. Her impressiveness is most successfully weighed, however, when she is treated as a writer with pressing social and political concerns. Her political attitudes are best understood, moreover, when she is considered as a writer whose satirical motives consistently drive her texts and frequently become explicit in them. The most important clue to these concerns, and the one that is most telling in the context of the caricatural themes and effects I will be discussing, is her fascination with anger. Much of her writing is charged with authorial anger sometimes only thinly disguised by her formidable talents for realist plotting and characterization. Many of her characters are driven by a rage that flares into vengeful violence.

A powerful insight into this aspect of Oates is provided by her book *On Boxing*[1] (1987) where she reveals her rueful fascination with the sport and draws a surprising analogy between boxers and writers arising from their shared 'fanatic subordination of the self in terms of a wished-for destiny' (26). Boxers, as Oates describes them, also share much in common with many of her most memorable characters because she sees them as responding to social disadvantage with calculated aggression, responding to impotence with a 'reckless expenditure of physical potency' (69). Oates stresses, above all, that this response arises from anger as 'a fully motivated and socially coherent impulse':

> Men and women with no personal or class reason for feeling anger are inclined to dismiss the emotion, if not piously condemn it, in others. Why such discontent? why such unrest? why so *strident*? Yet this world is conceived in anger – and in hatred, and in hunger – no less than it is conceived in love: that is one of the things that boxing is about . . . (68)

As Oates's career has progressed her belief in 'love' has increasingly attenuated and her emphasis on anger has widened and deepened. Her earliest literary criticism reveals her as preoccupied with 'love' in the sense that she is preoccupied with the human 'spirit': her first book of critical prose, *New Heaven, New Earth*[2] is subtitled *The Visionary Experience in Literature.* She already understands the spirit there in the modified terms of Lawrence and

Nietzsche and is anxious about the modernist loss of spirit; in her essay on Sylvia Plath her assertiveness already suggests that her spiritual assumptions are under threat: 'poetry – like all art – demands that its subject be made sacred. Art *is* the sacralizing of its subject' (131). When she becomes strident in this essay about the scornfulness and cynicism of modern poetry it is clear that her sense of the collective loss of the sacred in the twentieth century both deeply alarms and angers her. At the end of her essay on Plath she seems only to be whistling in the dark when she insists that the Plathian fragmentary self is merely 'romanticism in its death throes' and that 'Hopefully a world of totality awaits us, not a played-out world of fragments' (140).

It is clear, then, that one major source of Oates's own anger is the thoroughly secularized context in which the modern novelist must write. This also leads to her obsession with the extent to which the human has been degraded and reduced. In *Foxfire*[3] (1993), her novel about girl gangs published in 1994, Oates has her two central characters, Legs and Maddy, visit a natural history museum where they are attracted to a diagram illustrating evolution, shaken by the sense it conveys of vast stretches of time and of species extinguished in them, and baffled by the apparent purposelessness of those losses. They are bemused by the location of *Homo sapiens* in this scheme, the smallness and apparent vulnerability of that location; 'seeing *Homo sapiens* is no big deal!' (101). This moment acquires epiphanic proportions for Maddy in particular – she is the gang member who records the gang's activities and thereby reflects, from inside the text, Oates's own activity. She is also the object of authorial identification as a writer and a sensitive, intellectual member of Oates's own generation (the central characters are adolescents in the 1950s). This vision of the reduced spiritual circumstances of *Homo sapiens* thoroughly shakes Maddy's faith: 'her heart's broken? she can't take God seriously ever again?' (103)

The question marks indicate a reluctance fully to accept these spiritual losses, a reluctance which is the equivalent of the clinging on to the spiritual in Oates's essay on Plath. This is itself important and accounts for the tendency in Oates to search for hints of a vestigial sacredness: however, what is most telling is that it leads to a deep-seated spiritual frustration whose marks are everywhere in Oates's work. So she declares that boxing 'inhabits a sacred space predating civilisation', but then that it suggests, not only a savage rite of atonement, but also 'the futility of such gestures':

> For what possible atonement is the fight waged if it must shortly be waged again . . . and again? The boxing match is the very image, the more terrifying for being so stylised, of mankind's collective aggression; its ongoing historical madness. (*On Boxing*, 21)

This passage places a question mark after the idea of a sacred space and then erases it altogether with a counter-insistence that boxing matches follow each other with such mechanical repetitiveness that they cannot atone for anything, but merely reflect a purposeless violence.

Horror is aroused in Oates by what is left after the loss of the sacred – which for her is, in particular, cruelty and anger. Some of this can be explained by a 'Darwinian struggle for survival' (*On Boxing*, 109) especially in the political interactions between the powerful and those powerless individuals who are the repeated focus of Oates's novelistic scrutiny. Even to mention a spiritual dimension in Oates's sensibility may seem odd to readers who are most aware of her remorselessly realist characterizings of Detroit and its most disadvantaged citizens. This is her most powerful achievement: few contemporary writers have evoked poverty and its psychological consequences with such obsessive accuracy as Oates, and few have been as preoccupied with the difference that money makes. The mother of the first-person narrator of *Man Crazy* (1997) is typical of many of Oates's characters in her fear of being 'really poor, dirt poor':

> and men would know, always men can sniff out the degree of your desperation Mamma believed, and force you to do things you don't want to do at that time or in that place or in that way. When you have your own money, Mamma said, you have power. But you can lose it Goddamned fast.[4]

Similar economic imperatives motivate the girl gang in *Foxfire*: Legs, their leader, even formulates them in Marxist terms. She does so with the help of her friend the 'elderly Father Theriault, defrocked priest, bum-alcoholic' (202) – economics may be all that is left when religion is erased, when the spiritual is defrocked. When *Homo sapiens* can only be understood anthropologically, the spiritual is replaced by the material and human beings will regard each other as commodities: 'the tragedy is that men and women not only use one another as things but use themselves, present themselves, sell themselves . . . as things' (202–3). These politics drive the revenge which Legs takes on the farmhouse where the 'dwarf-woman' Yetta is tied to a bed and mounted night after night by a series of men, so that she is 'the woman-that's-a-body' (202). Legs burns down that household. Fire is the novel's controlling metaphor because it symbolizes the girl gang's attack on patriarchal capitalism: 'Foxfire' represents feminist revenge, but it also laments what the human has become because there is no afterlife. As Legs says in the novel's last passage, if we have a soul, it is 'Like a flame': she is above all concerned that such fire 'is real enough, isn't it, while it's burning? – even if there's a time it goes out?' (328).

Fire concedes the perishableness of the human but opposes its reduction to exchange value. The girl gang called 'Foxfire' is involved in similar opposition – in a reckless expenditure of themselves in response to their social impotence, and in an attempt to reject their political transformation into docile cogs in a machine. Their most symmetrical revenge for the commodification of young women comes when they kidnap the extreme conservative and anti-union businessman Whitney Kellogg Jr. who 'dealt in money and human-beings-as-money' (301). However, they fail in their attempt to make him an object of exchange and so fail to turn the political tables on him: he refuses to co-operate in their attempt to ransom him. When he is accidentally shot, Legs does her best to save his life even at the risk of being arrested: Oates seems determined to give 'Foxfire' the moral upper hand.

The themes of human perishableness and commodification, and the satirical anger that Oates directs at them, are the most important source of caricatural imagery in her work. They are also significantly paired in *What I Lived For*[5] (1994) where Oates puts herself inside the skin of Jerome Corcoran ('Corky') who might appear, as a misogynistic capitalist, to be her natural political enemy. Some fascinatingly dialogic tensions arise because of this novelistic impersonation: everything in the novel is seen from Corky's perspective but the sense that Oates's own perspective is entirely at odds with her central character's is a source of continual instability and questioning. At some points the novel seems to hesitate between realism and satire and Corky becomes a puppet in Oates's hands. This is of a piece with the decline of the spiritual because it implies that the human is more 'flat' than it was, that it has lost the roundedness that the spiritual bestowed. Corky is therefore merely a bundle of mostly selfish desires and energies – and the wages of sin is death. *What I Lived For* is haunted by death and bodily waste, which is presented as its small-scale equivalent.

When Corky visits the morgue, he gets into conversation with a pathologist called Wolf Wiegler who declares that he lost his religion because of his work with corpses and that what he now admires is the 'machinery' of brain and body, declaring that it is that machinery now which is 'God', but only while it is alive – once it is dead 'we're all shit' (246). The metaphor of fire that Oates gives to Legs and this one of machinery that she gives to Wiegler are roughly equivalent, but the associations of mechanism in Wiegler's metaphor are appropriate for the more pressing concerns with mere function and waste in *What I Lived For*.

The title of the last climactic chapter, 'Corky's Price', indicates why Corky is the object of realist sympathy as well as satire – he is, throughout, the victim of the system as much as its beneficiary. So, when he interposes himself between his daughter Thalia and his old friend Vic Slattery when she tries to assassinate him, he saves the life of the rising political star at the cost of his own. This brutally reinforces the political point that is continually made throughout: Corky is a rich capitalist but he is endlessly at the mercy of those richer and more powerful than himself, and of economic and political forces too complex for him to understand. One of the novel's most memorable achievements is its depiction of Corky's self-destructive energy, he is 'a man in motion' (79) who is 'happiest in his car, in motion' (232), and he arouses acute anxiety in the reader by his fretful and restless use and abuse of himself as he negotiates and networks and drinks and smokes. *What I Lived For* is so claustrophobically confined to Corky's perspective that the reader is made to worry about his financial risk-taking and his blithely hubristic trust in his own business instincts – especially because he is constantly revealed to be alarmingly crude in his perceptions.

The novel's headlong energy is unnerved by its obsession with death – and both are made political by the parallel themes of mere utility and being used up. The pace is repeatedly haunted by *memento mori* which hint that Corky and his narrative are wearing each other out. Corky's 'machinery' is compulsively watchable, but its progress towards becoming mere 'shit' is continually foreshadowed in references to Time and Death. As early as page 60 he is declaring that the world is nothing but motion, 'And, if you stop, the motion rolls over you indifferent as waves or clouds, you're dead meat'. Later he thinks of Time as 'a conveyor belt like in the slaughterhouse carrying us all along' (366). When he dies on the last pages a character called Tyde ('that little prick'), who has pestered him on and off throughout, is revealed as not a character at all but the personification of Death, or time and tide, who has been

> waiting to see him for days, weeks, God knows how long he's been waiting for what he's got in that briefcase to show Corky, Corky gives him a wave. – Hell, come on in, I'm Corky Corcoran, I'm your man. (608)

Cunningly here death and capitalism are associated with each other. When Tyde approaches Corky he appears to be offering him a business deal; Corky's 'I'm your man' is an idiom he has used before (451, 494), and indicates the mutual usefulness of one character for another.

The taken-for-granted maleness of the idiom is also crucial; this system which imposes an ideology preoccupied with use and exchange is also a gender ideology whose assumptions are patriarchal. *What I Lived For* is concerned more than most of Oates's writing with race issues, but it shares the preoccupation with gender which is a constant presence in her work, especially her later work. Corky's background is Irish American and he is embittered about how the Wasp hierarchy has regarded the Irish as 'shit on their shoes' (17). African Americans, the novel points out, are now similarly dismissed. The attitude to women is more complex and explicitly linked in the novel to commodification. Here the key device is the colouring of the women characters by Corky's perspective, which reduces them to commodities and then to waste. He is unable to see women as characters at all – his point of view automatically caricatures them. He cannot think of them as 'fellow citizens' and is baffled by feminist insistence on 'a woman's *personhood*' as opposed to 'tits and ass' (223). Oates's satirical point is that such thinking caricatures Corky himself. That there is a self-reflexive aspect to this is clear when Corky thinks about his father in the Second World War, and about a war veteran saying that the Second World War is not real to young people, and wonders 'Is anybody *real* to anybody else?' (462). The alienness of other races, classes and genders makes this problem more acute; the caricatural imagery in *What I Lived For* satirizes how the unrealness of others dehumanizes them.

It does this most predictably by suggesting that Corky's sexuality reduces him, and its objects, to the status of animals. He has a nose for 'women's secret smells, secretions. Underarms, cunt.' This turns him into 'Doggy-Corky' (186). Later his fantasies about the young 'cocoa-skinned Marilee' and her 'black clit' make him pant 'like an actual dog' (223) – leading to the anxiety that human behaviour can be thoroughly explained by reference to animal behaviour. Corky himself subscribes to this, so it acquires particular power; he has been reading a sociobiologist called Turke who explains human evolution entirely in terms of female reproductive physiology, which requires that human babies are born totally helpless because otherwise their brain size at birth would kill their mothers: 'All of civilization, culture, human history, why Corky's where he is at this moment in Time, because a woman's ass is designed in a certain way' (438). He consequently interprets his own behaviour in sociobiological terms so that, having slept with his ex-wife Charlotte in her current marital bed, he is unnerved not by the adulterousness of the act, which is routine for him, but by the infringement of male territorial boundaries: 'on another male's turf, spilling your semen, it's one tomcat spraying another's territory, it's *dangerous*' (449).

The major achievement of *What I Lived For* is its defamiliarized exploration of masculinity. The defamiliarizing is important because masculinity presents itself as a norm, presents its perspective as common sense, its values as universal – the normalizing of masculinity is the most potent ideological weapon of patriarchy. This is echoed in Corky's own outlook: some of his most disturbing views are presented casually as routine, as thoughts which are actually unthinking. *What I Lived For* reinforces this by testing the novelistic tendency to arouse sympathy and even identification with the protagonist. Breathing Corky's air and thinking his thoughts, the reader is made calculatedly over-familiar with him. Being lulled by identification leads, however, into repeated discomfort as the first-person narrator is caught in thought processes which are repellently and violently misogynistic, so that the reader is continually harassed by the sense of complicity with them.

Corky is so thoroughly and relentlessly masculine that he can appear more personification than person. He is as purely masculine as boxing is in Oates's account of it, and it is significant that Corky's earliest American ancestor, Dermott Corcoran, was a bare-knuckle fighter known as the 'Irish Charger' who was 'a man among men, and would live forever' (546). In boxing, according to Oates, values are 'evaginated' because 'a boxer is valued not for his humanity but for being a "killer" ' (74). The values in Corky's world are equally ruthless and aggressive. He will never explain or apologize, he must never show 'any sign of indecision, weakness', he believes that women 'despise that in a man' (42). He is most at home when competing in business and when surrounded by the male camaraderie of bars arguing over sport and telling dirty jokes, where the values reinforce his own (267–68). At times Oates deploys the novel's characteristic mode of free indirect thought to have Corky make explicit what this male bonding requires. Unsettled by the suspicion that Vic Slattery may have played some part in Marilee Plummer's death, Corky refuses to follow the line of thought to the point where he is in danger of breaking a taboo: 'For there's a bond of maleness that does not so much repudiate the female as transcend her: the anxious intimacy of brother-rivals who dare never accuse one another of any *manly* sin for fear of being expelled irrevocably from that intimacy' (327).

This bond may lead to guilty complicity, and the discomfort it arouses is intensified through Oates's cunning in enlisting the reader, via identification with Corky, to the same brotherly complicity: having established this, Oates increasingly turns up the heat on Corky's sexual aggressiveness. Even his nickname lulls the reader into accepting him as just a boy with boyish roguishness – as, when he was young, his Aunt Frances accepted him as her 'sweet boy' (542), not realizing (as Corky sees it) that because he had already acquired adult male sexuality he was guilty of what would have appalled her if she had known his secrets. Corky regards masculinity as inevitably guilty and wonders if women suspect what 'utter pigs, what filth we are' (405). He thinks that in gender interactions the male is 'supposed to be the aggressor', that women respect men when they 'fuck rough so it hurts' (393): it is this which leads inevitably to cruelty. Oates is persuasive here about male guilt, which fuels male anger and worsens the cruelty. Corky is aroused by his own guilty responses to his worst fantasies of sexual aggression which he half accepts as an inevitable part of his maleness, but simultaneously repudiates as only fantasy:

> now sometimes in a foul mood he'll fantasize raping sodomizing thrusting his cock down some female's throat deeper than *Deep Throat* so she's choked on his jism, some women piss you off they're asking for it practically begging for it some of these feminists for instance and that knockout blond bitch so gorgeous in *Basic Instinct* but that doesn't mean Corky really wants to do such things, hell no. (363)

Corky's sexual rage is the source of acute authorial anger and Oates repeatedly reveals how it caricatures both him and women. Twice in the book there is a reference to the *fight between an 'It' and an 'I'* (239, 304) which describes a key conflict for Oates between the idea of characters as fully human on the one hand and degraded objects on the other. Corky's step-daughter Thalia speaks for Oates when she attacks the compulsiveness in the male need to conquer women to prove themselves to other men; she says that that is the opposite of freedom: 'Where freedom's fire, that's muck' (295). Thalia's metaphors echo those of Legs at the end of *Foxfire* and Wiegler in the morgue scene of *What I Lived For*, and they associate women with the fire of freedom and men with the muck of compulsiveness. The implication is that male desire reduces the human to muck; Corky thinks of women as objects for use, and equates them, once used, with waste: 'with Kleenex, toilet paper, you use it and as soon as you're done, you're done' (96, and see also 156, 178, 342).

* * *

In order fully to understand Oates's later work it is necessary to understand how it develops out of her early novels, where the most powerfully rendered preoccupation is with the impact on the self of economic circumstances. The title of *them*[6] (1969) draws attention to how the lives of the poor can be dismissed as merely alien and therefore unreal, how that imposition of mere alienness dehumanizes them so that the reality of their lives need not be thought about. In *Foxfire* Oates speaks more explicitly about the desire to identify with a group that excludes others, because it is explored as a motive for the girl gang's existence. The third chapter of this much more recent novel is called 'They, Them . . . Others' (19) and indicates the collective strength they gather from imposing mere otherness on outsiders. More relevantly to *them*, however, their motives for forming their gang arise from their own sense of being excluded, their own sense of being 'them' to the rich. So when a Congressman makes a guest appearance at their school assembly and declares that any American boy or girl can aspire to be President or head of General Motors, they resent him and regard him as an 'asshole' for 'expecting us to believe there isn't a special creation of God, or of man, to which we didn't belong, here at the shabby south end of Hammond in the worst damn public school in the district, we didn't belong and never would' (7).

Oates's description, in *them*, of the Wendell family centres on the extent to which poverty makes them who they are. When Jules Wendell opens the door for his employer, he is 'responding as mechanically as if he'd been bred out of centuries of subordinate flesh' (231). It is paradoxical to equate the mechanical with flesh, but the paradox is part of a crucially satirical point – that historical subordination has made routine this reduction of the human to the machine, so that the equation can seem obvious enough to be made with that casual 'as if'. Jules's mother and uncle are 'diminished people' (251); Jules's father is entirely a vessel of anger:

> Yes, anger was at the core of him; his soul was anger, made up of anger. Anger for what? For nothing, for himself, for life, for the assembly line, for the cockroaches and the dripping toilet. One thing was as good as another.

> Anger. No money. Where had the money gone? Where would the money come from? Anger, money. His father. (135)

The repetitiveness of this passage indicates not only the relentless repetitiveness of his father's life but also how its three key terms – his father, anger, money – repeat each other, become each other's exact equivalents. His father is erased and replaced by anger: his life is entirely defined by lack of money.

However, the realist references, to the assembly line, cockroaches, the dripping toilet, are dismissed almost as soon as they are made. Oates does much obviously novelistic work to notate automotive Detroit where 'brakes are always squealing and the air stank and the Negroes were standing out on the street corners all day long' (315). But the parenthetical way this material is introduced reveals that the philosophical interests of the young Oates lie elsewhere. The reason she is so angered by the overwhelmingly heavy role that economic circumstances play in the lives of these characters – circumstances notated by this sort of realism – is that, at this stage of her career, she believes that human beings are spiritual creatures who are profoundly travestied by this reduction to mere economic material. For her to say 'his soul was anger' represents a shocking diminution of human potential. So she has a character called Mort declare, in a conversation with Jules, that everyone is searching for 'something more permanent, something transcendent' (421). In narrating the love affair between Jules and the mysteriously unstable Nadine, Oates describes how Nadine claws at him, wanting the 'divinity in him, so violently aroused' which was 'distant to her' (370) and refers to Jules being 'beatific' (356) with his love for her. Writing home to his mother and sister, Jules declares his belief that there is a 'Spirit of the Lord in us all, it makes us able to talk to one another and love one another' (306).

So Oates explicitly eschews a narrative too dominated by 'prodigious details of physical existence' and says that if Jules were writing his own story it would 'deal with the spirit exclusively' because he thinks of himself as pure spirit 'struggling to break free of the morass of the flesh' (255). Oates's preference philosophically is clearly for Nietzsche rather than Marx. Economic facts are there to be transcended and later in this passage the emphasis is on the spiritual effort Jules invests in his will towards commanding his own narrative and so achieving freedom and the breaking out of the spirit into 'beauty, in patches perhaps but beauty anyway' (255).

However, economic and social forces operate to frustrate this will to transcendence. These acquire increasing influence in Oates's novels as her career progresses so that the will to transcendence is increasingly marginalized, but in *them* the struggle between the two is more precariously balanced. This accounts for the novel's curious quality as two quite different novelistic discourses – social satire and realism on the one hand, and a form of aspirational idealism on the other – vie with each other. Jules himself is made to appear as a prisoner of textual constraints which he attempts to escape. Oates clearly regards these as also her own constraints which are imposed on her by the intractable nature of her material. So, having described Jules's spiritual aspirations, she declares ruefully that 'All of Detroit is melodrama, and most lives in Detroit fated to be melodramatic, but Jules's fate was to fall again and again into astonishing shrill spaces of craziness, all of it overdone physically and aborted spiritually, but somehow logical' (255–56). This reveals her own disquiet at the narrative hyperactivity of *them* which she tries to justify by confusing what is textual and what is 'real', declaring that the real is actually melodramatic and Jules's particular fate even more so. To say that his fate is 'overdone' is pre-emptively to co-opt a term that might easily be used to find fault with the novel, and use it to define what she insists happens to him – which happens because the times are 'physical' rather than 'spiritual'. Oates is claiming that it is because the time and place are 'aborted spiritually' that this narrative must be so 'overdone'.

Aborted spirituality requires that the subjective life also be aborted. Anything like a Jamesian subjectivity would be entirely inappropriate, and Oates reserves her evocation of Lawrentian subjectivity for those passages where Jules is in love – these are necessarily fleeting and fragmentary (though not fleeting enough, they are unconvincing partly because they are so obviously derivative). Hectic narrative action seems to be Oates's main recourse given that complex subjectivity is impossible for her spiritually stunted characters. Oates's explicit anxieties about this are crucial, however, especially when they lead her to show Jules trying to transcend his own narrative and being confronted instead by its power to constrain him, and even being implicitly humiliated, in one passage, by parodies of it. On the run, he enters a cigar store and looks at the covers of paperback books whose plots luridly reflect what has happened to his sister and himself. A story entitled 'My Baby's Father Was Killed in My Arms' (280) is, as Eileen Teper Bender has pointed out, the story of Jules's earliest life: 'One minute after my baby was conceived his father was shot to death in my arms – my ex-husband broke in and killed him, pumping five bullets into him!'[7]

Oates's point is that these narratives are sensational and lurid but also true, that such things really happen to these desperate others, to 'them'. This is shocking to conventional novelistic expectations because it insists that the real is actually not subtle and complex but crude and flat. So to Maureen Wendell the 'reality' of Detroit and her family appears less 'real', less 'convincing', than the world of Jane Austen (165–66). To her it seems that the suffering of a novelistic character is much greater than that of her grandmother, with whom no one really sympathizes. Maureen's life lacks the depths and sensitivities that are probed by Jane Austen. The impact of *them* is caricatural by contrast with realist novels of the Austen kind because it suggests that the majority of human beings are far less 'human' than the sophisticated and nuanced creatures evoked in such novels, being shallower and more insensitive than those creatures.

Above all they are more compulsive, and more compelled than realist characters. The generations repeat each other in *them*, not with the cyclic organicism of the generations in Lawrence's *The Rainbow*, but with mechanistic inevitability; so the first and last sections of the novel begin, respectively, with Loretta in August 1937, and her daughter Maureen in April 1966, being girls in love standing before a mirror (9, 383). Their lives are scripted in advance and their scripts are the exact opposites of those in the movies where the characters are enviably glamorous and free: as Loretta says, 'I want to be like people in that movie, I want to know what I'm doing, I don't want to be shoved this way then that way' (108).

All the Wendells are shoved this way and that because their world is dominated by 'infernal mechanistic energies' (Bender, 39), which come from both within and without. Their economic situation is a relentless mechanism, but they are also controlled by mechanistic drives. To Maureen, members of her family are less vivid than her daydreams; she sees them at supper as merely 'shapes inside clothes', her father 'a dense object', her mother a 'fluttery, insubstantial object' (128). She remembers having seen her sister Betty fooling around by a bus stop with a wild gang of girls, all uniformly dressed, and Betty out of control with laughter, 'a hard, wiry little object, like a puppet or even like a top . . . turning round and round on the sidewalk' (129). She watches Jules walking through the house and has no feelings for him, perceiving him as a 'shadowy object' whose passage into manhood is merely a series of actions he must perform like everybody else (129).

So Jules is described searching for Nadine and becoming interchangeable with his car 'whose mechanism was set for a certain fate and would not fail to get him there' (335). Earlier, on the run with Nadine, their need for money and food makes him act like a dog which is 'drawn to alleys and corners': 'His bowels felt sick but he acted out of habit. Mechanical movements seemed to Jules magical and therefore blessed, almost invisible' (286). Despite his desire elsewhere for transcendence Jules celebrates the mechanistic here – the implication, however, is that this is peculiarly masculine. Throughout the novel it is men who are most at home with the human as machine. When Jules thinks of women he thinks of their bewilderment, which he characterizes in terms of their lack of affinity with machines: how in a laundromat or a car they only appear to be in control, how their own 'machinery is as wobbly and nervous as the machinery of the car' (93). By contrast, it is the mechanistic nature of men which most makes women regard them as alien, as 'them'. There is a tendency throughout for the women characters to regard the males as thoughtless automatons, all disturbingly, or amusingly, mimicking each other. Loretta's brother Brock pushes his plate away after eating in the same way as his father and all other men – 'they were so predictable!' (17). Her husband Howard sighs 'with the sigh of Loretta's lost father'; when he loses his job as a policeman he walks 'like any man out of a job' (53).

Throughout *them* it is male compulsiveness which is dwelt upon as the cause of reductiveness, and of the depletion of a fully spiritual humanity. Male desire turns both those who feel it and those who are subjected to it into caricatures. When Maureen turns to prostitution she is doing what her mother has done before her, and the repetition stresses the inescapability of patterns imposed by oppressive demands that males appear compelled to make. 'A man was like a machine', Maureen thinks, 'one of those machines at the laundromat where she dragged the laundry' (194). The rituals of selling herself are as predictable and routine as washing cycles, including the client's orgasm where the declaration of love is urgent but 'familiar'. This is the most obvious of all the forms of commodification; it arises from Maureen's urgent desire for money (179) and leads to her hardening 'as if a shell were shaping itself out of her skin' (184). She hates the thought of intimate affection (189–90), and sex for her is defined by alien male faces contaminating hers with their roughness, imprinting her 'like shells enclosing her face' (196).

This repeated image of the shell may refer back to one of the first images in the novel, the comparison of the urban crowd with sea creatures drawn 'helplessly together' (15) where the emphasis is not only on anonymity, but on being attracted to anonymity, a wish to surrender the individual self. The shell further suggests a vulnerable inner being which needs protection and shrinks away from an external callousness, and which causes an increasing loss of identity on Maureen's part, arising because the poverty of the Wendells has always attenuated any identity she might have had. Her mother has always used Maureen's bed as a refuge from her husband, making Maureen sleep on the sofa. This lack of ownership of her own bed is the source of her current state where she finds herself in so many other beds she does not own (189), and which sharpens her loss of herself. The person she becomes when she is with a client is only fleeting (197–98). She is so 'empty' that she feels nothing and her body quickly forgets (200). Male bodies are oppressive; they have 'too much flesh', 'too much weight'. Masculine desire causes a form of dismemberment, a reduction – 'it only came to this: a hand or another part of the body' – and it leads to what Oates in her Plath essay calls 'a played-out world of fragments', and away from the 'world of totality' she fervently desires (*New Heaven, New Earth*, 140). The process of self-erasure culminates, in narrative terms, in Maureen being beaten unconscious by her stepfather so that she is left comatose for months, a state in which she 'sees her self step out of her body' (206).

* * *

The preoccupation in *them* with the body, and its relationship to the self, looks forward to the much more systematic discussion of this subject in *Wonderland*[8] (1971) which Oates published two years later, and in which her anxious anger about the loss of spirituality reaches crisis point. When Maureen remembers her career as a prostitute and thinks her body was like that of an animal, 'or one of those things that are just one cell, very tiny' (316) and when Jules thinks of the parts of his body as something that would be 'outlined . . . X-rayed . . . photographed . . . ill-smelling', they are thinking of themselves in relation to their bodies in precisely the way that unsettles the author of *Wonderland*. Whereas in *them* the self appears diminished because it is defined economically, in *Wonderland* it is diminished because it is defined biologically, the 'soul' may only be a 'cell' (384). The central character, Jesse Vogel, reminds himself that the brain is 'not sacred' but 'touchable', that it is 'matter', 'a weighable and measurable thing' (312). The radical project that *Wonderland* pursues is to treat this idea novelistically – that is, in the textual form which has historically been most concerned with the exploration of personality as precisely not merely a measurable thing, but complex and mysterious. Repeatedly, however, its characters question this assumption of traditional 'realism'. Jesse's boss, Dr Roderick Perrault, declares that the concept of personality is an illusion, 'a tradition that dies hard' (335).

The most memorable things in *Wonderland* arise from Oates's satirical anger at the implications of this reductively medical view of the self. It is a novel repeatedly characterized by a sense of horror and disgust arising from a profound disturbance at the way selves can be invaded and dismantled and transformed by other selves once there is no sense of any spiritual dimension in the self. Jesse himself is subjected to such a process by Dr Pedersen, who adopts him after Jesse's biological father kills himself and all the other members of the family. Pedersen sets out, calculatedly, to shape Jesse into a replica of himself, insisting that by doing this he will be correcting a defect of nature, 'modifying certain freakish twists of fate' (98). There is a sharp irony in this because he and his own children are the most freakish characters in the novel.

The Gothic monstrousness of the Pedersen family is satirical; it embodies the perverted ambition of the father to shape others to his own ends. That all the family are grotesquely obese may seem paradoxical given that their pursuits are so exclusively cerebral – the father a doctor and medical researcher, the son Frederich a composer, the daughter Hilda a mathematician. However, obesity is a physical rebellion against this unnatural exclusivity; the Pedersen family's obsession with eating is the body's revenge, an overpowering displacement activity. Even so, the focus on eating, digestion and body fat in *Wonderland* acquires a meaning of its own beyond the call of satirical duty, and suggests authorial horror at the extent to which the body has claimed human territory at the expense of the spirit.

Oates's disgust here is comparable with that of Swift, in the sense that it arises from the anti-humanist revulsion of an essentially religious person. The scene where the alcoholic Mrs Pedersen passes out naked in the bathroom and is rescued by Jesse is especially urgent with Swiftian horror. Her breasts are 'swollen, yellowish bulbs of flesh'; she has pendulous lumps of skin, a heat rash and the 'air of something fruity, yeasty, sour rising from her' (157); her head and face are dwarfed by her body which has become 'important, exaggerated' (158). According to traditional Christian values the body should keep its place, but in Swift's Brobdingnag and in Oates's *Wonderland* it swells to gigantic proportions. This reversal of the traditional ideal is accompanied in both Swift and Oates by another reversal which is thematically linked to it – the human spirit becomes mechanized, and machines are endowed with spirit. This satirical notion – the 'mechanical operation of the spirit' – is expounded by Swift in *A Tale of a Tub* and further explored in the 'Laputa' section of *Gulliver's Travels*. It is invoked by Oates in *them* and becomes a key idea in *Wonderland*. Jesse's spirit becomes 'automated, mechanized' (191). One of his professors in medical school declares that human beings are afraid of mechanisms 'because they do not understand that they are mechanisms themselves' (191).

Oates's main concern is that this view of the human spirit opens the way for one individual to turn another into a mere object of use – it is a psychological form of commodification. So Hilda is turned into 'an instrument to provide answers to questions' (144). Her freakishness arises from how much she is over-developed in one area and shockingly under-developed in every other, and also how much her father wishes to put her on display, as in the scene where she is wired up in front of a New York audience and made to answer mathematical questions in competition with an equally freakish boy, and while being monitored by a brain scanner (132–42). Frederich is a musical prodigy but his physical state is a sad contrast to his intellectual one: he has to have several teeth extracted, he has an infected gall bladder and he looks 'like a partly-deflated balloon' with pendulous skin like 'an intelligent frog' (148). When Mrs Pedersen finally rebels against her husband, enlisting Jesse's help to run away, she tells Jesse that Pedersen believes that once a patient has come to him, 'He owns the patient, he owns the disease, he owns everything' (171). He appropriates Jesse so that his adopted son hears him inside his own head speaking his own thoughts: 'Dr. Pedersen's being extended in Jesse's' (150). Pedersen acquires almost authorial power over the other characters, so that Hilda feels he may have 'imagined her into being' (128).

Pedersen's imposition on his children of an upbringing based entirely on mechanistic calculatedness is reminiscent of Dickens's Gradgrind, but he is not simply a rationalist. What motivates him above all is a form of territoriality, a drive to appropriate other selves, which is evoked caricaturally by his vast size because it embodies a grotesque ontological greed. A memorable scene depicts fanatical eating by the Pedersen family, culminating in the description of the father, with his face 'sharply handsome inside that pouched, bloated encasement of skin, his eyes sharp and glistening as the eyes of skinny, devilish birds' (127). As elsewhere in the novel, this suggests one self inside another as though the handsome self has been swallowed, and yet the handsome self is also, strangely, like a vulture. A long speech by Pedersen follows, in which he advises Hilda to allow him to interpret everything for her as he does for Jesse, and predicts that Jesse will 'become the complete form of the spirit I have imagined for him' (127). Pedersen's grotesque appetite for selves is made literal when Hilda declares – during her public display in New York – that her father wants to eat her: 'You want to press me into a ball and pop me into your mouth, back where I came from. You want to eat us all up!' (140). This combination of territoriality and eating also features in one of the most famous of political cartoons, 'The Plum-Pudding in Danger' in which Napoleon and William Pitt carve up the world, which sits on a plate in front of them.[9]

The crucial caricatural point here is that such obsessive greed is associated with the draining away of all those sympathetic feelings, and all that understanding, which are most closely bound up with how human beings like to perceive humanity. The transformation of humans into vultures is instantly recognizable as an image for this, drawn upon for example by John Heartfield in his photo-montage 'Madrid, 1936' (Lucie-Smith, 103) where two vultures in Nazi uniform tower gigantically above a cityscape dominated by three enormous bayonets, so that associations of vulture greed are conflated with those of aggressive territoriality. More broadly this is connected to an anxiety repeatedly expressed in the caricatural tradition about how definitively the human can be distinguished from the animal. Roderick Perrault declares that 'an animal has as much personality as a man' (335) and it is ironically appropriate therefore that the scene in *Wonderland* where the characters seem most inhuman is the one which deals with vivisection, when Jesse and his future wife Helene are taken by their friend Trick to visit the 'pathology farm'.

Part of what distinguishes this scene is its deadpan manner, especially in a novel with a tendency to overwriting. Trick says that Jesse aspires to 'a condition of personal bloodlessness', but that condition in the scene's characters is all the more horrifying because Oates keeps its style flatly bloodless as well, while staining the scene thoroughly throughout with blood. The characters' lack of response to the animals' suffering is so total that it is surreal because it opens a disorientating gap between that lack of response and the horrors that are described. It is the acrid smell they notice first and then the sound of laughter. They are greeted by a student called Peggy who brushes something at first unidentified out of her hair which is then revealed to be 'a small piece of intestine' (239). There are descriptions of experiments on cats, sheep, dogs and monkeys, three times referred to as 'fooling around'; the dogs are quiet because their barks have been removed, the monkeys quiet because they fire flamethrowers at them and they 'shoot some of the fire down the things' throats' (241). In a touch that anticipates the morgue scene in *What I Lived For*, one of the students is eating in the midst of all this (242), so continuing the motif of the mechanical relentlessness of human eating. It is joined in this scene, however, by a sexual element with Peggy's 'shrill flirting' with Jesse (245), and Trick's jealous competitiveness with Jesse in relation to Helene.

The juxtaposition of these appetites with satirically grotesque cruelties again indicts the thorough self-absorption induced by these forms of human greed. The extent to which this drains human beings of what is self-flatteringly regarded as 'human' capacities for fellow feeling is stressed in the scene because both Peggy and Trick see human behaviour reflected in that of the animals on this farm. The ewes are muscled out by the rams 'as in so-called human circles' (239) according to Peggy, and the only differences that Trick can see are that humans heal less well and are more likely to sue (243).

* * *

There is a harping throughout *them* and *Wonderland* on caricatural reductiveness. However, both novels call upon a Lawrentian idiom explicitly designed to oppose this with an insistence that a healing transcendence, achieved through sexual love, can redeem the economically or biologically reduced self. So, during his affair with Reva Denk, Jesse 'felt an immense, dangerous pulsation – as if the hot, hollow, radiant core of his being, the elusive Jesse itself, were very close to his grasp' (*Wonderland*, 355). This overheated style, and the sex mysticism that lies behind it, mar both novels and seem all the more unconvincing because the power of Oates's satirical writing makes the opposite case so thoroughly. By contrast, *Expensive People* [10] which dates from a similar period (1968), but lacks this Lawrentian dimension, is a much more complete, if less ambitious, success. The world of this novel resembles that of boxing in being thoroughly 'evaginated' because its presiding female figure Nada, mother of the first-person narrator, Richard Everett, is hardly womanly, let alone motherly. As one of her intellectual friends says 'you're *in essence* not really a woman and yet you've had a child. It's monstrous . . .' (243). In this she resembles Hilda in *Wonderland* who is said to have a secret self which is not Pedersen's daughter, 'or even a female' (128). Both women are so freakishly two-dimensional that femininity is almost erased in them. It is implied throughout *Expensive People* that it is largely Nada's lack of maternal feelings for her son that makes him mad and eventually makes him kill her.

However, her husband's role in this is also condemned, just as Pedersen's role is clear in the unsexing of his daughter. Nada's husband herds her around like 'an animal being driven into a pen'. It is this which makes her respond violently, and 'gift us all with a swift bite' (16), and which also turns her into a predictable mechanism – 'like a rag doll inspired by clockwork, ticking and clicking through tears and anger and exhaustion' (17). It may therefore also be her husband's treatment of Nada which partly accounts for her inability to respond to her son as a human being. She is turned into a mechanical doll and therefore, when attempting to interact with Richard, glances at him 'with the dim, mild surprise of a person noticing life in a store dummy or in a corpse' (110). This is all the more chilling because Nada is a successful writer who is credited at one point with having written one of Oates's own stories (194–211). Richard thinks that the sympathy she displays in her stories must have exhausted all her sympathy; when he tells her he has been reading her work she stares at him 'as if I had just crawled out of a crack in the wall' (222). Her name means 'nothing' (in Spanish) but her husband too knows 'nothing' and has an 'emptiness' where he should have had imagination, sensitivity and taste (43–44).

Nada seems to be the main focus of satirical anger in *Expensive People*: she is the shockingly bad mother whose lack of feeling dehumanizes everything around her. However, if the novel is seen in the context of Oates's other work it is clear that Nada is the product of her social circumstances. As Oates says in an afterword to the novel, *Expensive People* was imagined as the second of a trilogy comprising *A Garden of Earthly Delights* (1966) and *them* (1969). These novels were 'conceived by the author as critiques of America – American culture, American values, American dreams' (309). Her more recent novels can also be regarded in this way but what is conspicuously different is that their critiques of America have a much clearer feminist agenda and indict, above all, the carnivorousness of male desire. This is implicit, as I have shown, in *What I Lived For*, but it is much more the major concern of *Blonde*[11] (2000), which acquires its formidable power from combining in one novel all the satirical themes and caricatural techniques I have identified in her earlier work.

Like Nada, the Marilyn Monroe of *Blonde* is compared to animals and dolls. However, this novel – which deftly combines fact and fiction – makes the point much less ambiguously that it is not Monroe's own monstrousness but masculine culture which has turned her into a caricature. Her grooming for stardom is 'a species of animal manufacture, like breeding' (281). When her agent Isaac Shinn proposes marriage to her she is described, in a phrase that closely echoes phrases in *Expensive People*, as 'like a dazed ewe being herded expertly toward the pen' (283). The key point here, as in the earlier novel, is that the woman is dehumanized and imprisoned by powerful male manipulativeness. When Norma Jean is overwhelmingly upset at the decision of her first husband Bucky Glazer to go to war, and becomes sexually needy and aggressive, the horrified response of this young and unsophisticated man is by contrast not at all calculated. However, in calling her a 'sad, sick cow' he starts a refrain that echoes, with variants, throughout the novel (192, 308, 312, 477, etc.); misogynistic responses can be automatic and taken for granted, but can also be part of a larger systematic oppressiveness. A suaver version is in the habit of Marilyn's lovers Cass Chaplin and Eddy Robinson of calling her 'Fish'. These sons of famous fathers are her partners in a *ménage à trois*, but they are also a gay couple, and their nickname for her indicates their gay and supercilious squeamishness about female genitalia.

Blonde depicts, with relentless ferocity, Monroe's travestying by these masculine perspectives. It quotes another of her husbands, Arthur Miller, diagnosing her case as arising from the 'intersection between private pathology and the insatiable appetite of a capitalist-consumer culture' (542). Oates's own diagnosis concurs, but focuses the point about private pathology on that of the men in Monroe's life, including Miller, as much as on Monroe's own. She shows this private pathology also to be related to appetite by calling upon caricatural imagery of the sort that dominates *Wonderland.* Otto Ose is a clear descendant of Dr Pedersen in this respect. He was the man who, before Monroe was famous, took the nude photographs of her that would haunt her later career and contribute to her being belittled in some quarters as merely pornographic. Ose, as portrayed in the novel, is a freak of the *Wonderland* sort; he is not just misogynistic but mysteriously lacking in maleness so that his appetite for Monroe is purely commercial but powerfully defined as 'hawklike': 'He looked so *hungry*, so *predatory*' (228). Throughout the novel it is above all the camera that commodifies Monroe. Here it turns her, as Ose says, into 'a piece of candy, luscious enough to eat' (229). Ose cannot respond heterosexually to her but the camera provides a phallic displacement: he will not allow anyone to touch his camera because that would be 'Like touching Otto Ose's genitals' (201).

The dominant theme in *Blonde* is the gap between 'Marilyn Monroe', the construct created by the camera, and the 'real' woman and her life. Oates brings to bear all the caricatural techniques from her earlier work to explore the meaning of the cinematic construct and to reveal how much it is composed of male fantasies, and how it finally destroys her because 'The hunger of strangers is boundless and can never be appeased' (420). It is important that she is first called a 'sad, sick cow' when her first husband realizes that she has her own hunger, and is not simply the passive recipient of his own. The book dwells on the poignant differentness from the glamorous image of Monroe's actual femininity – for example, of 'her honey-brown curly hair' (194) as opposed to the artificial girliness of the painfully peroxided star. Part of this are the confrontationally detailed accounts of her heavy menstrual flows, her odours, her abject leakings: these are designed to oppose the Marilyn glossiness and also the sanitized fantasy of her as all surface and all fantasized metonymy, the Sugar Kane of *Some Like It Hot* who is 'the female body', the 'female buttocks, breasts' (613). Another important part of it though is Monroe as the subject of desire as well as its object, as the woman who responds to the male beauty and skilful love-making of Cass and Eddy G with astonishing sensations inside her in the place where the anatomical words are inadequate and the word 'cunt' has 'only a cartoon meaning, coined by the enemy' (327).

The implication is that the language itself contains masculine assumptions and has an inevitable, if implicit, tendency to caricature the most distinctively feminine experiences. Oates's strategic repetition, throughout *Blonde*, of stereotypical phrases – 'sad, sick cow', 'dumb broad' – draws attention to how the language insinuatingly imposes crude misogynistic labels on a woman whose sexuality is considered too conspicuous. To say that Monroe is defined by the male gaze is to make an obvious feminist point; Oates's more interesting insight is that Monroe was astonishingly adept at anticipating that gaze and inventing herself minutely in the terms to which it would most respond.

So, after she has learned her part, she becomes 'clockwork'; she transcends mere acting through her ability 'to see herself already on film, like an animation' (411). If 'cunt' is a cartoon word created by the enemy, this insight into Monroe's acting suggests that its power arose from her ability to construct herself, to splice herself together as the cartoon that the male gaze required. So it was partly this extraordinary skill that caused her downfall because it contributed to the crude simplifications of her image, and ultimately to the mistaking of that image for the 'real' woman. That there is something deathly in this and linked to her self-destructiveness is indicated by its juxtaposition with another motif in the novel, that of the ghost baby: 'I knocked on the door and bent my ear to the door, and I swear I heard a baby scream inside' (411). This Gothic idea is connected to the reality of Monroe's multiple abortions and miscarriages and also to her recurrent dream of a baby she never had, a dream in which her yearning is sometimes joyfully satisfied (567) but which is guilt-ridden at other times and terrifying because the baby wants to punish her for killing it: 'It's followed me here. It wants to devour me' (465). So, in the passage about her self-animation, this ghost baby is contrasted with her cinematic 'animated image' – stressing the gap between the mothering of life and the mere splicing together of an ideologically distortive construct in which she is 'displayed like a big animated doll' (425).

The repeated references to dolls (15, 43, 158, 256, 427, 615, etc.) also form a contrast to the ghost baby motif. Monroe's reduction to a mere object of use, a 'foam-rubber sex doll' (444) is the key source of the caricatural imagery in *Blonde*, and of Oates's authorial anger. Arthur Miller is accurate in identifying the origin of this commodification in 'capitalist-consumer culture' (542), but he himself is revealed to be not entirely innocent of it in his confusion of Monroe with his teenage lost love, a girl called Magda. Much worse, however – and clearly illustrating that the commodification of a woman like Monroe is thoroughly political – is President Kennedy's use of Monroe as a sort of sex toy which is then discarded. The implication that he was also indirectly involved in her death becomes even clearer when this part of the novel is understood in the context of Oates's novel *Black Water*[12] (1992) which condemns the involvement of another Kennedy in the death by drowning of a young woman.

5 *Muriel Spark's Puppets of Thwarted Authority*

In Muriel Spark's twenty-second and most recent novel *The Finishing School*[1] (2004), Rowland Mahler is unsettled by the talent of his seventeen-year-old student Chris Wiley. Both aspire to write novels but Rowland's has stalled and he feels increasing jealousy at Chris's self-assurance and apparent talent. This is especially humiliating because Rowland's literary ambitions are at the centre of his sense of himself; the 'whole point' of the school called College Sunrise which he runs with his wife Nina is to allow him to write. Nina believes in Rowland as a novelist as much as he does himself (7–8), and her investment in this self-image means that Rowland's marriage depends on his potency, or lack of it, as a writer. *The Finishing School* traces the collapse of their marriage, but it is characteristic of Spark that she makes this incidental to the novel's major concerns. The nature of their original attraction to each other suggests its fragility: Nina was impressed by Rowland's scholarship (his thesis on Rilke 'clinched the deal'); Rowland 'was in love, basically, with her practical dependability' (42). Husband and wife regard each other – as so many Spark characters have done – as objects of use rather than love.

Nina suspects that Rowland may be sleeping with the French teacher in the school, but this does not bother her 'unduly' (61), and she transfers her affections easily to a local art dealer. She is repelled by Rowland's growing obsession with Chris and finds it alien because she cannot understand a jealousy which is not sexual but aroused by 'a book, a work of art, a piece of writing' (69). She is less worried, however, about the damage to her marriage than about its impact on the school, especially when it arouses murderous thoughts in Rowland.

College Sunrise resembles institutions which organize the characters and narratives of other Spark novels, highlighting hierarchies and the consequent rivalries, ambitions, suspicions and mutual manipulations. These include the women's hostel in *The Girls of Slender Means* (1967), the nunnery in *The Abbess of Crewe* (1974), the film industry in *The Public Image* (1968) and *Reality and Dreams* (1996), and the school in *The Prime of Miss Jean Brodie* (1961). She is much less interested than most contemporary novelists in intimate and affectionate relationships, and much more drawn to interactions between characters which arise in professional contexts where careers are at stake. This set of Sparkian priorities reflects the preoccupation with power which has led her to adopt satire as her dominant mode. All of her institutions can be taken to represent much wider social and cultural structures which belittle her characters and attenuate their freedom to act.

The finishing school run by Rowland and Nina reflects contemporary culture because it is 'mobile'; starting in Brussels, it moves first to Vienna, then to Lausanne, and is now 'at Ouchy on the lake' (2). This, and the various nationalities of the pupils, indicates how unstable class and sexual identity have become. Confidence in the prosperity of parents of finishing-school students is undermined by references to their bankruptcies, and even to their crimes. When Princess Tilly is impregnated by the handsome gardener, she keeps her independence while the baby is assimilated by her aristocratic family. Chris appears to be rapaciously heterosexual: apart from his girlfriend, he also pursues the school's violin-playing neighbour, arouses the affection of Nina, and seduces a sixty-year-old female academic. However, he both relies upon Rowland's obsession and reciprocates it, telling Nina 'I need his jealousy. His intense jealousy. I can't work without it' (101). Nina wonders early on if a homosexual element is involved, but the relationship between the two writers appears to have literary motives, so it is the more surprising that by the novel's end they are running College Sunrise together, and come out in a 'Same-sex affirmation Ceremony' (155).

Such a conclusion needs to be seen in the context of Spark's satirical tendency to impose severe limits on her characters' range of responses and understanding. She is calculatedly reductive: a vivid example in *The Finishing School* is her ruthless cutting down to size of Chris, seen at first as a confident young genius but gradually exposed as merely a self-satisfied writer of popular historical fiction. Her habit, similarly, of assigning a single motive to her characters is clear as early as the fourth page: 'A faint twinge of that jealousy which was to mastermind Rowland's coming months, growing in intensity small hour by hour, seized Rowland as he looked'. Spark sees people as at the mercy of both internal and external forces: institutions mould their careers, but even their emotional lives are overwhelmed by drives beyond their control.

It is here that Spark's Catholicism is most obtrusive. The novel's eleventh chapter begins:

> According to the catechism of the Roman Catholic faith, into which Rowland had been born, six sins against the Holy Spirit are specified. The fourth is 'Envy of Another's Spiritual Good', and that was the sin from which Rowland suffered.
>
> Suffered is the right word, as it often is in cases where the perpetrators are in the clutches of their own distortions. With Rowland, his obsessive jealousy of Chris was his greatest misfortune. And jealousy is an affliction of the spirit which, unlike some sins of the flesh, gives no-one any pleasure.

> It is a miserable emotion for the jealous one with equally miserable effects on others. (80)

Such an intrusion is extremely unusual in contemporary fiction, which routinely eschews explicit moralizing, particularly when linked to declarations of religious faith. Nevertheless, it helps to explain the nature of Spark's fiction, and undermines recent, poststructuralist dismissals of her Catholicism as irrelevant. Martin McQuillan, for example, has insisted that the term 'Catholic writer' is an 'oxymoron' because

> Writing is not a theological activity, it purposely undermines essential and stable meanings, which presuppose and seek a single and authoritative centre. Meaning is always plural, writing is always cut adrift from its source and origin.[2]

McQuillan's point – a truism of contemporary theory – is unhelpful when applied to Spark because what distinguishes her as a writer is her resistance to plurality and instability. It is by now platitudinous to say that all language and all texts are endlessly open to multiple interpretations and to new subversions of any authoritativeness that they might claim for themselves. To discuss Spark in these terms makes her sound like any other postmodern writer, and distorts the extent to which her texts go against the grain of postmodern plurality.

A visible example of this procedure is the way *The Finishing School* ends with a list of the characters and their respective fates which strenuously resists any sense of open-endedness; its closure leaves no room for speculation about what has happened and what it means. Spark is not merely an author whose background is Catholic like the novelists McQuillan names in order to suggest that the novel as a form is more Catholic than Protestant: Joyce, Beckett, O'Brien, Ford, Conrad, McCarthy, O'Connor, Burgess, Hemingway, Fitzgerald, Dos Passos (2). The preoccupations of these writers are largely secular, whereas Spark's texts are repeatedly marked by spiritual concerns. Her satire is based on the premise that the human activities which she depicts are not what ultimately matters. Her comedy reveals the triviality of what is perceived by her characters as important. Most of them are deeply deluded: a number indulge in occult practices which Spark depicts as cheap and misdirected substitutes for authentic religion. Prominent amongst these are Patrick Seton, the medium in *The Bachelors* (1960), the satanists in *The Ballad of Peckham Rye* (1960), and Ian Tooley in *A Far Cry From Kensington* (1988) – characterized as 'Vegetarian, graphologist and astrologist'.[3] These two-dimensional cranks represent in flagrant form a general tendency in Spark's characters towards a conspicuous wrongheadedness which must be put down to profound spiritual disorientation.

The true corrective to such a state is in the quotation from the Epistle to the Philippians which Spark introduces into *The Bachelors*:

> All that rings true, all that commands reverence, and all that makes for right; all that is pure, all that is lovely, all that is gracious in the telling; virtue and merit, wherever virtue and merit are found – let this be the argument of your thoughts.[4]

Direct theological interventions are rare even in Spark's work but this one is framed in a way that explains why: the Biblical quotation is recited by Ronald Bridges, the novel's central character, as an antidote to 'melancholy and boredom'. It is described as 'meaningless to his numb mind' but only 'in the sense that a coat of paint is meaningless to a window-frame, and yet both colours and preserves it' (107). The minds of almost all Spark's characters are 'numb' in this sense: what should be most meaningful has become meaningless. It is also constantly implied that if their perspectives were coloured by this spiritual 'paint' then they would be 'preserved'. What defines them instead, and condemns them, is the wrongness of their colouring.

If the nature of Spark's fiction can be largely explained by this orientation towards spiritually perversity, her satire arises from the calculated contempt with which she displays her subject-matter. She is profoundly at odds with the humanist assumptions of the classic realist novel and holds her own characters at a disdainful arm's length: their lives are unalleviated by their fictional relationships because they are mostly incapable of the self-transcendence required to grow or develop in response to others. Spark's satirical vision is directed not so much at specific targets but at human beings as a species. From her Catholic perspective the merely human and worldly is inevitably flat and two-dimensional because the richest and most complex truths lie elsewhere. The pleasures of her fictions arise from the consequent fun she has with the incongruous weight which her characters attach to trivia, so that, as Helene Cixous says, 'A macabre cheerfulness springs up from the complete absence of values'.[5]

The most important premise of Spark's satire is accordingly the most hidden; what should be central is peripheral, and what should be marginal becomes central. This is already clear from the aggressive manner of Spark's first published work, her short story 'The Seraph and the Zambezi'[6] (1951), where a genuine seraph confronts a human dressed as a seraph for the performance of a nativity play. Samuel Cramer, the human fake, is the opposite of an archangel: he is directionless, a 'half-poet, half-journalist' (95) who claims to have chosen 'Life' (98) instead of literature, and now writes only occasional verses and conducts an inconsequential affair with a dancer called the Fanfarlo.

The inadequacy of his nativity play as a response to Christmas is implied, but it acquires a much more representative significance with the introduction of the seraph, whose spiritual reality is vividly evoked by contrast to the factitiousness of Cramer's fancy-dress: 'a toga-like garment made up of several thicknesses of mosquito-net, but not thick enough to hide his white shorts underneath' (99). The entry of the formidable archangel is a rebuke which reveals that the human world is shallow and meretricious, and it is presented on a scale which represents a form of transcendence in which instability and relativism no longer preside. It defies laws of perspective and so still looks the same size whether it is observed close up or from a distance:

> altogether unlike other forms of life, it had a completed look. No part was undergoing a process; the outline lacked the signs of confusion and ferment which commonly indicate living things, and this was also the principle of its beauty. (100)

The seraph stands for those theological meanings which are stable, essential and refer to a single and authoritative centre, and which, as Martin McQuillan insists, are impossible in writing. The seraph is the opposite of everything which Cramer has by implication expressed in his play: his toga'd version is merely textual and so embodies the degraded status that – from this spiritual perspective – writing must always occupy, and which it always, by implication, does occupy in Spark's work. Outside of writing there is Nature (represented in this story by the River Zambezi) and the world of the spirit, but these are unreachable: writing must focus on what is human and therefore unstable and relative.

A writer of fiction is bound to be preoccupied with human nature, but by constantly implying the inadequacy of that focus, Spark exposes the fatuousness of her characters' activities. After reciting the passage from the Epistle to the Philippians, Ronald Bridges becomes obsessed with the party he has recently attended, and thinks of the guests as 'automatic animals'. This may seem to be the stuff of 'comfortable satire' but his mood intensifies so that he finally perceives them as 'ridiculous demons' (*Bachelors*, 108). The sensibility lying behind this is clearly that which led Spark, in her prescriptive essay 'The Desegregation of Art', to declare that

> the art and literature of sentiment and emotion, however beautiful in itself, however striking in its depiction of actuality, has to go. It cheats us into a sense of involvement with life and society, but in reality it is a segregated activity. In its place I advocate the arts of satire and ridicule. And I see no other living art form in the future.[7]

It is this sensibility which links Spark to the version of Graham Greene presented in Richard Hoggart's essay 'The Force of Caricature'[8] which argues that the breath breathed into Greene's characters is so insistently the author's that his characters are merely puppets.

Hoggart's description of Greene's characters is accurate but he misses the extent to which the overt constructedness (in both genre and theological terms) of Greene's novels reinforces the powerful sense that his characters are trapped in structures of meaning which are so definitely not of their own making that their transformation into 'puppets' works ontologically. As Greene's Catholic successor Muriel Spark makes such designs far more explicit and explores their implications in more detail and with more postmodern licence. This licence is also increased because, unlike Greene, she is a satirist. The idea of characters as authorial puppets is present as early as Spark's first novel *The Comforters* (1957) where, as Frank Kermode notes, the heroine Caroline 'does her best to resist manipulation by the mind of the unseen novelist'.[9] Kermode also points out how this aesthetic issue is bound up for Spark with a theological one, involving a contrast between the novelist and God, who does not exercise artistic freedoms 'at the expense of his creatures' (268).

Spark's exploration of this ontological issue – although given a Catholic orientation in her work – links her to some younger contemporary novelists. Martin McQuillan and Bryan Cheyette are both right to oppose any tendency that the phrase 'Catholic novelist' might have to make her to seem 'marginalised'.[10] Catholicism is inherently at odds with postmodernism, but both modes of thought are profoundly opposed to liberal humanist assumptions about the autonomy of the individual, and it is in her satirizing of those assumptions that Spark has surprising affinities with other postmodern writers. The point is further confirmed by the influence which Spark has exerted on non-Catholic novelists, much of it insufficiently acknowledged. Martin Amis and Will Self are very different to Spark – preferring baroque elaboration to her astringent minimalism – yet both of them have deployed ideas similar to hers. The 'murderee' of Amis's *London Fields* (1989), in conspiring to effect her own murder, closely resembles the protagonist of Spark's *The Driver's Seat* (1970); 'Frank the Phone', who nags away at the protagonist of Amis's *Money*[11] (1984), is reminiscent of the telephone voice in Spark's *Memento Mori* (1959), which keeps reminding the major characters that they are bound to die. The surreal after-life setting of Will Self's *How the Dead Live*[12] (2000) is anticipated in Spark's *The Hothouse by the East River* (1973).

These two writers of the generation after Spark's are far more complicit with the postmodern phenomena they satirize than she is. This is partly because they have both become media celebrities so that they are, in a sense, postmodern phenomena themselves. It is also because they do not have a coherent moral system, such as Spark's Catholicism, to rely on when distancing themselves from the culture they indict. The effect of clinical detachment in Spark's fiction is aided by her deployment of the novella form: where Amis and Self characteristically write lengthy novels which are involved and involving, Spark's brevity is achieved through rigid control and efficient narrative lines. What is unpostmodern about her novels, and also entirely unlike 'ecriture feminine', is their refusal of open-endedness, their compact definitiveness, resembling the seraph in whom nothing 'was undergoing a process'.

The key characteristic of Spark's depiction of postmodern identity is her complete lack of nostalgia for the self in its earlier manifestations. Her early novel *The Public Image*,[13] centred on an actress called Annabel Christopher, explores the idea of the self as all postmodern surface, but there is no grieving over any consequent loss of ontological richness; instead the protagonist is remorselessly revealed to be entirely shallow. The novel does not satirize the loss of identity that Annabel suffers from becoming a puppet of the film industry. Its main satirical point is rather that the film industry gives her an identity where previously there was none. She is described in an objective third-person narration as 'stupid' (9) and her husband is entirely justified in telling her that she is unqualified to talk about 'significance' because she is herself so 'insignificant' (16). This moment resembles the later *Reality and Dreams*,[14] where the word 'redundant' is pushed beyond its economic meaning in order to raise the idea of a 'non-necessary person' (27). Here, Spark's Catholic satire is at its most ruthless – and disquieting – in wondering whether there may be some people who are simply spiritually worthless.

The caricatural effects of *The Public Image* evoke its heroine's complete emptiness. The key image in this respect – that of the shell, which reinforces the idea that Annabel is all lustrous surface – is introduced in a letter to Annabel from her husband Frederick. This is read to her, after Frederick's suicide, by her director Luigi Leopardi whom Annabel has earlier compared to Pygmalion (34), with the implication that backfires upon her that she is merely a stone image brought to life at his command. After Luigi has read Frederick's accusation that Annabel is 'a collector's item, perfectly formed, a pearly shell – but empty' (92), Spark confirms this image with the narrative information that Luigi, when he first recognized Annabel's potential as a screen actress, had noticed 'not Annabel, but her recordable image, eyes that would change with the screen's texture, something sheerly given in the face' (93). The crucial satirical point, however, is that Annabel's transformation in no way represents a travestying of any essential self she might have because, as Helene Cixous points out, 'Without a part, she stops being anything': she is nothing but 'a machine making movies'.[15]

As an empty shell and therefore literal nonentity, Annabel is the absent centre of *The Public Image*, but she is not alone because the whole world in the novel is equally shallow; the novel's satire impugns what Cixous calls the 'monstrous power' which the film industry bestows on 'these two-dimensional beings' (207). Frederick is more reprehensible than the wife he repeatedly criticizes. Marginalized by his wife's growing fame, he responds with a suicide aggressively timed to coincide with the arrival at their flat of a group of degenerates dispatched there by himself so that his wife will appear to have been dissolutely partying at the time of his death: 'He had sent that party, that intolerable party, to be blood on her hands, blood on her public image' (58). He is one of a series of characters in Spark's fiction who plot to ruin the lives of others, authorial puppets who attempt to make puppets of others. This point is confirmed by the image carefully applied to him near the start of the novel when he is described as 'like a tiny doll-man, his arms straight and sticking out from his sides as if they were made of cotton, filled with doll-stuffing and sewn-up' (13).

Such underhand manipulators in Spark's fiction are not shown as destroyers of human plenitude but as exploiters of a paucity which makes the human all too easy to predict and categorize. Spark enjoys placing her characters in reductive categories. Her deployment of what Hoggart calls the 'typical catalogue' (84) dominates *The Bachelors*, which begins and ends with a sweeping montage of the massed ranks of bachelors behaving in typically bachelor ways. The implication is that bachelors are especially two-dimensional because they lead lives of stalled and infertile singleness. Like the sterile automatons of *The Waste Land*, they can be summed up by reference to a few typical and automatic actions: 'they smoked a cigarette, slept, then rose at twelve' (129). Much of even Jean Brodie, the most complex of Spark's characters, can be explained by her membership of a similar category: 'for in many ways Miss Brodie was an Edinburgh spinster of the deepest dye'.[16]

In *The Bachelors* it is the authorial voice which makes sociological observations; in *Memento Mori*[17] this role is taken by Alec Warner, a gerontologist whose detailed scrutiny of the impact of old age parallels that of the novelist's concentration on people over the age of seventy. His card-indexes and files and cross-referencing (58, 139) represent another failed attempt by a Spark character to assume the God-like role of author. The key satirical point here is to show how unwilling human beings are to accept merely human status, to behave humanely, and how ready they are to aspire to God-like judgement and control.

It is also clear, however, that Spark believes there is an actual paucity about the human that makes this kind of reductive 'scientific' treatment all too easy to apply to it. The behaviour she focuses upon tends to be merely compulsive – sexuality, in particular, is regarded in this way throughout her work. Much of the very dry humour of *Not To Disturb* (1971) arises from its deadpan references to the casual and manic sexual activity which has taken place before the story starts, and it is in response to this that the character called the Reverend reads out a newspaper article about a new 'anti-sex drug'[18] used to control sex offenders, the implication being that the sex drive is a simple mechanism that can be simply regulated.

Spark's dismissiveness about sexuality is calculated to mock its routine aggrandizement. She frequently stresses its ability to turn those who experience its demands into unthinking machines. Godfrey, for instance, in *Memento Mori*, is at a loss to understand why he pays a young woman called

Olive to inch up her skirt and display her suspenders. But Spark is the least feminist of women writers and presents her women characters as the equal of men in their compulsiveness. This is presented with astringent definitiveness in *The Girls of Slender Means*, which centres on a hostel for well-bred young women in the years just after the Second World War. The shabby gentility of the May of Teck Club cannot conceal the ferment of desires which preoccupy its members: its own structure reflects their ape-like hierarchy which is revealed to be driven by instinct throughout.[19]

For Spark, sexual instinct is linked to other forms of compulsiveness that severely reduce the human capacity to choose freely. The young women in the May of Teck Club are insistently presented as frozen into habitual patterns of thinking. Her most characteristic way of indicating such mental rigidity is through the use of mechanically repeated phrases – a constant device in her novels, most famously in Jean Brodie's references to her prime, and to her pupils as 'la crème de la crème'. This further suggests that Spark's people are authorial puppets by implying, not characterization, but ventriloquism. *The Girls of Slender Means* offers an especially telling example:

> Dorothy could emit, at any hour of the day or night, a waterfall of debutante chatter, which rightly gave the impression that on any occasion between talking, eating and sleeping, she did not think, except in terms of these phrase-ripples of hers: 'Filthy lunch.' 'The most gorgeous wedding.' 'He actually raped her, she was amazed.' 'Ghastly film.' 'I'm desperately well, thanks, how are you?' (44)

The 'waterfall' here is akin to the metaphor of the cataract in an earlier passage about VE day (17): both indicate a subhuman drive, a herd instinct. Dorothy says only what her social position tells her to say and her 'phrase-ripples' indicate lack of individual volition. The phrase-ripples, which act as substitutes for thought, suggest the repetitions of a mechanism rather than the growth of an organism. They evoke, not the branching roads of the humanist self, but the cul-de-sac of caricature. Such patterns of repetition in speech and behaviour are deathly: the nuns in *The Abbess of Crewe*, for example, all behave like 'a programmed computer'.[20] This is linked to the looming presence of actual death; the characters in *The Hothouse by the East River* are introduced as living in 1960s Manhattan but they turn out to have died at the end of the Second World War.[21]

Spark's characters repeatedly choose deathliness. The most obvious of these is Lise, the protagonist of *The Driver's Seat*, who is engaged in a compulsive search for the man who will murder her. That the death instinct has replaced the sexual one in Lise is clear from the way she dismisses her most persistent suitor with the insistence that she has no time for sex and that 'Sex is no use to me';[22] she repeatedly refers to the object of her search as her 'type'. Her choice of this course is the logical consequence of the life-crushing control which subsumes her whole self in her job. Lise is defined by how thoroughly snapped shut she is, and therefore how unnatural. The novel's ironic title emphasizes her need to be completely in charge, resembling the monastic characters condemned throughout Spark's canon for the life-denying narrowness which they impose on themselves. Father Ambrose, in the recent novel *Aiding and Abetting* (2000), is 'very convinced of himself' and 'had arranged his life so that there was no challenge, no fear of any but the most shallow pitfalls'.[23] In the context of Spark's other work, Lise's fanatical self-discipline can be seen as one of many attempts to pull all the strings; she makes a puppet of herself so that she can exercise total control. The murderer she looks for will, in the process of killing her, be the agent of her desire for death, the two poles of submission and domination are combined in a paradoxical eroticism. In other novels the struggle for power is even more clearly the desire of one character to dominate others. So Fleur, in *Loitering With Intent* (1981), is, as Bryan Cheyette has pointed out, 'no different from Spark's other mythomaniacs – such as Jean Brodie, Lister, or the Abbess of Crewe – who, as novelists manqué, attempt to shape reality according to their abiding myths'.[24]

One of the distinctive features of Spark's work is the eerie lack of warmth between the characters: this also interposes a cold distance between them and the reader. This chill is intensified by those who repeatedly aspire to the role of author or God. Tom Richards, the protagonist of *Reality and Dreams*, the film director who is accused by his lawyer Fortescue-Brown of needing to play God, is typical. More interesting and more characteristic, however, are those who strive for God-like control in a more devious way, especially through blackmail, or plots related to it. Spark herself has commented on this: 'The terrorism in the novels is symbolic of everything that goes on like that, which is wrong. There's lots of blackmail in my work and unspoken blackmail . . . I can't stand it.'[25] However, what makes *The Prime of Miss Jean Brodie* Spark's most complex novel is that Brodie's puppeteering is much more ambiguous in its motives and impact. Jean Brodie is the exception that proves Spark's caricatural rule; she is treated far more humanely than is usual for Spark, and so her aspiration to the God-like role appears entirely different. It is true that she is authoritarian, even fascistic – her support for Mussolini and Hitler makes this obvious. She takes possession of her pupils and works tirelessly (and jesuitically) to bend them to her will: 'Give me a girl at an impressionable age, and she is mine for life' (9). Worst of all, she channels her frustrated sexuality into constructing the lives of those around her into a compensatory fiction in which Rose will have an affair with the art teacher Teddy Lloyd (with whom Brodie is in love) and Sandy will act as an informant.

Brodie's saving grace is that the impact of her activities is chaotically unpredictable. Even her faults turn out to have positive value: as Sandy is aware, 'Miss Brodie's defective sense of self-criticism had not been without its beneficent and enlarging effects' (86). Moreover, she does genuinely open the minds of her pupils, and is open-minded and absent-minded enough herself to be ineffective as a tyrant. Above all, she appears a force for enlightenment when contrasted with the oppressive atmosphere elsewhere in Marcia Blaine School and, especially, when contrasted with Sandy, the pupil who betrays her and develops into the most despised Spark type – that of the underhand manipulator. Sandy's moral wrongness is confirmed by her links with bribers and corrupters elsewhere, and by her 'insolent blackmailing stare' (122). Further proof of Sandy's more typically Sparkian status is provided by her becoming a nun. By contrast with this deathly fate, Jean Brodie represents the messiness of life and is therefore celebrated by an uncharacteristically complex, sympathetic and full treatment. She is Spark's most attractive character, even if her attractiveness is achieved against the grain of her author's predominantly caricatural sensibility.

6 *Magic Realism As Caricature: Angela Carter and Salman Rushdie*

The fantastical material in the work of Angela Carter and Salman Rushdie is deployed metaphorically in order to explore political issues. The premise behind their 'magic realism' is that traditional realism looks so closely at specific individuals in specific situations that it has severe difficulties in evoking the bigger picture – the political system – which ultimately determines what these specificities will be. The starting point of this fiction, then, is not with the autonomous individuals of traditional realism but with a wider political context in which individuals inevitably become puppets: Carter and Rushdie both self-reflexively present their characters as authorial puppets in order to reinforce this point. And because political context looms so large, characterization in this fiction is coloured with preoccupations and images which are shared with those of political cartoonists.

Carter and Rushdie intervene in their own texts to make explicitly political points. Elsewhere, they have their characters make these points for them; Carter reveals the premises of her own caricatural vision when she has the heroine of 'The Tiger's Bride'[1] (1979) reflect on her commodification and its consequences. Because her father used her as a bargaining chip in a game of cards and so lost her to 'The Beast' – because, therefore, she has been 'bought and sold, passed from hand to hand' (63) – she has been reduced to a similar mechanical state as the Beast's maid, who is not human but a 'marvellous machine' (60). Her commodification was possible because patriarchy had already denied her a fully human status: 'I was a young girl, a virgin, and therefore men denied me rationality just as they denied it to all those who were not exactly like themselves' (63). The patriarchal habit of promoting masculinity as the only acceptable and 'normal' mode of being condemns the feminine to a subordinate and worryingly alien status: this systemic misogyny reduces whatever is outside the masculine pale, whatever is not thoroughly like itself, to a caricature. The virgin is transformed by this dehumanizing perspective into a mechanical doll: she and the maid become each other's doubles, each other's 'clockwork twin' (60), because the virgin has 'been allotted only the same kind of imitative life amongst men' that the doll-maker gave to the maid (63).

These caricatural images put authorial anger fully on display and they are strikingly effective because of their confrontational directness, even crudity. Because patriarchy imposes itself as a norm, as unquestionable common sense, it requires in response this especially flagrant act of satirical defamiliarizing which loudly proclaims that the patriarchal vision is responsible, in fact, for degrading an innocent young girl into an object of use. Much more powerful than these abstractions is her transformation, like the maid, into a 'system of cords and pulleys' (60).

'The Tiger's Bride' is a re-telling of a fairy tale – so, too, are most of the stories in *The Bloody Chamber*. That collection is therefore a useful starting point for the discussion of magic realism which characteristically draws upon such re-tellings – though it generally incorporates them in a realist idiom in specific social contexts. This accounts for the self-consciously hybrid nature of magic realism, its combining of textual and oral narrative techniques, and also for its oxymoronic name. The fairy tale element amounts to a form of *faux naiveté* which disrupts realism and so deconstructs it: its childlike component points impudently at the emperor's new clothes and exposes his ideological nakedness.

There are crucial links between these methods and those of caricature, especially in the satirical confronting of the naive and the sophisticated. Magic realism incorporates an atavistic childishness, and so – as Gombrich and Kris point out – does caricature:

> Civilisation has taught us to renounce cruelty and aggression which once ran riot in atrocious reality and magical practices. There was a time in all our lives when we enjoyed being rude and naughty, but education has succeeded – or should have succeeded – in turning this joy into abhorrence. We do not let ourselves relapse into that state again, and if ever such impulses break loose under the influence of passion, we feel embarrassed and ashamed. In caricature, however, these forces find a well-guarded playground of their own. The caricaturist knows how to give them scope without allowing them to get out of control. His artistic mastery is, as it were, an assurance that all we enjoy is but a game.[2]

A key effect of caricature arises from the contrast between its often crude and aggressively energetic materials and how they are mastered by a thoroughly knowing and mature technique. The childlike content is exploited for its simplistic vividness: this is what the fairy tales supply in magic realism, where a sophisticated voice re-tells the simple story.

It is not surprising, therefore, that the same metafictional voice should also sardonically draw upon caricatural and childish crudity. This is especially appropriate because magic realism repeatedly satirizes the oppression of powerless, and mostly innocent, victims, by much more powerful figures who are cynical and meretricious. The prototype of this motif is in the prototype of the whole magic realist tradition, Gabriel Garcia Marquez's *One Hundred*

Years Of Solitude,[3] which was first published in Argentina in 1967 (in 1970 in Britain). This novel is centred on the isolated village of Macondo whose inhabitants live in a state of such pre-modern innocence that when modern technology finally reaches them they respond to it with childlike bafflement and wonder. A train is described as 'Something frightful, like a kitchen dragging a village behind it' (184). Their innocence leaves them entirely at the mercy of predatory outsiders such as Mr Herbert whose apparent harmlessness – he is 'chubby and smiling' (186) – helps him to colonize the village before its natives know what is happening. He personifies the impact in South America of United Fruit: his fascination with bananas is taken as an eccentricity but leads to Macondo being utterly transformed. The villagers, however, perceive the transformation as a form of magic or an act of God; their childlike incomprehension of technology leads to its being defamiliarized from this perspective: like 'Divine Providence', the colonists 'changed the pattern of the rains, accelerated the cycle of harvests, and moved the river from where it had always been and put it with its white stones and icy currents on the other side of the town, behind the cemetery' (188). The impact of these changes on the inhabitants of Macondo is particularly poignant because they are so bewildered by them; they are entirely vulnerable, and so unprepared for the colonists that they think they might be 'philanthropists' (188).

The paired motifs of innocent wonder and vulnerability are also recurrent throughout *The Bloody Chamber* and also refer to oral story-telling. Here, though, the innocent characters are all (except in 'The Lady of the House of Love') adolescent girls involved in their first sexual encounters, and Carter is anxious to stress their growing knowledge and power. This indicates the different political agendas of Garcia Marquez and Carter. Garcia Marquez is evoking and indicting wrongs that have already been committed: Carter, by contrast, is writing out of a gender context that is still evolving and can be influenced, so it is important for her to stress that women can acquire enough power to change their lives. For this reason her focus is not so much on shifts in historical circumstances as on profound transformations in her characters themselves.

These transformations are achieved as a result of the power struggles which preoccupy *The Bloody Chamber* and which involve a sense, on the part of its female and male protagonists, of a profound mutual alienness. However, the alienness of males, as it is perceived by the females, is stressed the most, and it is this which is vividly evoked by the fairy tale motif which represents the males as animals – the major motif of the whole collection. It is here, as well, that Carter's deployment of the resources of caricature is most in evidence. The transformation of the victim into an animal is one of the most common and enduring sources of imagery in the caricatural tradition: Edward Lucie-Smith identifies 'the tendency to endow human beings with animal forms, or to show animals engaged in human activities'[4] as one of the conventions of caricatural art.

In drawing upon this venerable tradition Carter achieves a brilliant satirical reversal. Patriarchal assumptions insist that the masculine is rational and therefore properly human, whereas the feminine is irrational and therefore related to Nature in all its disorder. Carter's animal caricature insists on the opposite by cunningly arousing an anxiety that the sexual appetite is so voracious that it makes human beings irrational and beastly. The men in these stories are animals because they are so sexually driven; Carter's satire is directed at the social requirement that these appetites be tamed, when it is in fact society's most powerful and respected members who are hypocritically licensed to satisfy them most freely. Her heroines repeatedly encounter males whose physical potency and social power are equally daunting, and who combine these features so exotically that they seem to be not even the same species as the female. As the Beauty in 'The Tiger's Bride' says: 'Nothing about him reminded me of humanity' (64).

As always with caricatures these beastly males are simultaneously larger and smaller than life; as the Beauty again says, 'I never saw a man so big look so two-dimensional' (53). In the title story, the heroine imagines that the Bluebeard figure has pressed his heart in the file where he stores mementoes of his past loves, but it is 'very thin' and 'pressed flat as a flower, crimson and thin as tissue paper' (26). Although this character is less explicitly beast-like than the other males, he turns out to be the most inhuman and is successively compared to a stone and a lily (26); his face resembles a mask (9); his bodily excretions are 'toad-like' (22).

He is so entirely defined by his desire for sadistic domination that he is incapable of any other response. This gives him the 'strange, ominous calm of a sentient vegetable' (9) and makes him – unlike almost all of the other male protagonists – incapable of being changed. He can prevent change by tyrannizing over time, which becomes his servant and traps the heroine in a seemingly endless night (30). He is what Carter calls, in *The Sadeian Woman*[5] – the key text for understanding *The Bloody Chamber* – an 'embodiment of that merciless excess, that overreaching will to absolute power that carries within it the seeds of its own destruction' (103). He is characterized by this single, repetitive 'excess' which requires him to lack any other characteristic: the scene where he peremptorily strips his wife is simultaneously multiplied in a 'dozen mirrors' and reduced to the monomaniac gaze of his monocle (15). His flatness is deathly; he is so simply an embodiment and so thoroughly confined to the role of 'puppet master' that, once he is deprived of it, and 'his dolls break free of their strings' (39), he must inevitably die.

The only extensively explored character who rivals this Bluebeard figure's flatness is 'The Erl-King', who transforms girls into caged birds: he, however, is capable of behaving affectionately and wreaks his damage inadvertently through his innocence. Carter vividly conveys his seductiveness and the frightening dilemma he poses to the heroine who declares that she loved him with all her heart but had no wish to join his 'whistling congregation' (90). This brilliantly evokes one of the most important issues in feminine identity formation because the temptation that the erl-king embodies is that of accepting a fate dictated by biology, of being thrust 'into the seed-bed of next year's generation' (88). The implication is that women who are willing to restrict themselves entirely to the role of wives and mothers accept the version of womanhood caricatured by the caged bird. So the erl-king's 'green eye' is a 'reducing chamber' that could make the heroine 'diminish to a point and vanish' (90).

There is a telling ambiguity in this story because the danger posed by the erl-king is one that arises out of a love which is, in both senses, captivating: in order to resist it the heroine must achieve the opposite transformation to the one he threatens and turn herself into a liberator. Carter signals this by one of her characteristic shifts in narrative voice, so that, when the heroine strangles the erl-king with his own hair and opens his cages, she moves from speaking as 'I' to referring to herself as 'she'. This narrative jolt enacts the heroine's acquisition of a new side to her character: in eschewing the fate which would condemn her to caricatural flatness she acquires a new potential to be multi-faceted.

By contrast, the limitations of the feline first-person narrator of 'Puss-in-Boots' are indicated by the single-mindedness of his narration: not only is the narrative voice consistently maintained but so is the single note he insists on striking – his tone of complacent levity is invincible. Where the erl-king represents the bondage of married and domestic love, this fashionable cat is fervently opposed to it and in favour of opportunistically acquired casual sex. He is shocked with disbelief when his previously rakish master falls in love – he himself is defined as a caricature precisely because he is incapable of this sort of human development.

As his master says, 'All cats are cynics' (71): this tomcat stands for the young male who cherishes his street knowledge and whose only values are those of loyalty to his friend, and who is otherwise amoral. His only concern is fun, so it is appropriate that he is the favourite animal of comic strips and cartoons. His levity is unperturbed because he is thoroughly lacking in emotional depth and sympathy; in this respect, also, 'Puss-In-Boots' contrasts with 'The Erl-King' which is heavy with melancholy and regret.

Carter's unusual strategy in 'Puss-In-Boots' is to allow a caricature to tell the story so that an increasing unease arises about the tomcat's lack of emotional response to what he is recounting. His world resembles that of Ben Jonson's *Volpone* which is solely directed to the dynamics of winning and losing, of domination and submission, and the tricks invented to ensure that winning is achieved at any cost. The narrative tone, however, is closer to that of comic opera – the story starts with an allusion to *Figaro* – and this appears to imply harmless romantic frivolity. The story is most effective in the lack of fit between these two components, especially when the cat decides to aid his master's access to the woman he loves by killing her husband. The trickery he uses to achieve this is described with blithe, self-congratulating frivolity, a tone related to his smiling mask that cats wear all the time: 'we have our smiles, as it were, painted on' (69). The narrative voice continues to smile even when the content has slipped into deep seriousness.

By contrast with this stubborn stasis and singularity, the emphasis in the stories based around 'Beauty and the Beast' and 'Little Red Riding Hood' is the surprising capacity of the characters to transform themselves. All of these stories are premised upon a single image: the encounter between the powerful, frighteningly alien male and the apparently defenceless female is compared to the encounter between a predator and his prey. But the stories all unsettle this by revealing the hidden strength of the young girl and the vulnerable humanity of the male.

A key effect of these stories, then, is to explore the boundaries of the human, especially the boundaries between the human and the animal. Carter makes this concern more explicit in *Nights at the Circus*[6] (1985), published five years after *The Bloody Chamber*. In this novel she repeatedly refers to the otherness of animals: she says that the howling of wolves is so chilling because 'of its distance from humanity' (228); she has Walser look into the eye of a tigress and discover there 'the entire alien essence of a world of fur, sinew and grace' (164). Elsewhere, though, the gap between the human and the animal seems worryingly small, as when the Educated Apes mimic human behaviour so convincingly while the Ape-Man is subhumanly stupefied by alcohol (163). The apes make 'studious observations' of human behaviour which they then subject to 'parody . . . irony . . . satire' (142): meanwhile, and in symmetry with this from the opposite direction, the carnival in which the clowns are involved exposes the animal underside of the human. This is why Fevvers, the novel's heroine, considers clowns 'a crime against humanity', and thinks that there is little distance between the Monkey House and Clown Alley (143), and why Buffo the head clown looks especially deplorable when his make-up starts to run and he looks 'hideously partly human' beneath his 'customary mask-like inhumanity' (173). It is therefore an especially unnerving moment when the chimpanzee called the Professor stares into the eyes of Walser, who is dressed as a clown, and produces in him 'that dizzy uncertainty about what was human and what was not' (110).

If there is really no significant difference between human beings and animals then human destiny is purely biological, and this is bad news, in particular, for women. *Nights at the Circus* counters this anxiety with the figure of Fevvers who is grossly physical but is also winged and therefore magnificently defeats biology – this makes her a more politically acceptable version of the New Woman that Guillaume Apollinaire sees personified by de Sade's Juliette. In *The Sadeian Woman* Carter quotes the French poet contrasting Juliette with her sister Justine who is 'enslaved, miserable and less than human': by contrast Juliette is 'a figure of whom minds have as yet no conception, who is rising out of mankind, who will have wings and who will renew the world' (79).

However, *The Bloody Chamber* repeatedly contemplates the worst biological destiny of all – the reduction to the status of predator's victim, the transformation 'from living flesh to dead meat', 'the dead status of thing' (*Sadeian Woman*, 138). This is the ultimate reification – beyond that described by de Sade in Minski's castle where living women are turned into furniture (94) and paralleling the fate of Marilyn Monroe in whose world 'women may be ordered like steaks, well-done, medium rare, bloody' (65). This fate threatens the heroines in *The Bloody Chamber* when they encounter their beastly mates; they will be 'horseflesh' (11), 'bare as a lamb chop' (15), 'Miss Lamb, spotless, sacrificial' (45), 'the cold, white meat of contract' (66).

Most importantly of all, however, Carter shows the Beauty and Little Red Riding Hood learning, through their bravery and cunning, to evade this reification: they are 'nobody's meat' (118). Each of these stories edges itself out of the caricature of the predator encountering its prey and shows both the male and the female characters in the gradual process of becoming more fully human. This is aided by an ambiguity which is already present inside the image of the males as predatory animals because it has an effect that Edward Lucie-Smith identifies in William Heath's caricature of the Duke of Wellington as a giant lobster, in which he finds a 'reluctant admiration': 'Wittingly, or unwittingly, this caricature conveys something of the old soldier's staunchness of character' (Lucie-Smith, 69).

The presentation of the males as wild animals implies power and energy as well as a potential for inhuman cruelty, and the stories show the males and females in a process of rapprochement in which the males are tamed by love and the females learn to understand their own capacity for sexual responsiveness. These stories move, then, increasingly out of a simplistic tableau (predator and prey) related to what Carter calls 'the black and white ethical world of fairy tale' (*Sadeian Woman*, 82) and into a much more messily human interaction which is morally neutral or ambiguous. This process shows the characters emerge out of caricatural flatness and into a greater individuality achieved through greater mutual understanding.

* * *

Angela Carter's repeated references to masks, and her preoccupation with role-playing and performance, lead a number of her critics to invoke gender theorizing about 'masquerade' in order to account for this aspect of her work. Mary Russo,[7] Sarah Gamble[8] and Linden Peach[9] all discuss the two essays by Mary Anne Doane[10] in which she draws upon Joan Riviere's 'Womanliness and Masquerade'. According to Doane:

> The masquerade, in flaunting femininity, holds it at a distance. Womanliness is a mask which can be worn or removed. The masquerade's resistance to patriarchal positioning would therefore lie in its denial of the production of femininity as closeness, as presence-to-itself, as, precisely, imagistic . . . Masquerade . . . involves a realignment of femininity, the recovery, or more accurately, simulation, of the missing gap or distance. To masquerade is to manufacture a lack in the form of a certain distance between oneself and one's image. (*Femmes Fatales*, 25–26)

Mary Russo is sceptical about Doane's theories, even in their revised form, because they involve a 'disavowal of the female body as a site of political activism' (168). But there are surely worse problems with masquerade than this: Russo is willing to concede that it dismantles 'essentialist models of femininity', whereas its tendency as a metaphor is in fact to suggest that the mask can be removed to reveal a 'real' face underneath. This implies that this face is, by contrast, authentic and therefore represents an essential self with an essential gender identity. A gender outlook that was consistently performative would not hinder itself with a metaphor that carries such associations of a depth versus surface model because the associations of depth will always imply the possibility of eventual access to an essential, underlying truth. A thorough performativeness would not imply a simple either/or (mask or mask removed) but an endlessly shifting range of nuanced possibilities.

A further problem with masquerade is evident from the ways that the mask has been used in the caricatural tradition. Caricature focuses on the face, probing and distorting it with satirical intentions: this leads it inevitably to the mask, which hints at a suspicious reluctance to allow the face to present its naked truth. Caricature is suspicious by nature, always ready to assume the worst and to imply underhandedness. Edward Lucie-Smith contends that theatrical masks played a key role in the pre-history of caricature (26–29). On the cover of his book is a powerful example of the role that masks play in political cartoons: in Gerald Scarfe's 'Nixon Is Right Behind You', which first appeared in the *Sunday Times*, a saturninely predatory and impossibly jowly Nixon peers one-eyed from behind a mask of Henry Kissinger, all fuzzy hair and rubbery smile.

Political problems hobble masquerade when it is proposed as a positive gender strategy. Doane focuses exclusively on masquerade as flaunting and ignores its equally powerful associations with sinister concealment. By invoking the mask, feminists run the risk of confirming sexist assumptions rather than subverting them, of endorsing the patriarchal stereotype of women as manipulators of cunning surfaces. Misogynistic suspicions that women have something to hide are disturbingly in evidence, for example, in Jonathan Swift's 'A Beautiful Young Nymph Going to Bed' which describes in appalled detail a woman dismantling herself: she is so thoroughly reduced to a mere mask that she 'Must ev'ry Morn her Limbs unite'. Swift finds his own art overwhelmed in the face of hers as he tries to show 'The Anguish, Toil, and Pain, / Of gath'ring up herself again'.[11]

Swift is a major participant in the caricatural tradition precisely because he is so finally attuned to what is loathsome in human character and behaviour; the unnerving misogyny of this poem confirms these credentials because it is part of a profound anti-humanism which drives an anger and hatred that regularly erupt into his texts. His attitude of fierce suspiciousness is shared by James Gillray, whose 'Weird Sisters; Ministers of Darkness; Minions of the Moon' of 1791 draws upon multiple images of the mask to express disquiet about the political impact of George III's madness.[12]

This etching is especially relevant because it is so preoccupied with gender. The king's incapacity leads his wife, Queen Charlotte, to acquire more power than Gillray thinks she should: the moon is composed of her face and that of her husband stuck together, but it is *her* face that is shining forth as the ascendant crescent. The associations of the moon with both madness and femininity are powerfully, if misogynistically, drawn upon, and the king's metaphorical overshadowing leads to the feminizing of others in power: the ministers are transformed (via a reference to Fuseli's famous 1783 illustration of the witches' scene from Macbeth) into 'weird sisters'.

There is a profound sense of disquiet in this etching which reveals the unsettling effect of sticking one face on top of another. Carter's own use of the mask far more closely resembles this caricatural deployment of it than the one implied in feminist masquerade – as such it reinforces her caricatural imagery, which I have already discussed. In *The Bloody Chamber* it is significantly always the male characters who wear masks, and they do so in order to deceive the female characters. In 'The Tiger's Bride' the Beast wears 'a mask with a man's face painted beautifully on it' (53): this story advocates the stripping away of mere social surface in order to find eroticized selves which will allow a passionate interaction between the genders. In 'The Bloody Chamber' the Bluebeard character's face seems 'like a mask' as though 'he had laid by the face in which he had lived for so long in order to offer my youth a face unsigned by the years' (9). The image is connected to that of the 'hideaway' which he can resort to when 'the yoke of marriage seems to weigh too heavily on [his] shoulders' (21): it represents a tendency in normal masculinity towards reserving part of the self, avoiding full commitment, and even full communication. Most disquietingly, this story questions the distinction between this ordinary masculine behaviour and the sensibility of the psychopath: it is the face of a killer which hides behind the mask, and his hideaway is actually the eponymous torture chamber.

* * *

The mask is important in caricature because it not only evokes the hiding of the 'real' self, but also interrogates the very concept of such ontological coherence and substance. In Salman Rushdie's work its most extensive role is played in *The Satanic Verses*[13] (1988), where it excites anxieties related to postcolonial identity. It is introduced naturally into the story because its two central characters, Gibreel Farishta and Saladin Chamcha, are actors: Chamcha inhabits 'the caricature of an actor's room full of signed photographs of colleagues . . . a room bought off the peg, by the yard, an imitation of life, a mask's mask' (174). Acting, though, is a metaphor in this novel for the roles that must be adopted by those – like Rushdie himself – who have had to learn how to adapt themselves to alien cultures. Chamcha has learnt a highly self-conscious adeptness in his multicultural role-playing. Excluded at his English boarding school, 'he began to act, to find masks that these fellows would recognise, paleface masks, clown-masks, until he fooled them into thinking he was *okay*, he was *people-like-us*' (43). Later, though, he plays the opposite role, wearing patchouli oil and 'a white kurta, everybody's goddamn cartoon of the mysteries of the East' (174) and this despite his more-English-than-the-English taste for 'Cricket, the Houses of Parliament, the Queen' (175).

This postcolonial masquerade is much more effective than the gender masquerade recommended by Mary Doane because it is not subverted by the associations of sinister underhandedness in the mask but strengthened by them because they represent the bewildering uncertainties that characterize postcolonial identity. The anxiety aroused by the mask hobbles its use as an image of empowerment, but it is very vivid in evoking Chamcha's sense of ontological powerlessness in his dream of 'a man with a glass skin, who rapped his knuckles mournfully against the thin, brittle membrane covering his entire body and begged Saladin to help him, to release him from the prison of his skin' (33–34). Rudely woken from this dream, Chamcha finds himself involuntarily slipping back into his Bombay persona and regards this as a disastrous 'regression', thinking '*I'm not myself*' and nightmarishly imagining serial regressions: 'Masks beneath masks until suddenly the bare bloodless skull' (34).

Masks also figure in *The Ground Beneath Her Feet*[14] (1999) where they are linked to its major theme of role-playing and (musical) performance. Their presence in that novel alongside references to feminist theory suggest that Rushdie may well be taking up themes from Angela Carter's later work. So he satirizes his heroine Vina Apsara for her belief that 'women no longer see men purely as individuals, but think of them as repositories and products of the ignoble history of their sex' (338). These concerns are consonant with those of Carter because they show that gendered perspectives can caricature both the masculine and the feminine. More characteristic of Rushdie, however, is that he ties this attitude to a questioning of 'the modern idea of the auto-determinant self'; Vina's reductive generalizing of men transforms individuals into 'culturally generated automata' (338).

The automaton is the key caricatural image in Rushdie's work and again a sign of his affinity with his friend Carter and her desire machines and mechanical dolls, although in his case the context of the automating of the human is rarely gender – overwhelmingly the context is political history, especially of a postcolonial kind. Rushdie dismisses the idea of the auto-determinant self as 'modern', and so stresses that what has become the common-sense view of the self is historically specific, and may disappear. This also explains much about the way that characters are portrayed in his own fiction. Where the classic realist novel assumes that individuals determine their own characters and destinies, Rushdie's magic realism portrays them (as in the passages from Marquez which I discussed earlier) as being thoroughly at the mercy of historical circumstances. It is this which turns them into automata.

This theme is most explicit in Rushdie's most recent novel *Fury*[15] (2001) in which the protagonist, Malik Solanka, is convinced that 'Puppet-masters were making us all jump and bray' and wonders, 'While we marionettes dance, who is yanking our strings?' (8). The novel takes this as its controlling metaphor, which arises from Solanka's own activities as a famous dollmaker. It is contrasted with the theme of Dionysian fury alluded to in the title and is further articulated by the contrast between that which is merely mechanical (and therefore doll-like) and that which is spontaneously creative and potentially ecstatic. These states of mind are allegorically represented in the country of Lilliput-Blefescu whose name refers to Swift's satirizing of the 'mechanical operation' of the human spirit. In Lilliput-Blefescu there is chronic conflict between the Big Endians, who believe in mathematics, and the Elbees, who believe in poetry; as Solanka's girlfriend Neela says:

> it's like the struggle inside human nature itself, between what's mechanical and utilitarian in us and the part that loves and dreams. We all fear that the cold, machine-like thing in human nature will destroy our magic and song. (158)

The invention of a country whose factions illustrate contrary states of the human soul is characteristic of a tendency towards allegory in all of Rushdie's novels, despite his own explicit rejection of that idiom:

> I usually resist the idea of allegory. In India there's too much of it, allegory is a kind of disease. People try to decode everything, every story or text allegorically, and although clearly there are elements you could call allegorical in *Midnight's Children* and *Shame*, the books are not allegories in the way that *The Pilgrim's Progress* is, where everything stands for something and the real story is a story that is not told. Allegories ask readers to make a translation, to uncover a secret text that has not actually been written. In that sense I don't think my books operate as allegories.[16]

This passage is interesting because it rejects allegory but acknowledges an

Indian obsession with it which, in fact, must have been an important shaping force on his work. What is clear from Rushdie's description of allegory is that it is not allegorical strategies which are repugnant to him but a sensibility which he regards as lying behind allegory, a sensibility which wants to explain everything systematically. Rushdie's response arises from his sceptical and libertarian mistrust of theocratic attitudes to life – that same mistrust which led to the satire in *The Satanic Verses* which caused him such terrible trouble. Rushdie's own deployment of allegory has the opposite of this totalizing effect: because he enlists allegorical strategies alongside numerous others they are far from suggesting that everything can be translated and explained – instead they contribute to the hybrid hotchpotch of his texts.

Rushdie's own allegory is very unlike that of *The Pilgrim's Progress.* Instead it resembles that mode of allegory which is related to caricature and whose political character is defined by Walter Benjamin in the passage I quoted at length in my chapter on Joseph Heller. Here the point is the exact opposite of that allegory which elaborates a systematic code which translates everything into a grand narrative: it is not about tyrannical wholeness but about 'the fragmentation behind the alleged order and causal evolution of history'.[17] This is the version of allegory which Fredric Jameson[18] sees as enjoying a revival in the postmodern period and identifies as one of the features of postmodern art which distinguishes it from the symbolist aesthetic of modernist art; it is associated with relativism rather than the moral and spiritual absolutes of *The Pilgrim's Progress*, it is 'provisional' and 'aleatory' and characterized by

> a generalized sensitivity, in our own time, to breaks and discontinuities, to the heterogeneous (not merely in works of art), to Difference rather than Identity, to gaps and holes rather than seamless webs and triumphant narrative progressions . . . The allegorical, then . . . can be minimally formulated as the question posed to thinking by the awareness of incommensurable distances within its object of thought, and as the various new interpretative answers devised to encompass phenomena about which we are at least minimally agreed that no single thought or theory encompasses any of them. (167–68)

This describes very exactly the mode of allegory which Rushdie deploys. The novel which is most dominated by it is *Haroun and the Sea of Stories*[19] (1990) which is allowed an extra licence of simple explicitness because it is a children's story, and which is specifically directed against the sensibility which produces allegories of the totalizing sort: its villain is Khattam-Shud who tries to erase story-telling because he believes the world 'is not for Fun' but 'for Controlling' (161). Rushdie's antipathy to allegory is an antipathy to theocratic control, and his own version of it pits Chup (quiet) against Gup (gossip, nonsense, fib); in a brilliant passage the two are joined in combat in the form of a man fighting his own shadow (123–26). The over-controlling tendencies of allegory are deflected in *Haroun* through comedy and, in particular, through what Catherine Cundy identifies as 'a particularly cartoon-like quality' in many of its scenes, 'where the words on the page scramble to convey the speed and particularity that a thousand sequenced animations flitting across a screen can provide'.[20]

Cundy rightly identifies this as a recurrent characteristic of Rushdie's prose (5), and its impact is to turn *Haroun* into a cartoon allegory, which self-reflexively presents the story via its gaps and holes. The seamless web of the cartoon is self-evidently constructed out of its separate components, the animation creates the illusion of movement conjured out of multiple stills.

The cartoon, then, evokes Differences rather than Identities: most crucially, and most obviously, because of the spectacular and comic wrongness of its picturing of the world. This is a characteristic of all caricatural art, and in cartoon the deliberate childishness is even more obvious: children are the principal consumers of cartoons, just as they are the intended readership of *Haroun*. Once again, though, the child-like is used as a device; *Haroun* is a political satire aimed at Rushdie's theocratic persecutors, and its child-like simplicity insists that the values it is championing ought to be so obviously worth championing, and the opponents of those values so obviously the villains, that even a child could see the moral point.

Cartoon allegory in a children's story is unproblematic; it is much more challenging when it is used in Rushdie's political novels, where the charge of irresponsible childishness might be thoroughly damning. Aijaz Ahmad makes a charge of this sort when he claims that the reader of *Shame* is 'in danger of forgetting that Bhutto and Zia were in reality no buffoons, but highly capable and calculating men whose cruelties were entirely methodical'.[21] Ahmad's literal-minded misunderstanding of the satirical method is instructive because it reveals how Rushdie's caricatural method depends upon confrontationally childish insult, and his use of the word 'buffoon' is telling because it indicates the habit that caricature has of turning political leaders into clowns. The whole point of this sort of political cartooning is an act of rebellion which energetically refuses to accord figures of authority the respect they are accustomed to receive.

This is a tradition which includes Charles Philipon's famous portrait of Louis-Philippe as a pear (or 'poire' – the French word also meant 'fathead'). This first appeared in Philipon's own magazine *La Caricature* in 1831 and led to a libel trial in which 'Philipon was acquitted of the charge of defamation after sketching the transformations from head to pear and asking the jury, "Is it my fault if His Majesty looks like a pear?" '[22] It is clear that Rushdie enthusiastically endorses this anti-authoritarian spirit because he quotes with approval the children of the Chilean film director Miguel Littin urging their father 'to pin a great long donkey's tail on Pinochet', and mocks the 'farcical trial and subsequent execution of Bhutto by that fearsome "cartoon", Zia ul-Haq'.[23]

Rushdie's political novels are most accurately seen as cartoon allegories in this tradition. In *Shame*[24] (1983) the eponymous personification is applied to Sufiya Zinobia who becomes the Beast of Shame because, as her mother points out (200), she incarnates the shame of her parents Bilquis and Raza Hyder, and she is transformed into something not human but 'something more like a principle, the embodiment of violence, the pure malevolent strength of the Beast' (242). But, as her husband is thinking this, he is observing what Catherine Cundy calls the 'body-shaped hole in the bricks' Sufiya has left behind as she burst out of the confines he imposed on her, and this hole is 'a stock image from the "Tom and Jerry" cartoons' (Cundy, 92).

It is the cartoon element which derides allegory, even in the course of its deployment, by insinuating a distinct edge of parody:

> Shame walks the streets of night. In the slums four youths are transfixed by those appalling eyes, whose deadly yellow fire blows like a wind through the lattice-work of the veil. They follow her to the rubbish-dump of doom, rats to her piper, automata dancing in the all-consuming light from the black-veiled eyes. (219)

The 'automata' indicate how Rushdie's use of allegory is linked to an emphasis on the powerlessness of individuals who are driven or erased by forces far more powerful than themselves. So one character in this passage is a beastly personification and the others are her dismissively and minimally characterized victims. The personification is comparable to those in Shelley's 'The Mask of Anarchy' where a powerful oppression has imposed itself on a whole country, and transformed individuals into impersonal forces, or 'masks', which disguise what Shelley's idealism takes to be true human nature. The personification is also reminiscent of how Honore Daumier uses the device in his lithographs of the Franco-Prussian war – these contain female figures labelled Liberty, Europe, Diplomacy and Peace.[25] Moreover, Rushdie shares Daumier's contempt for the political leaders who preside over these terrible political circumstances. The thoroughgoing depersonalizing of individuals which is evoked in cartoon allegory shows that Rushdie's political outlook goes well beyond what Richard Cronin considers his 'somewhat vague liberal prejudices'.[26] He is very far from the 'auto-determinant self' which dominates the fiction of liberal humanist writers but is preoccupied with how tyrannical rulers like Iskander Harappa cease to be human beings (*Shame*, 209) and how their influence dehumanizes and automatizes everyone around them. So the appropriate idiom for Rushdie's political novels is not the liberal and balanced extending of authorial sympathy, and even love, to all the characters which is required in realism, but that caricatural method which obsessively lampoons as much as it characterizes. This is what the animator Jack Brunel means, in *The Satanic Verses*, when he declares that 'Heartlessness' is the 'Only thing a cartoonist really needs. What an artist Disney would have been if he hadn't had a heart. It was his fatal flaw' (317). *Shame*'s peripheral hero, Omar Khayyam Shakil, is therefore contrasted with the poet after whom he is named:

> he remembered with hatred instead of love; not with flames, but icily, icily. The other Omar wrote great things out of love; our hero's story is poorer, no doubt because it was marinated in bile. (40)

So *Shame* incorporates its own synecdoche in the form of the eighteen shawls embroidered by Rani Harappa and entitled 'The Shamelessness of Iskander the Great'. Each depicts a scene from the tyrant's life, each of them marinated in the bile of Rani's horrified perspective which further cartoons Harappa's already caricatured life. The imagery Rani draws upon is traditional in political cartoons. In the 'badminton shawl', the reference to the sport works metonymically to expose Harappa as a 'man of pleasure masquerading as a servant of Duty' (192), the juxtaposing of badminton and sex (racquets, shuttlecocks, frilly underpants) mocks Harappa's seigneurial womanizing. In the 'slapping', 'kicking' and 'hissing' shawls complex political acts are represented by simple physical actions: the first two translate Harappa's oppressiveness into personal acts of violence, and the third translates the creation of a police state – its spies, and its carefully orchestrated atmosphere of paranoia – metonymically into the action of whispering and then metaphorically into a web with Harappa as the 'head spider'.

The 'torture' and 'election' shawls resemble those cartoons of Hogarth and Gillray which form synecdoches of the political culture of their day: in the 'election' shawl even the tiniest figures are recognizable and nameable. But there is also a marked tendency for the imagery to become increasingly less realistic and more outlandish so that the horrors of Harappa's regime are shown to intensify. The shawls come to resemble those kinds of caricature which reveal its kinship with the grotesque: in the 'swearing' shawl, Harappa's oaths are transformed into 'foul creatures crawling from his lips'; in the shawls of 'international shame' he is shown 'riding an atomic bomb' and 'slitting the throat of an emerald chicken and plucking the feathers from its east wing'. And the 'white shawl' is surreal, its whiteness (white policemen on a white background) evoking the difficulty of properly discerning what Harappa is up to (193).

This leads, in the later shawls, to a preoccupation with death and apocalypse. Firstly, in the 'allegorical' shawl, it is only the death of a Daumier-like personification: Harappa is strangling a female figure called 'Democracy' which then acquires more complex associations because it resembles Sufiya as a child so that 'Democracy' and 'Shame' get entangled with each other. Secondly, in the 'autobiographical' shawl the artist herself is shown as an old crone but with a body composed of 'wood, brick, tin . . . she was earth and cracks and spiders' (194) – a common idea in the caricatural tradition, certainly since the work of Giuseppe Arcimboldo (1537–93). As Edward Lucie-Smith says, 'Even after Arcimboldo's time, the technique of constructing a human creature out of inanimate objects remained popular with designers of fantastic prints' (49). However, this idea is much more telling when it has less to do with a fantastical frisson than (as here with Rushdie) an anxiety about the degrading of the human to the status of fragmentary objects. So the last two shawls culminate in an apocalyptic landscape:

> the people hanging upside down with dogs at their open guts, the people grinning lifelessly with bullet-holes for second mouths, the people united in the worm-feast of that shawl of flesh and death . . . and Little Mir Harappa . . . [whose] heart had been removed . . . and there was a villager standing beside the corpse, with his bewildered remark sewn in black above his head, 'It looks as if,' the fellow said, 'his body has been looted, like a house.' (195)

* * *

The dehumanizing invasion and disintegration of the self and the body that dominate the climactic imagery of Rani Harappa's shawls are also key motifs of Rushdie's *Midnight's Children*[27] (1981). The major source of these motifs is the self of the first-person narrator Saleem Sinai who personifies post-colonial India because its birth coincided with his own, and he was therefore 'linked to history both literally and metaphorically' (238). So, early in the novel, when he says 'I have begun to crack all over like an old jug' (37) it is clear that this mirrors what has happened to his country, and even clearer when it is soon followed by the cracking of the earth: 'huge gaping fissures appeared in the midst of macadamed intersections' (39).

Saleem disintegrates because he is helplessly tied to a disintegrating nation; his helplessness is most graphically illustrated when the sadistic schoolteacher Emil Zagallo victimizes him, and in the process re-emphasizes his unshakeable link with India. Singling Saleem out from his classmates, he drags him by his hair to the front of the class then tugs the boy's nose, and laughs: 'You don't see? . . . In the face of thees ugly ape you don't see the whole map of *India*?' (231). Then he further elaborates the conceit, finding the Deccan peninsular in his nostrils and Pakistan in his facial stains, the East Wing in the birthmark on his right ear and the West Wing in his stained left cheek. This provides Saleem's classmates with a whole new set of taunts; the most significant one, 'map-face' (232) evokes a recurrent motif in caricature in which the face or body is transformed into a map: Johann Michael Voltz's 1804 portrait of Napoleon (Feaver, 64) is one such example. Here, there is a connection to the transformation of the body into a thing or conglomeration of things, but more specifically to the traditional concept of the 'body politic'.

Zagallo's heartlessness illustrates some of the crucial characteristics of the caricatural method. The schoolmaster's status permits him to assault Saleem in physically intimate and torturous ways: caricature can normally be excused because the power relationship is the opposite of this, and the victims are assaulted only metaphorically in revenge against their authority. Still, the emphasis on power is instructive because it reveals why political questions are always at least implicit whenever caricature is deployed. The fact that the caricaturist Zagallo is the powerful character allows him to add physical injury to insult and so enhances the feeling of cruelty that the passage arouses (when he pulls out Saleem's hair it increases the ugliness which he has already drawn attention to, and makes the boy vulnerable to new insults). As an adult Saleem becomes 'an unfortunate fellow with a face like a cartoon' (322).

All of this stresses Saleem's powerlessness. What caricature does is to seize a part of its victim's person – the nose, as here, is its most common target – and dwell upon it with distortive focus so that it looms large and ugly. It is as though the victims have an alien mask forced upon them against their will, so that caricature deprives the victim of power over that which should be most intimately their own; it is an act of aggressive metaphorical colonizing. Rushdie's use of these techniques fits very appropriately with his thematic preoccupation with the lack of 'auto-determination' of the self, and his repeated image of puppets and automata. Saleem's self is so thoroughly tied to the state of India that he is entirely under occupation by it. His magical telepathic abilities, bestowed on him because the hour of his birth coincided with the independence of India, mean that even his brain is not his own because it is overwhelmed by other voices, other thoughts: 'multitudes are jostling and shoving inside me' (9).

The magical abilities of the children of midnight make them resemble the superheroes that feature in 'cheap comics of a most unliterary nature' which Rushdie says he devoured as a child; these were 'almost always mutants or hybrids or freaks' (*Imaginary Homelands*, 425). Like Batman, Spiderman, Aquaman and Superman, Rushdie's eponymous children are all 'freak kids' (*Midnight's Children*, 221) who, as a result of an accident, have acquired special abilities. But their powers are paradoxical; while they constitute a superhuman potency, they also lock the heroes into mechanical patterns of repetition, and turn them into the puppets of their own power.

The potency of the children of midnight must also be stressed, however, especially because it makes them exceptional and so connects them, self-reflexively, to the potency of the novelist. It is the quality of 'unlikeness' which Rushdie sees as being shared by the comic superhero and the novelist: this is 'the thing that makes it impossible for a writer to stand in any regimented line . . . a quality novelists share with the Caped Crusaders of the comics' (*Imaginary Homelands*, 426). Saleem, in particular, embodies the struggle against regimentation because his mind contains such swarming multitudes. The multiple voices inside Saleem's head are also the multiple voices inside the novel are raised against the uniformity that the regime of Indira Gandhi tries to impose. By contrast with the untidy polyphony of the children of midnight, the child of Indira Gandhi is associated with the tidiness of cloning: 'certain high-ups in that extraordinary government (and also certain unelected sons of prime ministers) had acquired the power of replicating themselves . . . a few years later, there would be gangs of Sanjays all over India' (395).

The struggle against deadening uniformity is the most consistent theme in Rushdie's work. It is still present in *Fury* where it takes the form of that struggle within human nature 'between what's mechanical and utilitarian in us and the part that loves and dreams' (158). The key motive for Rushdie's caricatural strategies is vividly to satirize those repressive tendencies which transform human beings into automata. His use of nicknames throughout *Midnight's Children* and *Shame* confines the characters to a single aspect or role, and traps them in patterns of inhuman repetition. Calling Indira Gandhi 'the Widow' associates her with death and loss and so implies that this is her major influence on her country (especially by contrast with the alternative title of 'Mother', which is equally accurate biographically and which Rushdie only applies to her with heavy irony). Characterizing her by reference to her hair is also self-consciously reductive:

> if the Mother of the Nation had had a coiffure of uniform pigment, the Emergency she spawned might easily have lacked a darker side. But she had white hair on one side and black on the other; the Emergency, too, had a white part – public, visible, documented, a matter for historians – and a black part which, being secret macabre untold, must be a matter for us. (*Midnight's Children*, 420–21)

The equation of the Emergency with Mrs Gandhi's hair is deliberately simplistic, and is part of a highly elaborated pattern of such equations which characterize Rushdie's political novels. This is his greatest strength as a writer and is one he shares with the best political cartoonists. It requires a talent for the continuous production of witty ideas, a talent rarely required of traditional novelists who sustain their narratives much more through character development and plot construction, qualities less dwelt upon by Rushdie. His creative problems arise when the ideas show signs of flagging, as they do in *The Satanic Verses*, and when he tries to write more conventionally, as he does in *The Ground Beneath Her Feet* and, much more damagingly, in *Fury*.

There are signs of the latter problem, however, as early as the later chapters of *The Satanic Verses* where Rushdie writes about the death from cancer of Saladin Chamcha's father Changez (520ff). Theoretically, given that

Rushdie's novels pride themselves on incorporating multiple discourses, it ought to be possible for him to shift into a thoroughly realist idiom at this point. Theoretically, too, it ought to be possible to slow down the narrative rhythm and dwell upon a single individual and his suffering, and this ought to produce the sense of an ending that Rushdie clearly wants. Rushdie works hard to notate the naturalistic details of Changez's physical decline: 'The cancer had thickened Changez's blood to the point at which his heart was having the greatest difficulty pumping it round his body' (522). However, it is very difficult to get involved with this death at this late stage because the overwhelming tendency of the novel's political focus has been on the operation of large-scale forces metaphorically expressed; and this flat-footed account of unmetaphorical fact therefore seems entirely unconvincing. The rest of the novel is defined by caricature rather than characterization, so it is too late now to engage the reader's interest in Changez's suffering which must depend on our believing in him as a 'real' person to begin with.

The far more damaging problem in *The Ground Beneath Her Feet* and *Fury* is that the subject-matter that gave Rushdie such creative authority and gave his work such multiple resonances – the postcolonial condition of India and Pakistan – is thoroughly marginalized. The subject-matter that replaces it – mostly popular culture – is comparatively trivial and unable to carry the weight of significance he tries to bestow on it. Unmoored from postcolonial issues his work wanders about and stumbles into postmodern platitude, as when Vina Aspara is said to be

> a rag-bag of selves, torn fragments of people she might have become. Some days she sat crumpled in a corner like a string-cut puppet, and when she jerked into life you never knew who would be there, in her skin. (*The Ground Beneath Her Feet*, 122)

Some of the same preoccupations are present here as those which drove the political novels, and some of the same uses of cartoon allegory. However, when applied to popular culture this device meets no resistance of the sort that made its political deployment so formidable. Used politically, the cartoon effects invoke a satirical tradition whose self-conscious triviality subverts the pomp and pretentiousness of power. Applied to pop stars and other postmodern celebrities, the cartoon effects merely suggest a doubling of trivialities:

> Here is a Gary Larson cartoon of Vina and Jesse Garon Parker, the grotesquely Vegas-rhinestoned Fat Jesse of his latter, pill-popping, burgerizing days. They're alone in a motel room, looking out at the world through the slats of a venetian blind. What's this supposed to be, the dressing room of the undead? A zombie transit zone on the Far Side? Ha ha ha. (482)

The play with the notion of alternative realities (exemplified in this passage by an alternative Elvis who has adopted his manager's name) is entertaining and witty. *The Ground Beneath Her Feet*'s recurrent earthquake motif carries associations of historical and personal upheaval which are further articulated through references to 'variation' related to the musical meanings of the word 'ground'; these might have achieved a fruitful stylistic departure for Rushdie into something less allegorical, and more symbolist, and linked to the Rilkean associations of the novel's Orpheus allusions. Unfortunately, though, none of this makes the impact that it might have done because the central subject matter is so superficial – and this is even more the case in *Fury*, which lacks even the failed promise of its predecessor.

7 *The Caricaturist As Celebrity: Martin Amis and Will Self*

Martin Amis and Will Self share a belief that comic satire is the most appropriate idiom for the depiction of contemporary life. In a conversation first published in the *Mississippi Review*, Amis refers to his own 'essential comic crudeness as a writer'; Self replies that this is because Amis is a satirist and that satire 'is a form that depends on comic exaggeration, and on stereotyping'; then Amis asks if Self also considers himself to be a satirist and Self agrees that he is:

> one critic said about *Quantity Theory*: I don't think Self is interested in character, or in narrative, he's interested in conceits and language – and I took this on the chin . . . It's true I'm not really interested in character at all. Indeed, I don't even really believe in the whole idea of psychological realism. I see it as dying with the nineteenth-century novel.[1]

For both writers this is linked to an anti-humanist outlook and, more specifically, to a sense that humans are less human than they used to be – though this (and its attendant hints of nostalgia) is much more important in Amis than in Self. John Updike characterizes this perceptively:

> Amis writes out of a sensibility uncomfortably on the edge of the post-human. His characters strikingly lack the soulful, wilful warmth that he admires in Saul Bellow: they seem quick-moving automata, assembled of mostly disagreeable traits.[2]

Updike has modestly not noted here that Amis also admires Updike's own writing; yet Amis writes in a very different manner to these two senior American writers to whom he has been anxious to pay homage (as, for example, in the essays collected in *Visiting Mrs. Nabokov*[3]). Bellow and Updike are surprising role models for Amis because his own writing conspicuously lacks their superabundant enjoyment of human diversity and energy. By contrast, Will Self's proclaimed affinities with William Burroughs, Joseph Heller and J. G. Ballard (*Junk Mail*, 49–62, 167–72, 329–71) are much more predictable.

Updike is profoundly out of sympathy with Amis's 'post-human' satire: nonetheless it has been in this mode that Amis has achieved his most effective writing. Its motivation is best understood by reference to Amis's essay 'RoboCop II' where he explains why the RoboCop films are so successful in evoking a characteristically contemporary affectlessness. The eponymous cyborg incarnates this, but not quite 'because he is part machine', and he is 'not quite affectless, because he is still a man' (*Visiting Mrs. Nabokov*, 167). So, describing the actor who plays RoboCop, he says:

> He is *the man.* Like the creation he plays, though, Weller is only partly human now; to some extent, inevitably, he is *product.* The lost-self theme works so powerfully on us – perhaps we all feel it. Perhaps, as we speed into the future, we all feel that something has been left behind. (168)

This lost self is the absent centre of much of Amis's writing: what replaces it is the 'stereotyping' Will Self refers to, or the 'automata' whose dominance is regretted by Updike. The world of RoboCop is relevant because, as Amis points out, 'its imaginative origins' are in 'comic books' (164): the post-human in Amis's fictions is represented by the self-conscious cartoon flatness of his characters. It is effective, however, precisely because its context reveals how such flatness evokes absence and loss – so making that flatness all the starker: his comedy resonates because its origins in desperation are so apparent. More surprisingly, the lost values which Amis laments are consistently located in a Romantic sensibility apparently at odds with the yobbish loucheness with which his novels are obsessed. But Amis's caricatural vision is most accurately seen as satirizing a contemporary state of affairs in which Romantic values have been thoroughly trashed.

Most central is an ideal of innocence which is the starting-point of his indictments of corruption and depravity. Amis's autobiography is significantly called *Experience* (2000) and contains a number of reflections on childhood and children which reveal how large the subject looms in his outlook: one of the reasons he is drawn to Saul Bellow is because in him 'the sense of a child's vision is supreme and defining'.[4] This is partly an aesthetic concern involving an 'innocent eye' effect which may also explain why Amis was drawn to the techniques of 'Martian' poetry, especially, as Blake Morrison has pointed out,[5] in his novel *Other People* (1981).

More importantly, though, this is a key thematic concern and Amis quotes a passage from Bellow which reveals a belief in the pre-existence of the soul and deploys imagery of light and darkness. These both feature in Wordsworth's 'Immortality' ode, one of the major Romantic texts which treats the theme of innocence and experience. Moreover, the soul's descent from heaven and eventual return to it (a neo-Platonic concept implicit in both Wordsworth's poem and in the passage from Bellow) is a basic premise of Amis's *Time's Arrow* (1991). Here it supports the reversed narrative, the telling of the protagonist's story from his death backwards to his birth, so that the idea of a life before birth is made to work symmetrically with the more conventional idea of a life after death. This introduces imagery which contributes to the systemic disorientation that characterizes the novel, as when the inmates of Auschwitz are described as staring upwards into the sky, 'looking for the souls of their mothers and their fathers, their women and their children, gathering in the heavens – awaiting human form'.[6]

At a thematic level this concept is combined with the novel's most central preoccupation, its bewildered evocation of the Holocaust as a World Upside Down where torture masquerades as medicine. Innocence and the pre-existence of the soul are invoked in order to defamiliarize the evil and extreme corruption associated with the Nazi 'Final Solution'. So, on two occasions they are juxtaposed with the nightmare figure of a gigantic doctor towering over the world: on the first occasion this is a dream and the 'storm of human souls' is introduced as a simile for a 'blizzard of wind and sleet' (16), but on the second occasion he has become ominously literal and the 'queue of souls' appears between his legs like a grotesque (and gender-reversing) birth. It is the focus on innocence, and the adoption of an innocent eye with all its attendant vulnerability (here again there are suggestions of 'Martian' influence), that magnifies the impact of the damage inflicted and further defines the extent of the corrupt horror.

Time's Arrow also indicates why Romantic assumptions about innocence lead Amis to conceive its corruption in caricatural terms. The novel operates from the premise of an originally uncorrupted state which is then sullied: when he refers to 'snowdrops to be restored like white souls to the heavens' (122) he is imagining the soul at birth as tremblingly fragile and pure. Just before this, similarly, he imagines the land where Auschwitz was situated, but prior to its becoming a concentration camp, as conspicuously pristine: 'The land is innocent. It never did anything' (122). However, once corruption sets in, it leads to a thorough withering of both natural and human resources: 'at the railway station in Treblinka, the four dimensions were intriguingly disposed. A place without depth. And a place without time.' (151) Similarly, the protagonist's work takes 'so much of what is essential in [him] that there is nothing left' (152): his capacity to love is literally disabled and he is left impotent.

So the human is flattened to the status of a thing, an animal or a machine. The protagonist's boss, 'Uncle Pepi', has a 'feline' face and 'was only playing the part of a human being' (136). The Germans in the camp are transformed into a single personification who 'worked like a dream, like a brilliant robot you switch on and stand back and admire as it does all the hard work' (127). The organizational triumph of Auschwitz consisted of finding 'the sacred fire that hides in the human heart' – and then building 'an autobahn that went there' (132). Later a 'ruined god', who resembles the surreally gigantic doctor, has taken 'human beings apart – and then he put them back together again' (156).

There is a sinister kinship between such *disjecta membra* and Amis's use of the phrase '*cracked up*' (93) in which his use of italics draws attention to the pun. This indicates Amis's ruefulness about comedy, whose sources he questions on a number of occasions. Here the context is the protagonist's later activities as a doctor in the USA (but therefore earlier in the novel) and it is revealing about the extent to which laughter in Amis's work is associated with guilt and pain: their patients are in pain but the doctors experience 'the mortal hilarity that sniggers' (93) behind everything they do. Laughter is important to Amis because he is above all a satirist who wants to arouse it in response to his targets, but he is also highly conscious that laughter is rarely innocent, and never innocent in satirical contexts. He is conscious, in other words, that laughter is at odds with one of the most cherished values in his work – that it can be regarded as a response to the incongruities, often sordid or even evil, which arise because the world we inhabit has been so thoroughly drained of its innocence.

So Amis's recent book on Stalin is subtitled *Laughter and the Twenty Million*:

> Russia, 1917–53: what is its genre? It is not a tragedy, like *Lear*, not an anti-comedy, like *Troilus and Cressida*, nor yet a problem comedy, like *Measure for Measure*. It is a black farce, like *Titus Andronicus* . . . It seems that humour cannot be evicted from the gap between words and deeds.[7]

His own work also tends in this generic direction because he is especially concerned to express a late twentieth-century sensibility that has emerged in the wake of modern horrors like the Holocaust and Stalinist murders. Laughter for him arises from the attitude of shocked irony that responds to the collapsing of an earlier, and innocent, idealism. He draws upon Nietzsche's definition of a joke as 'an epigram on the death of a feeling' (*Koba*, 247), and his satirical novels dwell upon a sense of sometimes apocalyptic belatedness, an afterwards of sceptical exhaustion which hurts us into a self-contempt that is guiltily combined with furtive amusement.

Innocence has been made impossible, but the sense of its previous existence is indispensable if laughter is to be successfully aroused. Remembering a political meeting in 1999 in Conway Hall in Holborn, Amis describes how his friend Christopher Hitchens said that he had spent many evenings there with 'many "an old comrade" '. Amis meditates on the laughter this caused, describing it as 'the laughter of universal fondness for that old, old idea about the perfect society' but also as 'the laughter of forgetting' (*Koba*, 256). The acquisition of the knowledge that replaces innocent hope is painful, but laughter anaesthetizes the pain.

Amis is sceptical about the role of laughter – and yet he also places an extremely high value on it. When, in *Experience*, he describes the dementia that afflicted his father, Kingsley, towards the end of his life, what most horrifies him is the thought that his mental deterioration might lead him to laugh at 'unfunny things' (322). When, in *Koba*, he declares that he has no sympathy with his father's youthful desire for the 'Just City' (let alone the atrocities that were committed to achieve it) he invokes, as his two principal reasons for this lack of sympathy, his inability to imagine either what Just City laughter or Just City writing would be like (273). It might seem bizarre to place greater value on comic writing than on political justice – but the latter ideal is barely considered in Amis's outlook.

This partly accounts for the sense of moral ambiguity that Amis's novels arouse, because he often appears so anxious to be funny that other values take a back seat. To put it more broadly, though: there is often a preference in his work for the aesthetic over the moral. Even *Time's Arrow* is infected by this at times, which may be why Tom Paulin was so ferocious in his attack on it, on television, when it was shortlisted for the Booker Prize. Paulin described it as 'bone-headed', 'stupid' and 'morally obtuse'.[8] The novel does arouse an anxiety that it is unseemly, and even narcissistic, for an author to be performing such technical tricks when the subject-matter is so sombre. In this case, however, the stylistic tricks have become familiar to the reader by the time that the most morally unsettling content is broached, and those tricks have brilliantly created a context which is thoroughly disorientating.

For example, the description, early on, of a car crash happening backwards produces a visceral upset, a shocked queasiness:

> With a skilful lurch he gave the bent hydrant on the sidewalk a crunchy shouldercheck – and we were off, weaving at speed back up the street. Other cars screamed in to fill the sudden vacuum of our wake. (28)

The combination of these effects with the invocations of spiritual notions of innocence and guilt, which I have discussed, give *Time's Arrow* moral substance and weight especially because those notions are associated with another of the novel's key metaphors – Catholic doctrines of eternal punishment. In particular, the fate of the protagonist's soul can be accurately compared with that of the damned in Dante's *Inferno* where they are subjected to a punishment whose condigness is imagistically configured. So, for example, in Canto XX those who have been found guilty of superstitious divination – because their superstitiousness constitutes an overturning of true religion – walk backwards and with their bodies turned almost back to front. Amis's metaphorically damned Nazi suffers an analogous fate: because he turned medicine on its head, and became a torturer and killer, his soul must relive his life, but backwards.

It is precisely because Amis is preoccupied with twentieth-century horrors that he is drawn towards notions of innocence. Throughout *London Fields*

(1989), there are repeated invocations of a lost pastoral – the novel's title imagines a time pre-dating the city's urban decay and corruption, a time when the land was innocent, before it *did* anything. Whereas now 'there are no fields. Only fields of operation and observation, only fields of electromagnetic attraction and repulsion, only fields of hatred and coercion. Only force fields.'[9] Constantly troubled by this loss, the narrator Samson Young repeatedly fantasizes about returning to the London Fields and its 'innocuous sky' (463) where he played as a child with his brother – but this is heavily ironic because this London Fields is the place in America where significant developments took place in research for the atomic bomb, and the narrator is dying as a result of his early exposure to radiation there (161). So Samson Young (whose name is a stage elbow in the ribs) is turned into a personification: as Nicola Six says, 'you're at the heart of all this' (which, as a reference to first-person narration, is one of Amis's quieter metafictional moments), 'In a way, you are the Crisis' (161).

There is another heavy irony, which is similarly based on Romantic assumptions about innocence, in the novel's interest in 'Little Boy', the euphemistic name bestowed with astonishing insensitivity on the bomb dropped on Hiroshima. This acquires more resonance through the novel's treatment of the theme of childhood and its contrasting of two babies: Marmaduke, the son of Guy and Hope Clinch, and Kim, the daughter of Keith and Kath Talent. The female baby is made to carry all of the associations of pastoral innocence and is treated with a lyricism that contrasts significantly with the dominantly satirical writing; she has 'sweet breath and faceted roundnesses, as tender as an eyeball' (138), she is 'an *angel*' (102). The novel ends in this mode, poetically punning on the word 'impressions' – a baby's psychological impressionableness being physically represented by the imprints made on its body by fingerprints and clothes and a carpet's 'crenellations' (470).

Because this constitutes the novel's close it suggests that Kim embodies the possibility of hope, but her impressionableness is ambiguous – it also implies vulnerability. Moreover, the lyrical tributes to her have been tinged throughout with implications that her innocence is constantly withdrawing, as when she has stopped saying 'Enlah' because 'Time *takes* from you, with both hands' (239). This whittles away most of that possible optimism and replaces it with the theme that overwhelmingly dominates where innocence is concerned – the theme of loss.

The male baby Marmaduke personifies that loss, the impossibility of any longer giving credence to the Romantic concept. His contrast with Kim encapsulates the origins of the caricatural vision in Amis: Kim is the Romantic ideal and Marmaduke is the cartoon that substitutes for the ideal when it has been corrupted by our post-human times. He is an almost sleepless and relentless engine of domestic destruction, and a blithe source of fevered parental anxiety, who wins endless victories over a series of despairing nannies. His destructiveness is linked to his robust masculinity and his contrast in this respect with Kim indicates an aspect of Amis's outlook that has been little discussed – his location of contemporary social problems in a specifically masculine aggressiveness. Feminists have been rightly troubled by his simplifications of women,[10] but they have paid too little attention to how these are joined, to some extent with self-conscious symmetry, to caricatural simplifications of masculinity. That this is associated with one of the key themes of *London Fields* is clear from the 'Little Boy' motif, and its further explication in the passage where Samson Young remembers playing as a five-year-old with his brother in London Fields:

> Oh boys, you are heartbreaking and mysterious. The way you cock your weak bodies – to essay something, to dare something. Your love of war. Look! Watch! Oh, boys, why do you have to do this?
>
> But boys have to do this. (323)

Children playing in fields ought to be the most pastoral of images, but the boys' cocking of their weak bodies represents their striving to acquire fully phallic power, and their compulsive aggressiveness transforms the scene so that it foreshadows all the massively cruel and sordid consequences of lost pastoral which the novel laments.

The caricaturing of Marmaduke works by a similar reversing of the innocent ideal so that he is already not only 'sexual' but even pornographic in his tastes (158). He leers over a swimsuit advertisement, fellates his bottle, gropes his nannies and aspires to 'a career in child pornography: he knows it's out there, and he can tell there's a quick buck in it'. His aggression is not so much boyishly boisterous as a sinister foreshadowing of actual war: his nursery contains 'howitzers and grenade launchers and cartridge belts'. This paragraph escalates in characteristic Amis fashion so that a realist (if exaggerated) premise about boys' toys builds towards an outrageous climax in which Marmaduke is associated with nuclear war and said to favour the pre-emptive strike: 'Fight like hell for three days and then blow up the world' (220).

This is confrontational satire of such an extreme kind that its status as comedy is in doubt, but it is important because it weighs the magnitude of the loss that is being mourned. Corruption of innocence on a scale that produces both pornography and nuclear war in the nursery is the result of the entropic 'planetary and twentieth century' circumstances (141) which are diagnosed just after the domestic devastation inflicted by Marmaduke – 'broken glasses, chipped china, childblood, spilt milk, spilt milk' (140). The entropy identified by Amis combines the trashing of two Romantic values: innocence and Nature. The polluting of the natural environment is a repeated motif in *London Fields* where it is associated with the obsessive theme of death, and is also made a routine part of the setting – many of the scenes take place against the backdrop of metropolitan violence inflicted on the natural. Early in the novel this theme is connected to that of childhood when the narrator laments the number of animals threatened with extinction, then says that even dogs 'aren't living as long as they used to' and:

> How will we teach the children to speak when all the animals are gone? Because animals are what they want to talk about first. Yes, and buses and food and Mama and Dada. But animals are what they break their silence for. (97)

One of the most striking features of the style of *London Fields* is displayed in those passages where Amis brings to bear his *fleur du mal* poetry to describe the symptoms of massive hurt suffered by the abused planet. Such appalled magniloquence indicates that Amis has in mind the corruption of yet another Romantic value, for it invokes a kind of perverted sublimity. Guy Clinch in love resembles Shelley in believing that the planet is surrounded by a 'love force' (413); he has a vision of the moon, a revelation in which he penetrates beyond its 'mask' and seems really to apprehend the moon's truth as a heavenly body (344). All of this is subverted, however, because the love Guy feels has been aroused by Nicola Six for her own perverse ends, and his lunar epiphany is succeeded by the disquieting image of a 'dead cloud' which Guy thinks is an 'Awful sight'. The isolation of this phrase increases the sense that it is a pun in which the older meaning is present – but only to be superseded in order to stress the loss of that Romantic capacity for awe.

Samson Young has also seen a dead cloud and describes its behaviour – it 'oozed and slurped' (345) – as though it were a human with bad personal habits. Amis is arguing that the sublime has been lost because what humans have done to the planet has humanized it in all the worst senses, and to such an extent that the feeling of an encounter with awesome alienness has been depleted. So he imagines the planet having a human face – 'a *man's* face, because men did it' – whose ravages reflect the damage inflicted by drug addiction, its 'scalp churns with boils and baldspots and surgeon's scars' (369). The flattening of complex vitality into a single quality is caricatural: Nature has been travestied because it has been forced to resemble a starkly limited person – in particular, a gross and exploitative male. This satirizes the overturning of natural order, the unnatural mingling of diverse elements that has horrified moralists since the Middle Ages (it is such a staple of moral disgust that it is parodied as early as Chaucer's 'Pardoner's Tale' where the pardoner condemns cooks on these grounds). The contamination of Nature by necrotic human materials is a symptom of a world which is apocalyptically sick.

The proliferation of the human is the consequence of the refusal by humans to be confined to their proper sphere: one prime example for Amis is the arms race. The language he uses to talk about this, in the culminating paragraph of his journalistic essay 'Nuclear City', is of a piece with the venerable satirical premises that underlie his planet-with-a-human-face. There he speaks of 'mortal shame' and the need to acquaint 'our children' with 'the status quo, with the facts of life, the facts of death' (*Visiting Mrs. Nabokov*, 33). It is this too which leads to the post-human condition which Amis anatomizes in *London Fields*: it is the arms race that leads to the cultural dominance exercised by 'the satellites, triumphantly affectless' that seem 'to exclude everything human from their diagrams of the dead – corpse fields, skull honeycombs' (142).

In a similar passage a little later in the novel Amis also refers to the 'diagrammatic' (215), which is significant because the plot of *London Fields* implies that the post-human condition reduces human relationships to a diagram. So Samson Young proclaims that the protagonists in his story form 'a black cross'; close to the conclusion, as he comes to understand the plot fully, he realizes that 'I should have understood that a cross has four points. Not three' (466). Relationships, that is, have been radically simplified because they have been thoroughly drained of affection, and all that remains are struggles for power and ascendancy.

Amis is explicit about the causes of this in his autobiography, where he is frank about his own lack of emotional responsiveness in his early sexual relationships. He says that Tina Brown, an early girlfriend, identified 'a lacuna in [his] emotional repertoire' (*Experience*, 50) and he later declares that such lacunae in his generation have their origins in the threat of nuclear war (as exemplified in the Cuban missile crisis):

> The children of the nuclear age, I think, were weakened in their capacity to love. Hard to love, when you're bracing yourself for impact. Hard to love, when the loved one, and the lover, might any instant become blood and flames, along with everybody else. (138)

Amis says in a prefatory 'Note' that one of the titles he considered for *London Fields* was 'The Death of Love'. It is Nicola Six who contemplates the concept most explicitly because she wants to deploy 'love' as an essential component of the perverse game she is involved in: 'the equation she was working on' requires it. She has taken Guy Clinch as her principal victim because he seems old-fashioned and innocent enough to be still susceptible to this nearly defunct emotion. But she starts to have her doubts even about him because 'Perhaps love *was* dying, was already dead' (132). Imagining '*love* as a force', she imagines it sickening in the face of the prospect of the collective death threatened by nuclear war – because love has two opposites, 'One is hate. One is death.' (297)

Here, too, Amis is elegizing one of the key Romantic values, and his assumptions about it are very close to those of the Romantics themselves who, as Raymond Williams has pointed out, placed their 'emphasis on love and relationship' as a political act against the forces exerted by capitalism and the 'primarily economic relationships which the new society embodied'.[11] What horrifies Amis above all in his lamentations over the death of love is that it has been inflicted by the power of large-scale political forces entering the private life. This is the point of the impotence of the protagonist of *Time's Arrow* when his political work renders him incapable of responding to his wife. It is the point, too, that lies behind Amis's horror at how Stalin implanted lies in the hearts of children, and performed massacres, a crime that 'feels like some form of rape: a travesty of love, prosecuted by force' (*Koba*, 214).

For Amis to 'feel' these public events he has to feel them, not as social catastrophes, but as an infringement on intimacy: for him, the personal should never be political and things have gone badly awry when it becomes so. The extent of the priority he gives to the personal is at times astonishing and the explicitness of his statements astonishingly ingenuous. So, in his autobiography he conducts a lengthy discussion about Israel in terms of the conflicting attitudes towards it of two of his most valued friends, Saul Bellow and Christopher Hitchens. It is clear throughout that his most urgent response relates to his discomfort about their disagreements and, in particular, his anxiety that Hitchens's scepticism about Israel will alienate Bellow. Far worse, though, is that he allows the discussion to culminate with his explanation of his own pro-Israeli stance which he relates straightforwardly to his feelings of warm nostalgia towards his first girlfriend, who was Jewish: 'So I will never be entirely reasonable about Israel. I will always think about her with the blood. Not *my* blood. The blood of my first love.' (*Experience*, 265)

An extreme privileging of the personal over the political also explains why he fusses about what he calls 'The Politicization of Sleep', and is appalled that Lenin thought about revolution even in his dreams. He is disgusted by the 'steely ones' who want 'politics to be going on everywhere all the time, politics permanent and circumambient' (*Koba*, 14). All of this is based on a very limited view of politics, the same view that leads him to consider himself (by contrast with his father) as not 'ideological' (272) and that quotes with intense approval (twice!) a review in which V. S. Pritchett proclaims Aleksandr Solzenitsyn to be 'not a political; he is without rhetoric or double-think; he is an awakener' (261).

In fact Amis has a very specific ideology: atavistic Romantic individualism (but sick with savage disillusionment). Amis's failure to recognize the nature of his own political outlook, or even to recognize it as political, is a severe limitation on his work and part of his ultimately conservative sensibility. Nonetheless, this ideology functions very consistently within his best work and bestows a powerful coherence upon it, and it is because the times are so at variance with his Romantic premises that his satire works so sweepingly and savagely. Like Guy Clinch, Amis believes that 'Love and war – love and historical forces – [do] not sit well together' (216). But what the twentieth century imposes on Amis is a vision of the personal repeatedly invaded: it is above all his consequent discomfort which motivates his satire. The frustration of his Romantic values drives him towards an art of angry comedy which is profoundly unRomantic.

The death of love reduces all the relationships in *London Fields* to a stark diagram that merely illustrates a power struggle which is conducted through cunning subterfuge, an 'equation' (to use Nicola's word) where forces are starkly ranged against each other in exchanges that produce simple pluses or minuses. In this the novel resembles Ben Jonson's *Volpone* which is diagrammatically defined by the image of a (seemingly) dying animal besieged by predators, an image which is then overturned by the superior scheming of the apparent victim, who turns out to be a conniving fox. Jonson's caricatural diagram in all its austere precision contrasts tellingly with the superabundant, if at times messy, complexities of Shakespeare's dramatic structures. A similar comparison can be made between Amis's diagrammatic plot and the generous energies of fiction by Bellow and Updike.

The motif of the power struggle is recurrent in Amis's novels where competitiveness is often dramatized in games of tennis and chess; so, too, in *The Information* (1995), the plot is driven by the rivalry between two writers. This preoccupation means that, in the relationships which he imagines, the participants are often easily divisible into winners and losers, the cheaters and the cheated. Guy Clinch resembles the 'gull' in Ben Jonson's ferocious comedies: he is so easy to deceive that Nicola gets bored, and can hardly concentrate properly on the role she is assuming. He is an upper-class liberal who is endlessly earnest in his pain about social inequalities but significantly ignorant about 'Enola Gay' and 'Little Boy' (*London Fields*, 124): he is badly out of touch with what the real problems are. Given the savagely un-innocent world in which he lives his own innocence makes him vulnerably out of place; Nicola – in the process of effortlessly gulling him – eats a succession of oysters which flinch as she squeezes lemon onto them: 'After all, you eat them alive' (125).

Just as Volpone is the opposite of the dead meat he pretends to be, Nicola is the opposite of the unworldly young woman she invents in order to lure Guy into her trap. Guy can be eaten alive because he is 'the fool, the poor foal . . . the fall guy' (126) – like Jonson and Dickens, Amis enjoys caricatural names. Nicola is the predator who pretends to be easy prey; she is a 'simulacrum' (131), she looks in a mirror and feels 'in succession, like a chorus girl, like a horse, like a cartoon' (129). She is mercurial in a way designed to inspire intense male passion, she is a 'Sack Artist', 'a Vamp' and 'a Ballbreaker' (260) but, in a satirical reversal, her most effective deception is her simulation of innocence, which involves a pretence of sexual inexperience, so that she describes her sexual being as like a little sister she has to protect. She then associates this sister with the flowers in Gray's 'Elegy' that waste their sweetness on the desert air, which are in turn glossed by Guy with a reference to Empson on pastoral (286).

But Amis takes the plot beyond this into a further reversal. Nicola's cheating is meant ultimately to turn *her* into the victim: she will win by losing her life. She self-consciously constructs a plot which will lead to her being murdered, and the self-consciousness is multiplied when she discusses the plot with the first-person narrator. In this scene Samson Young anticipates the strictures of Amis's feminist critics by saying that Nicola will be called a male fantasy figure, but she counters this by converting it into a form of metafiction. She does embody all the male fictions about women – because she has learnt how to do that from 'hot books'. She rejects the idea that she is a Femme Fatale because she is above all fatal to herself, she is 'a Murderee' (260).

Amis is very cunning in this deployment of metafictional layers which work as an immunizing irony against the feminist charge that Nicola is a masculinist construct. The immunity would be fully achieved if his work ever genuinely invented a woman who seemed both fully believable and identifiably feminine – who was convincing, that is, as a fully realized and specific person and who the narrative dwelt upon extensively and substantially with an interest which was not mostly sexual. The nearest he comes to this is in his 1997 novel *Night Train* which is narrated by a female police officer, but this is too much an exercise in genre fiction to answer these charges fully. The problem with the flat or insubstantial roles given to women in Amis's fiction is that female characters like Nicola are rendered as caricatures in the negative sense – their flatness produces a conservative effect in that it perpetuates predictable stereotypes.

However, the failures of range in Amis's work are linked to his most important strength. Nicola is a male fantasy, but this becomes one of the premises upon which the novel's exploration of destructive masculinity is based. Amis's representation of women is conservative in tendency, but his explicit focus on masculinity is unusual and challenging. Masculinity tends to be hidden in plain sight; its values promote themselves most potently by not promoting themselves explicitly at all, but by imposing themselves as a universal, non-gendered norm. In *London Fields* and *Money* (1984) Amis makes masculinity repeatedly speak its name; this defamiliarizes its assumptions and anatomizes the cultural and social impact of its appetites.

His most effective device for achieving this is comic satire, whose starting-point is in the relentless caricaturing of the male protagonists of the two novels. Keith Talent, in *London Fields*, is a small-time crook and a compulsive womanizer who is entirely indifferent to his wife, negligent about his child and more at home in the pub than at home. He is obsessed with playing darts, which he sees as the sacrosanct arena where his masculinity is most gloriously expressed. So he contemplates the brotherhood he shares with his hero Kim Twemlow:

> Kim and Keith: they were men. Men, mate. Men. All right? Men. They wept when they wept, and knew the softnesses of women, and relished

> their beer with laughter in their eyes, and went out there when it mattered to do what had to be done with the darts. Take them for all in all. (314)

This free indirect thought is a device that Amis uses throughout, alongside free indirect speech, to satirize Keith's repetitive language and his crude values and assumptions. He is a *reductio ad absurdam* – so simply one thing because he is male and 'modern': he is a symptom of the horrifyingly reduced times, and acquires paradoxical charisma from his unshakeable singleness. His pub mates above all respect and pay tribute to his 'indifference', his 'not caring about anything' (59).

Keith's sexuality is mocked by animal caricature. His sex drive turns him into a dog in a 'cartwheeling canine frenzy' (334), he has a 'reptile mind' (335). Pornography is one of the few things that arouses strong feelings in him: watching one of the videos that Nicola has made of herself for him he is driven to tears: 'He really did think it was beautiful' (332). This taste connects him most obviously to the protagonist of *Money*, John Self, who is another *reductio ad absurdam* because 'all [his] hobbies are pornographic in tendency'.[12] So he is reduced to the status of 'an animal – eating and drinking, dumping and sleeping, fucking and fighting – and that's it' (277). The flatness of the fictive world in both novels is the product of too much dominance by masculinity, by 'femalelessness' and 'unalloyed testosterone' (254). Pornography has taken control because of the death of love, but in *Money* that death is not the consequence of the nuclear threat, but of obsessive commercial greed, and the commodification of sex. Although Amis is ideologically conservative, no one was more eloquent than him about the impact of 1980s greed. There are passages in *Money* that resemble Ezra Pound on the blight inflicted by usury, except that Amis's writing contains none of Pound's portentous indignation, and is characterized instead by postmodern dismissiveness. Ossie Twain works exclusively in money, he is not even involved in 'stocks, shares, commodities, futures', instead

> he buys money with money, sells money for money. He works in the cracks and vents of currencies, buying and selling on the margin, riding the daily tides of exchange. For these services he is rewarded with money. Lots of it. (120)

Amis's disillusioned Romanticism is again at work here because the emphasis is on the unnaturalness, or even anti-naturalness, of money, which makes things propagate using destructively artificial, and therefore deathly means: 'dollar bills, pound notes, they're suicide notes' (116). As part of its systems of exchange, money can change itself into sex: in a brothel John Self is unsure whether it is his credit card or his penis that the prostitute is going to frank, 'Now, sir, I'll just take an impression of your penis here' (104). In bed Self and his girlfriend Selina talk frequently about money and he likes 'that dirty talk' (151).

John Self is a caricature who is aware of his own flatness and thinks that there are parts of his life 'that would take on content, take on shadow, if only [he] read more and thought less about money' (223). He finds it reassuring that Selina stays with him out of economic necessity, and exciting that when he has even more money he 'can kick Selina out and get someone even better' (24). He uses pornography obsessively but he also sees Selina as the personification of pornography (72): personification and commodification are two sides of the same corrupting coin which causes humans and things to contaminate each other. This is why Self's 'head is a city' by analogy with New York: in both there is a constant sick throbbing and threat of terminal explosiveness (26). Selina is compared at length to an aeroplane (233), and people and cars become indistinguishable from one another (241).

It is above all pornography that colours the narrative in this way. Looking into the sky, Self sees a cloud that looks 'like a pussy' (249). Erotic dancers pretend to be 'marionettes' (57). Celly, a nineteen-year-old woman who performs for Self and his associate Fielding in a fake audition which they stage for their voyeuristic pleasure, resembles, as she is getting dressed, 'a pornographic cartoon, a comic strip' (222).

Pornography, like the dominant threat of nuclear war in *London Fields*, produces a thoroughly 'post-human' culture which determines the novel's caricatural methods. These are necessitated because a post-human world renders obsolete any notions of psychological realism; 'motivation' as a way of understanding human behaviour is 'pretty well shagged out' (359): 'Even realism, rockbottom realism, is considered a bit grand for the twentieth century' (248). So human beings come to resemble RoboCop: a veteran TV presenter is called 'an aged android' (18); Lorne Guyland is one 'of the all-American robot-kings . . . all zinc and chrome and circuitry coolant' (185). John Self has a recurrent fantasy that he can have his self completely transplanted: with the help of money he will have his 'whole body drilled down and repaired, replaced' (5–6) and later he feels 'prosthetic', he is 'a robot', 'an android', 'a cyborg', 'a skinjob' (329).

* * *

Amis introduces into *Money* a character called Martin Amis and places him in conversations with John Self in which, amongst other things, he discusses the nature of fiction. During one of these interviews, Amis refers to the distance between author and narrator, and the implication is that the distance between Amis and Self is very wide (despite, ironically, their physical proximity at this point). Amis clearly regards Self as possessing all of the qualities that widen the distance: 'wicked', 'deluded', 'pitiful' and 'ridiculous' (246). The greater this distance is, the more likely it is that the character will be caricatured, but an important insight into the nature of caricature is provided when Amis declares that the greatest liberties can be taken with the most contemptible characters, that the author can 'do what the hell' he likes with such unfortunates, and 'This creates an appetite for punishment. The author is not free of sadistic impulses' (247).

The sadistic treatment inflicted on caricatures contrasts markedly with the sympathetic identification which realist characters are accorded. The cruel enjoyment of authorial control is repeatedly explicit throughout *Money* and more subtly implied in those interventions by the mysterious 'Frank the Phone' who torments John Self with his omniscience about Self's activities. He personifies Self's conscience (e.g., 217–18) and eventually engages him in a sort of allegorical battle (348–50). The conflict between the protagonist and the author is sadistically uneven – there can be only one winner – and the spectacle of the protagonist's blackly comic suffering is enjoyed by the reader with complicit voyeurism.

This is an even more obsessive theme in the work of Will Self, where it is repeatedly accompanied by a struggle on the part of the characters to acquire authorial control over each other. It takes a realist form in the short story 'Tough Tough Toys For Tough Tough Boys' (1998) where the protagonist, Bill, plays a manipulative game in which he elicits as much of a hitchhiker's life-story as he can while giving away as little about himself as he can manage. Bill is in the position of surrogate author literally because he is the centre of consciousness and metaphorically because he drives the car where the story is mostly set. His refusal to divulge information about himself makes him resemble the impersonal artist strived for by modernists but also indicates a desire to immunize himself against the narrative while also mastering it. He feels superior to the hitchhiker who is comparatively inarticulate and whose life is chaotic – but the story's central irony turns on Bill's eventual realization that he and the hitchhiker are disturbingly similar in the ways that most matter. Thinking of the hitchhiker's 'lousy, drink-raddled body', he decides: 'In that they were alike – in that and perhaps a lot else as well.'[13]

That irony arises from the unexpected collapsing of the distance between the author surrogate and the hitchhiker who therefore evades the fate of being his caricatural victim and emerges instead as the object of sympathetic identification. However, this is an unusual moment in Self's fiction; it also explains his uncharacteristic use, here, of a realist idiom which is appropriate to this moment of surprising affinity (however unwanted). Much more characteristic is the stark reversal of power relations that takes place between the brothers Danny and Tembe in the stories that begin and end this collection. In the first, 'The Rock of Crack as Big as the Ritz', it is Danny who discovers the seam of crack cocaine in the cellar of their house, and who sends his younger brother out to peddle the drug, and it is Tembe who, as a result, becomes dependent on it. In the last, 'The Nonce Prize', it is Danny who has become helplessly addicted and Tembe who has kicked the habit and taken charge, sending Danny out on the errands that he used to run. Danny is further humiliated when he is the victim of a set-up which makes him appear to have been the perpetrator of a paedophile murder, and is sent to prison. The affectlessness that characterizes this power reversal between two brothers arises only partly from the loss of normal responses caused by drug addiction.

Affectlessness anyway characterizes the relationships which Self regularly depicts: feeling is mostly replaced in his work by the will to power, the will to command the role of the author rather than be reduced to that of the character. His novella 'Cock' makes this most explicit in a framed narrative in which the first-person narrator tells the story related to him by a character he takes to be 'a slightly faggoty, fussy middle-aged don'.[14] These roles arouse a contest between them about the ownership of the narrative, which leads eventually to a physical struggle in which the narrator is raped, a concluding episode that grotesquely symbolizes (with the black comedy that characterizes the whole story) the power struggle which has preceded it. So, the don insists on his 'right to centrality – to be the pro- as well as the an-tagonist' and the narrator feels that this insistence marginalizes him (71).

This is a key moment in Self's fiction because it reveals how characters are caricatured when they are invented by narrators whose preoccupation is above all with imposing their world view. As early as his first intervention, the narrator adopts the role of literary critic when he dismisses the characters in the don's story as 'flat' and circumscribed by his 'underlying snobbery' (11). His metafictional point is that the narrowness of the don's outlook has prevented him from understanding his characters enough to portray them as 'fully-rounded' human beings. Even though these points are made only through the narrator's free indirect thought, they are themselves called into question by the don, who makes a similar charge against the narrator when he says: 'You're typing me, boy, aren't you? You're turning me into something that I'm not. An amusing character, an oddity, a type!' (38) The don shows all the symptoms of being driven as a story-teller by the sadism Amis identifies. In his case the sadism arises out of the anger and hatred he feels for his characters; he is far more involved in the story than first appears and his involvement has aroused violent feelings in him which the narrator glimpses intermittently (38, 49).

When the narrator and the don criticize each other for stereotyping they are applying the assumptions of liberal humanist criticism that expects fiction writers to distribute their sympathies broadly and equitably. However, the way that each charges the other with this fault reveals that no story-telling is free of the ideologies that inevitably distort characterization. The tendency of Self's fiction is to uncover such hidden agendas in order to insist that human beings are capable of very little imaginative extension of themselves beyond the narrow confines of what is hard-wired into their psyches.

In the case of the paired novellas 'Cock' and 'Bull' the stress is on the hard wiring of gender identity: they are especially rich in the exploration of this very powerful source of distortively ideological thinking because they are fables in which a woman grows a penis ('Cock') and a man grows a vagina ('Bull'). This means that they question aspects of masculinity and femininity that usually remain taken for granted, but they do not do so in a way that evokes multiple gender possibilities. These gender fables are not 'liberating' – instead, their protagonists are the helpless victims of a process that frightens, bewilders and even imprisons them. Both protagonists start to acquire the stereotypical qualities of the opposite sex and so to find themselves unlike themselves. The woman in 'Cock' becomes increasingly aggressive and turns into the angry, hateful don. The man in 'Bull' becomes increasingly vulnerable and loses 'some element of [his] basic bottle' (141).

The confrontational satirical reversal that dominates *Cock and Bull* (1992) shows that the narrator and the don are both wrong when they condemn each other for stereotyping – because stereotypes are true. It is the expectation about 'fully-roundedness' and complex unpredictability which is untrue. What has happened to the two protagonists is outrageously unexpected: however, once it is established as a premise, the gender results are all too predictable because there really are people whose lives 'are as flat as those of characters in a slight fiction' (40) and whose drives turn them into mechanical puppets. In 'Cock' the protagonist's husband constantly repeats the same phrases, and his 'conscious will' is 'an impotent flopping marionette' (36). In 'Bull' the doctor who seduces the protagonist has a 'sexual being' which is 'a dull thing, a lifeless thing, a mass-produced marionette with chipped paint and fraying strings' (160). In 'Cock' there is a character called 'Dave 2' who is 'a universal type' (30) and whose name links him to the eponymous hero of the story 'Dave Too' which features a series of clones called Dave who are united 'like so many Stickle-bricks' (*Tough Tough Toys*, 77).

It is significant that Will Self has worked as a professional cartoonist because he brings to his fiction a cartoon vision of self-consciously flat figures acting inside plots which are starkly illustrated diagrams. The ontologically reduced circumstances of his characters are explicit, most extremely in *How the Dead Live* (2000)[15] where they are, in fact, dead – but the key satirical point is that death merely, as it were, illustrates their previous lives. What they did in life haunts their persons, so that their abortions and miscarriages float like multiple foetuses around their heads (see e.g., 14) and the body fat they have gained and shed accompanies them like obese doppelgangers (179, 188). The characters seem travestied by death, so that the men attending Personally Dead meetings are mere 'cut-outs of men, snipped from old knitting patterns in *Women's Realm*' (193), but the point is that these characters were no livelier when they were alive. Death has taught them what an insubstantial thing the human self is, it has made them realize 'that style was personality, and that our sense of self was nothing but mannerisms and negative emotions' (196).

Because the self is so superficial and weak, the concept of self-determination, which is so cherished, is an illusion, and the self is constantly manipulated by more powerful internal and external forces. So 'lust makes puppets of us all' (322). But Self deploys his puppets and marionettes obsessively in order to emphasize the absence of autonomy in those areas of the self we conventionally regard as most intimately our own, and to anatomize what he regards as a powerful human drive to control, manipulate and dominate others, to colonize other selves. The implications of the struggle, in 'Cock', to appropriate the role of the author, extend well beyond fiction because they incorporate all the associations of the will to power – including, most specifically, the power to impose a vision of the world as though it were inevitable truth.

This is expressed even more explicitly in *My Idea of Fun* (1993) with its (literally) controlling metaphor of *Thomas the Tank Engine*. As a child the protagonist, Ian Wharton, is described encountering the Island of Sodor for the first time:

> The engine people zipped this way and that, buffeting the coaches. They were apple-cheeked, their pink-fleshed humanoid faces tore out of the metal of their boilers as if they were some early form of bio-engineering.[16]

This central motif in the novel carries with it several crucial caricatural effects: it has the vividness of childlike simplicity and it combines the human and the mechanical ('engine people'), but above all it is connected to the image of the puppet and the puppet master because it prepares the ground for the role of The Fat Controller. This grotesquely evil character is endowed with superhuman powers that allow him to manipulate minds and, in particular, allow him to enslave the mind of Ian Wharton; as he says: 'I control all the automata on the island of Britain, all those machines that bask in the dream that they have a soul' (75).

The Fat Controller is a fantastic creation but his role as puppet master has its obvious analogues in the political behaviour of real human beings. Self's harping on the role of psychiatrists can readily be understood from this perspective, and the role of Wharton's therapist Dr Hieronymus Giggle is clearly meant to be compared to that of The Fat Controller – this becomes even clearer when it is eventually revealed that they are in league. A psychiatrist also plays a key role in the plot of *Great Apes* (1997),[17] which seems to me to be the most successful of Self's novels so far. Here there is a brilliant construction of a world where chimpanzees are the dominant species. The psychiatrist Zack Busner is accused of having carried out illegal drug experiments which have led to the major narrative thesis of the novel, for they have caused the protagonist, Simon Dykes, to suffer a mental breakdown that has led him to believe that he is human although he is in fact a chimp in this chimp world (271). Busner becomes Dykes's guide to the horrifyingly alien world in which he finds himself.

This reference to supposedly therapeutic mind control repeats those in *My Idea of Fun*, but here it is part of a larger context which deals much more broadly with the impact on identity of hierarchical structures that determine at every point how individuals will behave and think. The evocation throughout of chimp hierarchies – in which 'arselicking' (176) becomes grotesquely literal – defamilarizes similar human structures whose operations are soft-pedalled by discretion and obscured by tradition. Self invents a fascinatingly original 'chimp' language to describe the structures of power and obeisance. It is the source of expertly timed comic moments, as when Simon's girlfriend says to her boss Martin Green: 'I acknowledge your employment suzerainty, I worship your adamant penis, you are the rising scut in my ischial firmament' (129).

The dominant satirical device of *Great Apes* is to target many of the most prestigious intellectual and cultural expressions of humankind – literature, art, philosophy, anthropology, psychiatry – and to refigure them in chimp terms. This is effective because the novel dwells on those expressions which most reflect on what it is to be human, so that their chimp transformations are especially disorientating. Desmond Morris's thesis in *The Naked Ape* – that modern problems are caused by being cut off from the natural world – leads the journalist and art critic Tony Figes to speculate that this is why magazines are full of cartoons that transform chimps into other animals. The verb for this, 'primatomorphise' (173), is the chimp version of 'anthropomorphise', and is a good illustration of the systematic chimpifying of the language throughout, its reorientation towards a chimp perspective.

So the novel has a lot of fun recasting famous quotations and even names into chimp form. Wordsworth's line about the child being father to the man becomes the 'infant' being 'alpha to the male' (172). A famous lawyer is called Carchimp, and a TV celebrity is Lloyd Grosschimp. Towards its end, the novel recasts the whole of primate history to explain why humans lagged behind chimps – which is attributed to the superiority of sign language to speech in the generating of large and efficient brains (298).

Tony Figes's speculations are particularly important, however, because they form part of the novel's self-reflexive exploration of its own caricatural premise. He ponders how *The New Yorker* 'was always full of cartoons that primatomorphised and often in the most ridiculous way; signing dogs, wise-cracking moose, speculative bison, philosophic humans' (173). Throughout *Great Apes* there is an unsettling oscillation between chimp and human perspectives that continually subverts any secure sense of where the human stops and the chimp begins.

The repeated references to ape imagery in human culture (in inverted form, so that they become allusions to humans made by chimps) continually interrogate what these allusions mean, and why their effect should be so insistently satirical. For chimps, the human form is automatically perceived as caricatural: novelty balloons are painted with 'Mickeys, Minnies and Mr Blobbys' but also with 'other, stranger caricatures, pale-muzzled, with exaggeratedly large proboscises' which turn out to be human (242). *Great Apes* accordingly incorporates a self-reflexive history of animal caricature which brilliantly explores the ontological meanings of the ape/human contrast and comparison, as when Simon and Zack Busner discuss 'the *Essay of the Learned Martin Scriblerus, Concerning the Origin of Species*'. This was composed by Pope and Arbuthnot, and was 'the precursor of the grand line of eighteenth-century satires, pitting evolved humans against primitive apes. A line that culminated in Swift's Yahoos' (273).

8 *Caricature Versus Character: The Self As Cartoon*

Will Self's self-reflexive history of animal caricature draws attention to the lineage which has been the premise of this book. His reference to the Yahoos is telling because Swift's assaults on humanism, especially in *Gulliver's Travels*, lead him to caricatural strategies which evoke (like Self's ape comparisons) a sense of ontological shrinkage. Swift makes this literal in 'A Voyage To Brobdingnag' by surrounding his hero with giants, but the point is metaphorical in his portrait of the Yahoos, an identifiably human creature which is nonetheless degraded by its miring in bodily drives and functions.

Swift's microscopically vivid descriptions of the body reflect the queasy distaste for it which he shares with James Gillray, whose assaults on the human body are a particularly significant example of how caricature works to insist on the unbreakable connection between individuals and the state. His individual bodies can often be read as a metaphor for the 'body politic', but they also insist on the terrible vulnerability of the body and its humiliating abjectness in both its literal and metaphorical forms. As Roy Porter has written, bodies are the 'butts of violence and violation' and

> they also serve as counter-agents of contempt and hatred – witness the explosive power of the fart in cartoons and low humour generally. In Gillray's 'The French Invasion' (1793), England is thus turned into a person, the map of the realm doubles as a portrait of George III, and he shits the Royal Navy into the face of France.[1]

Postmodernist writers draw upon these traditional resources of caricature as a form of raspberry-blowing at 'liberal humanist' conceptions of the self: comic crudity is one of caricature's most conspicuous effects and can be made to gesticulate rudely at the elegant discretion behind which that ideology hides. The metaphorical link which Salman Rushdie makes, in *Midnight's Children*, between his hero's snotty nose and the map of India[2] is directly in the line of body politic imagery which Porter finds in Gillray.

Elegant discretion is precisely what caricatural writers do not display: their personal investment is all too obvious and they make no effort at all to hide their prejudices. The venom expressed can often seem explosively excessive so that the reader is worried enough to question what authorial motives are driving such malicious energy. Pope even starts his 'Sporus' portrait (in his 'Epistle to Dr. Arbuthnot') by wondering whether his victim is worth attacking, but then brushes these concerns aside and launches into a tirade that compares him in turn to an insect, a spaniel, a puppet, the devil and finally to a hybrid monster. It is the gender associations which he introduces into the latter image which are most unsettling and which imply a homophobia which Pope does not seem to have under control.

This form of portraiture, then, shows no respect for the 'inner being' of the character being portrayed. Nonetheless, it could still be used by Charles Dickens, for example, even though he maintained a broad allegiance to a form of Romantic humanism. Caricature was an important device for Dickens because he was a profoundly political writer who was preoccupied with the impact of industrial capitalism on human character: for him, the loss of inner being was the grievous point. So, at the start of Chapter 21 in *Little Dorrit*, he satirizes the reifying impact of money by comparing the guests at Mr Merdle's dinner party to houses; in his number plan Dickens had written 'People like houses they inhabit'[3] as his note for this chapter.

Merdle is a great financier and his name suggests the traditional association of money and excrement. His dinner party is distinguished by the lack of any human interaction that occurs there; Dickens draws upon caricature to convey this because caricatures, unlike characters, are inhuman in their isolation – which is perhaps the major difference between the two. The guests are more personifications than persons: they are 'Horse Guards', 'Treasury', 'Bar', 'Admiralty', 'Bishop'[4] – impersonal representatives of the establishment. When they are seated they face each other transformed into brick and mortar:

> The expressionless uniform twenty houses, all to be knocked at and rung at in the same form, all approachable by the same dull steps, all fended off by the same pattern of railing, all with the same impracticable fire-escapes, the same inconvenient fixtures in their heads, and everything without exception to be taken at a high valuation – who has not dined with these? (292)

The capaciousness of these houses is commensurate with their emptiness. Merdle's wife is called 'the bosom' paradoxically because she is characterized by her lack of feeling; the bosom is 'extensive', but only physically, and requires room but only 'to be unfeeling enough in' – a phrase so carelessly clumsy it implies that its author thinks she is not worth the effort of polishing his prose. Dickens, unlike Swift, has great affection for bosoms and his satire is directed at an economic system that has produced one devoid of all the warm humanity associated with this body part, and dedicated instead to its exchange value: 'Mr. Merdle wanted something to hang jewels upon, and he bought it for the purpose' (293).

Mrs Merdle's bosom is a caricatural metonymy. As such it makes a telling contrast with the multiple metonymies which characterize realist writing and which serve to define the setting of the action and the physical appearance of the characters. Realist metonymies are assigned a self-consciously neutral significance – they suggest verisimilitude by appearing to be starkly unliterary, they invoke the 'real world' by how thoroughly they are not symbolic or allegorical, how much they are flatly ambient. Any significance they acquire arises from that which is bestowed upon them, not by the author, but by the characters and their responses to the physical environment in which they think and feel. By contrast, Mrs Merdle's bosom is the object of heated authorial attention: it summons up associations of feminine nurturing and warmth – and then frustrates them with explicitly satirical thoroughness by reference to frigid commodification.

Dickens's general faith in bosoms is a premise of this passage and indicates his humanist sympathies. However, he found caricature appropriate to his purposes because he was not a liberal individualist like his realist contemporaries: his novels are dominated by a collectivist vision which insists on the impact of systemic forces on the lives of individuals and their families. This differentiates him from that liberal humanist tradition which receives its fullest fictive expression in the realist novel whose sophisticated techniques evoke human personality as complex, organically developing, and engaged in subtly nuanced social interactions which are mutually influential and synecdochic of the network of relationships out of which society is thought to be composed. The greatest practitioners of this form in English were Jane Austen, George Eliot and Henry James, whose theorizing about its techniques was as influential as his novelistic practice. The enormous achievements of these writers, and the powerful persuasiveness of their idiom, has meant that their example has stamped itself very forcefully on literary consciousness. In fact their example has been so powerful that it has established itself as a norm against which other idioms are inevitably tested – and even test themselves.

The classic realist norm has been systematically deconstructed by modernist and postmodernist writers, and has been extensively analysed by critics. Three assumptions of realism, however, are crucial when its practice is contrasted with caricatural practice. The first is that human character is a kind of organism which develops and ramifies: this is an idea that realism shares with Romanticism (it is also the assumption, for example, behind Wordsworth's *Prelude*). Realist authors behave accordingly towards their characters; they treat them sensitively, discreetly and sympathetically as organisms should be treated – they are meticulous nurturers, skilful gardeners. By contrast, caricaturists treat their characters roughly, dismissively and often cruelly. And the contrast in their attitudes is often explicit and self-reflexive because they often describe their characters as machines or mechanistic constructs, the very metaphoric opposite of an organism.

Linked to this first realist assumption is the second: realist authors assume that the constant trajectory of human character is towards the acquisition of a maturity whose social and even aesthetic value is taken for granted. Repeatedly they depict an ingenue who is likeable and energetic but simple-minded and who must acquire the extra dimensions, the wider understanding, which are required of a fully adult person. There are further assumptions behind this of a politically conservative kind: the maturity that these characters acquires equips them to fit more fully into an adult society whose values are largely sanctioned. The process is generally sadder and more politically ambiguous in the work of Henry James: nonetheless, his characters can give the impression of being more adult – in the sense of being more labyrinthinely nuanced and more sophisticatedly oblique in their responses – than any adult has ever actually been. This emphasis on 'fully rounded' maturity in realism contrasts with the deliberate and confrontational childishness that marks caricature, which often dwells on arrested development and ontological stasis and is restless with uproarious rebellion and crude insult.

Realist assumptions about maturity are tied to the third assumption, which is that the fully mature person has reached a deep understanding of the nature of love as a supreme human value. The most substantial and explicit exploration of this is in John Bayley's *The Characters of Love* which articulates, with fascinating thoroughness, the ins and outs of the liberal humanist ideology of love, its celebration of the ontological expansiveness which love bestows. Bayley is especially instructive for my purposes because his stress is not just on love between characters, but between authors and their characters; writing about love as a theme, he says:

> The most important thing I hope to show is that an author's success with this theme is closely linked with his attitude towards his own characters – that author, in fact, is best on love who best loves his own creations . . . What I understand by an author's love for his characters is a delight in their independent existence as *other people*, an attitude towards them which is analogous to our feelings towards those we love in life; and an intense interest in their personalities combined with a sort of detached solicitude, a respect for their freedom.[5]

It is significant that such a vivid formulation of this ideology comes at a point when its author is aware that it can no longer be regarded as a 'truism' (8). What Bayley is above all trying to do is to assert this set of values in the face of others, terribly alien to him, which are overthrowing it: 'many forces are at work', he says, 'helping to dissolve the uniqueness of the personal existence' (37). It is Bayley's anxious sense that he is fighting a losing rearguard action that leads him into dogmatic prescriptiveness: 'the great conventional character can only be created by love, by our delight in the existence of another person' (39).

This belief is closely associated with Bayley's assertive belief in individualism, which is evident, for example, when he reprimands Lionel Trilling for adopting too social a view of Jane Austen's *Mansfield Park* whose 'richness', as Bayley sees it,

> starts from Jane Austen's instinct for feeling herself into the character and world of Fanny, just as in her next novel she feels herself into those of Emma. She does not begin with insights into the nature of society. (215)

Bayley's ideology is entirely coherent and explicit and so forms a very useful contrast to the ideologies of the caricaturists whose work is the subject of this book. These ideologies do vary considerably but what they share is a marked emphasis on the impact of social and political forces which transcend the power of individuals. Connected to this is a profound scepticism on the part of these caricaturists about the value, and even the existence, of that love which is such a transcendent value for Bayley and others in the liberal humanist tradition. Martin Amis even goes to the extent of making what he calls 'The Death of Love' the major theme of one of his novels.[6]

The preoccupation with love as a theme, and the concept of love between author and characters, are combined in Bayley's account of the tradition he wishes to describe and even revive. The opposites of these qualities, however, are equally in evidence in the caricatural tradition where the emphasis is on coldness between the characters, or even on loathing and contempt, and where the authors themselves aggressively express consistent coldness, loathing and contempt only relieved by humour. These authors take no delight in their characters as other people, and they have no interest in what Bayley calls 'the indefinable interior man' (45). Instead the relationship between the characters and the world they occupy is starkly simplified in order deliberately to avoid the 'expansiveness' (47) which Bayley identifies in his favourite texts.

Bayley chooses finally to define this expansiveness by reference to its opposite which he finds in a 'puppet show' he says that Henry James once witnessed and by which he was at first enthralled, praising its 'economy of means' (47). In the end, however, James was struck more by its limitations, and Bayley's point clearly relates to its lack of that expansiveness which he and Henry James most prize. What is telling here, from my point of view, is that the puppet show is a very accurate analogy for the caricatural texts I am concerned to explore: the reduction of the characters in these texts to puppets is extremely common and puppetry as a metaphor is frequently explicit. Henry James is finally dismissive of the puppet show and what he wittily calls its 'economy of ends' (47) – but, for the writers I am concerned with, it is precisely this economy which (satirically and often misanthropically) they want.

Bayley complains about the growth of a literary criticism which 'creates a language for reflecting on a work of the imagination which is fundamentally different from the language of the work itself' (268). This critical activity has for a long time been regarded as entirely legitimate, but my own practice in this book accords well with Bayley's traditional assumptions because I am concerned above all to identify a caricatural language which has hardly been noticed as such. This is not to say that all the authors studied here would be happy with the term 'caricature' – especially because it is often used in an unthinkingly pejorative way. However, I do think these authors would quite readily recognize the satirical contexts in which my definitions of caricature place them.

Above all I hope that my use of this term and my definitions of it in relation to specific passages and texts will make available a language for talking about postmodern fiction which will enable this dimension of it to be more fully comprehended and more accurately placed in its historical context. Although it would be inappropriate in this book, the term 'caricature' could also be usefully applied outside the bounds of postmodern fiction. The anti-humanist attitudes which are implied in its use are widespread throughout the modern period so that much twentieth-century poetry, when it creates a character, also draws upon caricatural imagery.

So the early poetry of T. S. Eliot is better understood when his use of caricatural effects is properly noticed. Sweeney is his most obviously relevant creation because Eliot explicitly imagines him in opposition to that Emersonian Romanticism which glorifies human sensibilities and potential: he juxtaposes Emerson's remark that history is the lengthened shadow of a man with the image of Sweeney's silhouette 'straddled in the sun'.[7] The title of this poem, 'Sweeney Erect', indicates that Sweeney is nothing more than a man-sized penis: he personifies the reduction of love to mere sexuality. This is illustrated by his callous treatment of his epileptic sexual partner, by the obsessive naming of parts of his body and by the animal epithets both here – 'Gesture of orang-outang' – and in 'Sweeney Among the Nightingales' – 'Apeneck', 'zebra stripes', 'maculate giraffe' (56).

Reductiveness is the key caricatural theme. Given the explicitness of Eliot's ideology, as expressed in both his poetry and prose, reductiveness can moreover be seen as aimed with satirical directness at its opposite, the 'expansiveness' celebrated by the liberal humanist tradition. This is all the clearer because Eliot's most important target is the concept of love as it is celebrated by that tradition. His early work is haunted by the absence of love. In the two dramatic monologues, 'The Love Song Of J. Alfred Prufrock' and 'Portrait of a Lady', the characters occupy a social milieu so stifling that mutual responsiveness has been rendered impossible. Eliot's references to animal caricature in these poems suggest how thoroughly this has diminished the characters. Prufrock's imprisonment in his self, imposed by his abject lack of sexual daring, shrinks him so far that he can be compared to a crab scurrying across the sea-floor and to an insect pinned to a wall. The repeated word 'formulated' stresses that he is the victim of a stereotypical kind of thinking (by himself and others) that rigidly limits his range of possible responses.

One of these formulations, paradoxically, is a notion of romance that is shown to dominate the expectations of men and women in their relationships to each other and which are contrasted with the actual modern and urban context in which the expectations are being held and which disable them. This is vividly illustrated in the contrast of registers in lines two and three of 'Prufrock', the second line invoking the evening sky and parodying the language of a love poem, the third comparing that evening to a patient awaiting surgery. These lines, which open Eliot's poetic career, establish the symptomatic theme of love subverted by that anaesthesia and systemic sickness which Eliot associates with the modern condition.

Animal caricature is ambiguous in its meanings because it can depict shrinkage of being, as in the insect and crab images, but it can also imply that the human is in many ways inferior to animals. When the speaker of 'Portrait of a Lady' wishes to assume the shapes, successively, of a bear, a parrot and an ape, he is bursting with frustration to break free from the restrictive bounds of over-formulated 'civilised' behaviour. This arises out of Eliot's diagnosis of a decadent unnaturalness in the modern sensibility – the theme that dominates 'The Waste Land'. The poem's controlling metaphor of sterility evokes a profound alienation from the natural world which has resulted in an equally profound isolation of individuals. The tradition celebrated by John Bayley believes in a substantial interconnectedness between people which contributes to their expansiveness of self – by contrast, the disconnectedness in 'The Waste Land' imposes a stark flattening and loss of ontological dimensions. 'The Hollow Men', with its scarecrow imagery, makes this even more explicit.

Loss of naturalness is associated with the transforming of the human into a barren mechanism. The scene where the typist is coerced into sex is preceded by a reference to the 'human engine' (68) which resembles a waiting taxi: this foreshadows the sterile sexuality of this scene and insists that it is as merely 'automatic' as the hand which the typist uses to smooth her hair and start up her gramophone. The typist's lover is treated by Eliot with a haughtiness that draws upon obviously caricatural resources: he is defined dismissively by his physical appearance (he is 'carbuncular') and by his social class (he is 'one of the low'). The one personal quality which is bestowed on him, his self-assurance, is taken away again with Eliot's patrician insistence that this quality is held generally by men of his kind.

Most significantly, this quality, his sexual self-confidence, sits on him like a 'silk hat on a Bradford millionaire' – an equating of a personal characteristic with a piece of clothing which is a staple of the caricatural tradition and part of its satirical tendency to equate essence with appearance. Here, however, it is especially telling about how the caricatural effects in early Eliot originate in his diagnosis of the impact of commodity capitalism. This is evident from the huge metaphoric jump which the silk hat requires: its link to its nominal starting-point, the typist's lover, is self-consciously tenuous because its purpose is to serve patterns of association more generally established in the poem as a whole. The imaginative leap from the young man's sexual swagger to a Bradford millionaire draws attention to the generalness of the association that is being made, an association between modern sex and modern money, with all its crudely dehumanizing vulgarity. Caricature is highly appropriate in this context because it indicates how this dehumanizing process reduces human essence to mere appearance, transforms the human into a thing, a personal quality into a hat.

The most important influence on Eliot in this context was Charles Baudelaire, who was so quick to explore the impact on urban life of the new capitalist culture, and to diagnose – as Walter Benjamin pointed out – the fetishizing of the commodity and its personification in the figure of the prostitute, 'who is seller and commodity in one'.[8] 'The Waste Land', like Baudelaire's Parisian *Fleurs du Mal*, diagnoses the sterilizing impact of capitalist culture on human sexuality, and the transformation of human beings into commodities and machines. The urban crowd that Eliot describes (62) is composed, like those of Poe and Baudelaire, of automatons, and they are possessed by the kind of uniformity which Benjamin notes is imposed by Poe on such crowds. Benjamin connects this to the uniformity enforced by the mechanical processes in factory work.[9] His insights into this aspect of modern culture are highly relevant to my discussion of the widespread deployment of caricature in the postmodern period. They help to account for the occurrence, before and during that period, of profound ontological shifts which explain why caricature has come to seem such an appropriate form.

The most helpful essay for these purposes is 'The Work of Art in the Age of Mechanical Reproduction' (*Illuminations*, 211–14). This analyses the ontological impact of technology and concludes by indicating its most extreme impact in modern war: Benjamin quotes Marinetti's Futurist celebration of war which he considers beautiful 'because it initiates the dreamt-of metallization of the human body' (234). Coming near the end of Benjamin's essay, this is envisaged as merely the logical consequence of subtler reifications of 'human material' (235) that arise from a culture increasingly based on mass reproducibility which withers away what Benjamin calls the 'aura' that attaches itself to that which is unique. As a result of technological advances, the work of art can be more and more easily copied and disseminated, but so, also, can human material. Exemplary here is what happens to the film star whose cult, 'fostered by the money of the film industry, preserves not the unique aura of the person but the "spell of the personality," the phony spell of a commodity' (224). Just as the work of a factory worker is fragmented by the division of labour, so the role of a film actor is fragmented by the necessities of cinema production: the film actor's 'creation is by no means all of a piece; it is composed of many separate performances'(223).

These cultural features have enormously expanded since Benjamin published this essay in 1936. For postmodern culture the role of the animated feature could be taken as occupying that exemplary role which the film star's spliced-together performance occupies, in Benjamin's account, for modern culture. Animated features are much more self-evidently mechanical splicings together of visual bits and pieces: in these 'cartoons', movement is simulated by the multiplying of separate stills. Crucially, also, for my purposes, the characters in these cartoons are caricaturally drawn. The huge success of *The Simpsons* is symptomatic of the satirical attitude to human identity which has been widespread in contemporary culture, and which has been widely expressed in fiction.

Its representation in the visual arts has been even more conspicuous, especially in 'pop art'. Roy Lichtenstein is especially relevant because he drew upon comic strips which are obvious descendants of the more popular versions of caricatural art. Moreover his treatment of these strips involved, as Hal Foster has described in a recent essay,

> a layering of mechanical reproduction (comic), handwork (drawing), mechanical reproduction again (projector) and handwork again (tracing and painting) to the point where distinctions between hand and machine were difficult to recover.[10]

Discussing Lichtenstein's comic-strip depictions of combat between fighter aircraft, Foster seems to be alluding to Benjamin when he says that in these works Lichtenstein was pointing

> to a connection between the perceptual attitudes prepared by Modernist art and those demanded by modern war, a continuum between 'art vision' and 'machine vision'. In some respects art and war encouraged not merely a fast 'pop' eye but a Futurist 'killer' eye, and Lichtenstein brings out the aggressive nature of this way of seeing in his pictures of fighter pilots and the like. (7)

Andy Warhol's multiplying of pictorial clones, and his camp take on commodification, can also easily be explained by drawing upon Benjamin's account of mechanical reproduction. The camp element is important, however, and so is its link to loss of affect. Warhol's mass-produced Elvis Presleys and Marilyn Monroes diagnose not just the commodifying of film stars, but the sense that identity has been profoundly shifted by the impact of a technology of endless reproducibility.

The campness of pop art makes it determinedly apolitical: political responses to these same phenomena polarize around attitudes to Nature. T. S.

Eliot's satire arises out of his horror at the unnaturalness of modern culture; in the postmodern period, ecological attitudes espoused by writers as different as Ted Hughes, Adrienne Rich and Martin Amis lead to expressions of a similar horror combined with calls for a return to biological roots which arise from essentialist attitudes to the body and to gender.

By contrast, writers with Marxist leanings respond more ambiguously: Benjamin analyses the reifications involved but also sees in the culture of mechanical reproduction the possibilities of a transformative politics which might lead to new, post-capitalist identities. Donna J. Haraway's half-ironic praise for 'cyborg' identities is similarly optimistic about the potential of the changed identities that technology might bring. She opposes the organicism of radical feminists such as Susan Griffin, Audré Lourd and Adrienne Rich, their 'ecofeminism and feminist paganism'[11] with a celebration of the ontological potential of late-twentieth century machines which call into question the boundaries between the organic and the mechanical, because they

> have made thoroughly ambiguous the difference between natural and artificial, mind and body, self-developing and externally designed, and many other distinctions that used to apply to organisms and machines. Our machines are disturbingly lively, and we ourselves frighteningly inert. (152)

* * *

Astonishingly little has been written about caricature and its history, and what little there is mostly focuses on defining its place in the history of visual art. I have drawn upon this at a number of points where there is a striking congruence of imagery between the visual and the literary. Commentators on the visual tradition are helpful because they are not distracted by the pejorative connotations which bedevil the term when it is applied to literature, and which hinder an understanding of the resources which caricature provides. At times those resources are belittled by an unexamined doublethink which recognizes, in passing, that the use of caricature in Dickens and others is a powerful device, but which fails to explore the sources and nature of that power and which otherwise continues to think of caricatures as generally inferior to characters.

This unexamined preference is part of an unexamined ideology. So in his essay on Graham Greene, 'The Force of Caricature' (which I discuss in my chapter on Muriel Spark), Richard Hoggart dismisses Greene's methods of characterization as deeply flawed as though this were an objective aesthetic assessment unconnected to the difference between his own liberal humanism and Greene's Catholicism. Hoggart's complaint about a lack in Greene of 'submission from within to the difficult and subtle matter of characterization'[12] reveals Hoggart's adherence to the same outlook as that which leads

John Bayley to dwell on the importance of authors delighting in the sense of the interior life of their characters, their independent life as other people. Hoggart's phrase 'submission from within' is especially telling because it sounds theological, it sounds analogous to a Christian discipline requiring saintly self-erasure in the face of the higher demands imposed by God. This suggests that Hoggart, under pressure from Greene's Catholicism, is inventing an alternative humanist discipline: self-erasure in the face of human otherness. His disparagement of caricature in comparison to character is tied to a similar disparagement of allegory in comparison to symbolism (80), which is significant because – as I show in my discussions of Joseph Heller and Salman Rushdie – the use of allegory has important links with the use of caricature in the postmodern period.

Baudelaire and Benjamin are again key figures for the discussion of the role of allegory in the twentieth century. Christine Buci-Glucksmann in her book *Baroque Reason* is astute in her account of that discussion: for Benjamin, she says,

> Allegory makes its appearance only where there are 'depths which separate visual being from meaning'. As the language of a torn and broken world, the representation of the unrepresentable, allegory fixes dreams by laying bare reality . . . Through a veritable fragmentation of image, line, graphic art and even language, it breaks up reality and represents time by hieroglyphs and enigmas . . . As in Klee and Kafka, it brings on stage the reverse side of assertive humanism: 'the individual can appear here only in the form of enigma'. In contrast to medieval symbolism or the beautiful totality of future classicism, allegory anticipates the role of shock, montage and distancing in the twentieth-century avant-garde: it shatters its object and fixes reality by a kind of alienation effect similar to the logic of the unconscious.[13]

The aesthetic motives behind these self-consciously broken forms also lie behind the deployment of caricature: in particular the drive to evoke the ontological tornness inflicted by commodification. In my discussion of Joseph Heller I explore this point at some length with the help of Michele Hanoosh's political analysis of these themes in her fascinating book *Baudelaire and Caricature*.[14]

What most indicates the break from modernism into postmodernism is the loss of those 'depths' to which Buci-Glucksmann refers. As I point out in the Introduction, Fredric Jameson takes the loss of 'depth models' as one of the most characteristic symptoms of this break; he specifies four of these: the model of essence versus appearance; the Freudian model of latent and manifest; the existential model of authenticity; and the semiotic model of signifier and signified. All of these are lost and replaced 'by surface, or by multiple surfaces'.[15] I would want to add a fifth depth model to Jameson's list: that of a novelistic character's 'inner being', the concept of subjective essence. The postmodern loss of this concept is precisely what leads to the prevalence of caricature, in which characters are portrayed by mere surfaces.

* * *

The books I found most useful in applying the satirical concerns of visual artists to those of fiction writers were *Caricature* by E. H. Gombrich and E. Kris, and *The Art of Caricature* by Edward Lucie-Smith. I was able to find very little discussion of the relationship between the visual and the literary, although Peter Wagner's *Reading Iconotexts: From Swift to the French Revolution* [16] is a brilliant account of the interpenetration of visual image and text in *Gulliver's Travels* and Hogarth's engravings, amongst other works. I found this book of limited use for my purposes, however, because it is not concerned, as I am, with the ontological meaning of caricature. By contrast, Lucie-Smith's historical perspectives and Gombrich's theoretical explorations are both helpful because they both, in their different ways, indicate the different shapes that satirical distortiveness can impose on human identity.

Lucie-Smith's first chapter is a useful introduction and provides some helpful definitions. His second chapter traces the earliest historical roots of the subject, declaring that 'classical art has many of the externals of true caricature, but little of its genuine spirit' (21). When he moves on to discuss medieval art, however, and refers to gargoyles and other Christian carvings, it is clear that caricature shares much of its earliest history with the history of the grotesque, so that an understanding of the roots of the grotesque will also help with the understanding of the roots of caricature. So, for example, the artist Giuseppe Arcimboldo (1537–93) clearly belongs to both traditions and is discussed by both Lucie-Smith and by Geoffrey Galt Harpham in his book *On the Grotesque* where he describes that artist's 'Wasser' in which a man's face is composed of various fish:

> From the close-up view, 'Fish' appears an appropriate designation and 'Man' a mistake; from far away, the reverse is true. But there is a point in the middle distance, the point of the grotesque, when there appears to be equal evidence for both titles . . . At this point our understanding is stranded in a 'liminal' phase, for the image appears to have an impossible split reference, and multiple forms inhabit a single image.[17]

That point in the middle distance where humanity and fishiness overlap is also the caricatural point because it is the pictorial place where the ontological boundaries are interrogated. So Harpham is illuminating when he briefly considers the adjacency of the grotesque and caricature and says:

> Caricature and parody become grotesque by uniting the 'moral idea'

> (which I have been calling the perfect original) with the representation, in such a way that the two are fused into one. With caricature this unification occurs through the original's resolving itself into a single trait, without proportion or balance. Hitlerism, for example, is a grotesque caricature of the Germanic admiration for order and national pride. (127)

This self-conscious uniting of the moral idea and the representation, especially in parodic contexts, suggests an affinity with the metafictional techniques of postmodernist authors: for there, too, the relationship between the subject-matter and its expression is openly interrogated.

Michael Hollington, in his book *Dickens and the Grotesque*, helpfully provides another context for understanding the adjacency between caricature and the grotesque when he divides his account of the influence on Dickens of the grotesque popular tradition into three categories. These include his debt to the tradition of popular theatre (especially *commedia dell'arte* and pantomime) and the influence of literary tradition mediated through popular sources. His third category, the influence of visual satire, is illuminating when it demonstrates the ubiquitousness in Dickens of allusions to Holbein's *Dance of Death*, notices Gillray's John Bull appearing in *Barnaby Rudge* in the guise of John Willet, and identifies Mr. Bumble the beadle and Mr. Fang the magistrate as stock figures of visual satire. Hollington also provides a useful account of the influence of concepts of physiognomy and phrenology, especially where it relates to

> The supposed resemblance between human faces and animal heads – in physiognomical thought people with particular physiognomies are imagined to have the slyness of a fox, the servility of a dog, the ferocity of a tiger, etc – finds its counterpart in Dickens' regular habit . . . of developing animal analogies as indices of moral natures.[18]

These ideas constitute a major motif of the caricatural tradition and continue to loom large, as I have shown in my discussion of Angela Carter's *The Bloody Chamber.*

* * *

As Ernst Kris says, 'caricature is not only a historical phenomenon, it concerns a specific process and this process is repeatable and describable, for here we are in the field of psychology'.[19] Kris and Gombrich, especially in collaboration with each other, have been best at describing this process, drawing upon Freudian concepts to examine the detail of the mechanisms at work. They focus upon the origins of caricature in infantile life, and the wish to regain childhood freedoms which adults are required to renounce:

> Civilisation has taught us to renounce cruelty and aggression which once ran riot in atrocious reality and magical practices. There was a time in all our lives when we enjoyed being rude and naughty, but education has succeeded – or should have succeeded – in turning this joy into abhorrence. We do not let ourselves relapse into that state again, and if ever such impulses break loose under the influence of passion, we feel embarrassed and ashamed. In caricature, however, these forces find a well-guarded playground of their own. The caricaturist knows how to give them scope without allowing them to get out of control. His artistic mastery is, as it were, an assurance that all we enjoy is but a game. In this sphere, the sphere of artistic freedom, we are allowed to indulge our impulses free from fear. Willingly we may yield to the caricaturist's temptation to us to share his aggressive impulses, to see the world with him, distorted.[20]

This emphasis brilliantly illuminates the contrast between caricatural childishness and classic realist maturity, and suggests why postwar writers, in the process of deconstructing the hidden agenda in classic realism, have drawn upon caricature in order to uncover that ideology and rebel against it. It also suggests a defamiliarizing angle on postmodernist 'play', indicating (as with other aspects of the caricatural) a much older provenance for those strategies in postmodernist texts which have subversive fun with the aesthetic norms which are dictated by traditionally sanctioned cultural hegemonies. Here, too, these postmodernist writers can be seen to be drawing upon key aspects of the caricatural tradition in order to rebel against earnestly imposed, or unthinkingly followed, authoritarian values.

This point is confirmed by Kris's discussion of the element of serious play in caricature:

> Caricature is a play with the magic power of the image, and for such a play to be licit or institutionalized the belief in the real efficacy of the spell must be firmly under control. Wherever it is not considered a joke but rather a dangerous practice to distort a man's features, even on paper, caricature as an art cannot develop. (*Psychoanalytic Explorations*, 201)

The caricaturist is allowed to play around with a man's image when magical beliefs about that image are no longer held: and yet what he is doing depends upon an act of regression in which the magic is now only metaphorical. Philipon's famous transformation of Louis-Phillippe into a pear ('poire', which in French equals 'fathead') can be perceived as merely a form of rebellious wit, but its impact on his victim depends upon more primitive ideas that the king can actually (that is, physically and spiritually) be damaged by an attack on his image. This is not dangerous play, but primitive danger is being invoked, and the play is serious because the king's image (in the metaphorical sense of reputation) can suffer a damaging mutation. The aggressiveness of the act is real enough.

Gombrich's 'well-guarded playground' resembles those notions of 'carnival' theorized by Mikhail Bakhtin and drawn upon repeatedly by critics of postmodernist texts. These are meant to account for liberationist impulses which draw upon the concept of a set-aside time and space in which rebellion is sanctioned or even encouraged, and which confront established authority with a loudly or grossly populist disruptiveness often involving references to the grotesque body. *Nights at the Circus*, by Angela Carter, is frequently written about in these terms; her circuses and clowning, and her dwelling on her heroine's ample body, with its abject functions, hint that Carter herself was thinking in explicitly 'carnivalesque' terms when she wrote it.

Caricature, as Lucie-Smith shows in his chapter 'Popular Allegory and the Printing Press', has, from time to time, been deployed for the purposes of populist anti-authoritarianism. Like carnival, however, it could easily be seen as merely contributing to a form of repressive tolerance – as providing a safe release for popular energies that might otherwise be more dangerously channelled. Moreover, it contains within it those strands of the reactionary which are a constant within popular feeling. Lucie-Smith mentions, for example, caricatural handbills in the late fifteenth century which expressed aggressively anti-semitic attitudes: one showed 'Jewish scholars, in the pointed hats they were forced to wear by law, being suckled by the devil's pig' (33).

The caricatural impulse can easily be condemned as a refusal to understand otherness, or a refusal to grant fully human status to women, minority groups and those beyond the Caucasian pale. A number of swear words, obscene epithets and racial and gender insults can be deconstructed as a form of caricature at its most basic level: 'nigger', 'queer', 'cunt', etc. But one of the most significant cultural developments recently has been that oppressed groups have taken their caricatural label and worn it as a confrontational badge of pride – calling each other individually and themselves as a group, 'nigger', 'queer', etc. Two African American writers, Ralph Ellison and Toni Morrison, and one feminist writer, Joyce Carol Oates, have responded similarly to the caricatural imagery applied to their own groups. As I have shown in my chapters on them, Ellison and Morrison have explored the reifying of African Americans and its origins in slavery, and Oates has explored, in her novel *Blonde*, the commodifying of Marilyn Monroe, her transformation by Hollywood into a sex doll. All three writers deplore the caricatures that have been applied to their respective victims, before they deconstruct them.

It is significant, then, that Henri Bergson was a key thinker for Ralph Ellison.[21] For Bergson is another of the most useful theorists of caricature; his book *Laughter* purports comprehensively to explain humour and its mechanisms, but it refers repeatedly to caricature for its illustrations and it works much better as a specific account of caricature than as an explanation of the much larger and more complex subject. It has, essentially, one thesis which it keeps repeating – that laughter is produced where human beings are shown to resemble machines. Laughter, Bergson says, is aroused wherever a person appears to lack spontaneity and naturalness or 'suppleness'[22] and to behave like a rigid automaton:

> it might be said that all *character* is comic, provided we mean by character the *ready-made* element in our personality, that mechanical element which resembles a piece of clockwork wound up once and for all and capable of working automatically. It is, if you will, that which causes us to imitate ourselves. And it is also, for that very reason, that which enables others to imitate us. Every comic character is a *type*. Inversely, every resemblance to a type has something comic in it. (148)

Jonathan Miller is dismissive about Bergson's theory because it 'deals with so little of the topic'[23] but his dismissiveness is undermined because the example of humour he provides, immediately after his lucid account of Bergson's theory, actually supports that theory rather than his own sniffiness about it. It is a cartoon from the *New Yorker* which

> portrays two African explorers in a swamp. They are wearing pith helmets, and are surrounded by lianas, creepers, serpents and so forth. They are obviously in trouble because they are up to their necks in the swamp as they proceed from left to right of the cartoon. The figure at the back is saying to the figure at the front: 'Quicksand or no, Carruthers, say what you like. I have half a mind to struggle.' (12)

Miller interprets the humour of this cartoon as derived from its play with customary notions of the voluntary and the involuntary, which he regards as a fundamental concept for understanding social structures as they relate to distinctions between what we praise and what we blame (13). This is interesting, but the further Miller extends it the more tenuous it seems as a reading of the cartoon: once he gets beyond the theory about exercising will he seems merely to be rehearsing a subject that currently interests him.

Miller's point about distinctions between voluntary and involuntary actions contradicts him by confirming Bergson's emphasis on the mechanistic. As he rightly says, 'struggling is not the sort of thing about which one could be in half a mind' (12). The comedy arises because the two cartoon characters are such extreme adherents to an English 'stiff upper lip' attitude that an emotional response to adversity is almost inconceivable to them. Bergson's thesis, about comic characters being 'types', is thereby confirmed, and also his idea of the humour being produced by the 'ready-made' – which in this cartoon is a national stereotype. The stereotypicality of these African explorers is mocked with an exaggeration which certainly refers to a notion of the mechanistic: these English types behave so very typically that they resemble 'a piece of clockwork' more than they resemble human beings. Their reluctance to struggle even in these terrifying circumstances implies their apparently inhuman inability to respond in an unprogrammed way.

Miller is too dismissive about Bergson's emphasis on the mechanistic, which certainly explains the *New Yorker* cartoon very helpfully. My own point would be, though, that Bergson's model would be less helpful in explaining other, non-cartoon kinds of humour. It works here because it is explaining humour directly related to the caricatural tradition where transformations of the human into machines (and, connected to that, into dummies and puppets) amount to an obsession. This is a major reason why caricature has been such an important idiom in an age in which the mechanistic (as both Benjamin and Haraway emphasize) has had such a key impact on human identity.

Notes

The following texts are referred to repeatedly throughout this book:

Gombrich, E. H. and Kris, E. *Caricature.* Harmondsworth: Penguin, 1940.

Lucie-Smith, E. *The Art of Caricature.* London: Orbis, 1981.

Hill, D. (ed.) *The Satirical Etchings of James Gillray.* Mineola, NY: Dover Publications, 1976.

Feaver, W. *Masters of Caricature: From Hogarth and Gillray to Scarfe and Levine.* New York: Alfred A. Knopf, 1981.

Introduction

1 J. Hillis Miller, *Ariadne's Thread* (New Haven, CT: Yale University Press, 1992), 97.
2 Leo Bersani, *A Future for Astyana* (London: Marion Boyars, 1978), 5.
3 Thomas Docherty, *Reading (Absent) Character* (Oxford: Oxford University Press, 1983).
4 Fredric Jameson, *Postmodernism, Or, The Cultural Logic of Late Capitalism* (London: Verso, 1991), 12.
5 Philip Roth, *Sabbath's Theatre* (London: Vintage, 1995), 198.
6 Angela Carter, *The Bloody Chamber And Other Stories* (London: Penguin, 1979), 63.

1 Subverting Racist Caricature: Ralph Ellison and Tony Morrison

1 Ralph Ellison, *Invisible Man* (London: Penguin, 2001). Unless otherwise stated all references to Ellison are to this volume.
2 Toni Morrison, *Beloved* (London: Pan Books, 1988).
3 John S. Wright, 'The Conscious Hero and the Rites of Man: Ellison's War', in *New Essays on Invisible Man*, ed. Robert O'Meally (Cambridge: Cambridge University Press, 1988), 162.
4 Toni Morrison, *Jazz* (London: Picador, 1993).
5 Elizabeth Deeds Ermarth, *Realism and Consensus in the English Novel: Time, Space and Narrative* (Edinburgh: Edinburgh University Press, 1998), 65.
6 Ralph Ellison, *Juneteenth* (London: Penguin, 1999).
7 Tony Hilfer, *American Fiction Since 1940* (London: Longman, 1992), 45.
8 Joseph Trimmer (ed.), *A Casebook on Ralph Ellison's* Invisible Man (New York: Thomas Y. Crowell, 1972), 254.
9 Berndt Ostendorf, 'Ralph Waldo Ellison: Anthropology, Modernism and Jazz', in *New Essays on Invisible Man*, 104.
10 Craig H. Werner, 'The Briar Patch as Modernist Myth: Morrison, Barthes and Tar Baby As-Is', in *Critical Essays on Toni Morrison*, ed. Nellie Y. McCay (Boston, MA: G. K. Hall, 1988), 155, 152.
11 Toni Morrison, *Tar Baby* (London: Triad/Panther Books, 1984), 309.
12 D. Hill (ed.) *The Satirical Etchings of James Gillray* (Mineola, NY: Dover Publications, 1976), plate 30.
13 Missy Dehn Kubitschek, *Toni Morrison: A Critical Companion* (Westport, CT: Greenwood Press, 1998), 139.

14 Michele Hannoosh, *Baudelaire and Caricature: From the Comic to an Art of Modernity* (Pennsylvania: Pennsylvania State University Press, 1992), 163.
15 Toni Morrison, *Playing in the Dark: Whiteness and the Literary Imagination* (London: Picador, 1993), 71.
16 Angela Burton, 'Signifyin(g) Abjection: Narrative Strategies in Toni Morrison's *Jazz*', in *Toni Morrison: Contemporary Critical Essays*, ed. Linden Peach (Basingstoke: Macmillan, 1998), 184.
17 Toni Morrison, *Paradise* (London: Vintage, 1999).
18 Jill Matus, *Toni Morrison* (Manchester: Manchester University Press, 1998), 154.
19 Henri Bergson, *Laughter: An Essay on the Meaning of the Comic* (London: Macmillan, 1921), 34.
20 E. H. Gombrich and Ernst Kris, *Caricature* (Harmondsworth: Penguin, 1940), 14.

2 Joseph Heller's Allegories of Money

1 Joseph Heller, *Catch-22* (London: Vintage, 1994).
2 Joseph Heller, *Something Happened* (London: Vintage, 1995).
3 Joseph Heller, *Good As Gold* (London: Jonathan Cape, 1979).
4 Joseph Heller, *God Knows* (London: Jonathan Cape, 1984).
5 Joseph Heller, *Picture This* (London: Macmillan, 1988).
6 Joseph Heller, *Closing Time* (London: Pocket Books, 1995).
7 Walter Benjamin, *Charles Baudelaire: A Lyric Poet in the Era of High Capitalism*, trans. from the German by Harry Zohn (London: Verso, 1997), 165–66.
8 Michele Hannoosh, *Baudelaire and Caricature: From the Comic to an Art of Modernity* (Pennsylvania: Pennsylvania State University, 1992), 163. This book henceforth Hannoosh.
9 Jess Ritter, 'What Manner of Men are These', in *Critical Essays on Catch-22*, ed. James Nagel (Encino, CA: Dickenson, 1974), 56.
10 Judith Ruderman, *Joseph Heller* (New York: Continuum, 1991), 37. Henceforth Ruderman.
11 See Edward Lucie-Smith, *The Art of Caricature* (London: Orbis, 1981), 31.
12 David Seed, *The Fictions of Joseph Heller: Against the Grain* (Basingstoke: Macmillan, 1989), 52.
13 Paul Krassner, 'An Impolite Interview with Joseph Heller', in *The Best of 'The Realist'* (Philadelphia, PA: Running Press, 1984), 79–80.
14 Thomas Blues, 'The Moral Structure of *Catch-22*', in *Critical Essays on Catch-22*, 103.
15 Paul de Man, *Blindness and Insight* (London: Methuen, 1983), 188.
16 See for example Robert Merrill, *Joseph Heller* (Boston, MA: Twayne, 1987), 43. Henceforth Merrill.
17 Barbara Gelb, '*Catch-22* Plus: A Conversation with Joseph Heller', *The New York Times Book Review*, 28 August 1994, 18.
18 George Plimpton, 'How it Happened', *The New York Times Book Review*, 6 October 1974, 1.
19 Kurt Vonnegut, Jr., 'Something Happened', *The New York Times Book Review*, 6 October 1974, 1.

3 Philip Roth's Vulgar, Aggressive Clowning

1 Philip Roth, *Reading Myself and Others* (London: Jonathan Cape, 1975), 82. Henceforth *Reading Myself.*
2 Philip Roth, *Sabbath's Theatre* (London: Vintage, 1995); *American Pastoral* (London: Vintage, 1998); *I Married A Communist* (London: Vintage, 1999).

3 Tony Hilfer, *American Fiction Since 1940* (London: Longman, 1992), 74. Henceforth Hilfer.
4 Philip Roth, *The Ghost Writer*, collected in *Zuckerman Bound* (London: Vintage, 1998).
5 Philip Roth, *Zuckerman Unbound* and *The Anatomy Lesson*, collected in *Zuckerman Bound* (London: Vintage, 1998). This collection of novellas henceforth *Zuckerman*.
6 Philip Roth, *The Counterlife* (London: Jonathan Cape, 1987), 160.
7 Irving Howe, 'Roth Reconsidered', reprinted in *Philip Roth*, ed. Harold Bloom (New York: Chelsea House, 1986), 77.
8 Philip Roth, *The Prague Orgy*, collected in *Zuckerman Bound* (London: Vintage, 1998).
9 Philip Roth, *Operation Shylock: A Confession* (London: Jonathan Cape, 1993), 248.
10 Philip Roth, 'The Conversion of the Jews', collected in *Goodbye Columbus* (London: Corgi Books, 1964), 101.
11 Philip Roth, *Portnoy's Complaint* (London: Vintage, 1995), 36.
12 Philip Roth, *The Breast*, first published in Britain by Jonathan Cape, 1973 (London: Vintage, 1995).
13 Philip Roth, *Deception* (London: Jonathan Cape, 1990), 113–17.
14 Philip Roth, *The Human Stain* (London: Jonathan Cape, 2000).
15 Julia Kristeva, *Revolution in Poetic Language*, trans. Margaret Waller (New York: Columbia University Press, 1984), 26.

4 Joyce Carol Oates's Political Anger

1 Joyce Carol Oates, *On Boxing* (London: Bloomsbury, 1987).
2 Joyce Carol Oates, *New Heaven, New Earth: The Visionary Experience in Literature* (New York: Vanguard Press, 1974).
3 Joyce Carol Oates, *Foxfire* (New York: Plume, 1994).
4 Joyce Carol Oates, *Man Crazy* (London: Virago, 1998), 101.
5 Joyce Carol Oates, *What I Lived For* (London: Picador, 1995).
6 Joyce Carol Oates, *them* (New York: Fawcett Crest, 1969).
7 Eileen Teper Bender, *Joyce Carol Oates: Artist in Residence* (Bloomington: Indiana University Press, 1987), 42.
8 Joyce Carol Oates, *Wonderland* (New York: Fawcett Crest, 1971).
9 Draper Hill, The Satirical Etchings of James Gillray (Mineola, NY: Dover Publications, 1976), plate 83.
10 Joyce Carol Oates, *Expensive People* (London: Virago, 1998).
11 Joyce Carol Oates, *Blonde* (London: Fourth Estate, 2000).
12 Joyce Carol Oates, *Black Water* (New York: Plume, 1993).

5 Muriel Spark's Puppets of Thwarted Authority

1 Muriel Spark, *The Finishing School* (London: Viking, 2004).
2 Martin McQuillan, 'Introduction: "I Don't Know Anything about Freud": Muriel Spark Meets Contemporary Criticism', in *Theorizing Muriel Spark: Gender, Race, Deconstruction*, ed. Martin McQuillan (Basingstoke: Palgrave, 2002), 4.
3 Muriel Spark, *A Far Cry From Kensington* (Harmondsworth: Penguin, 1989), 77.
4 Muriel Spark, *The Bachelors* (Harmondsworth: Penguin, 1963), 107–8.
5 Helene Cixous, 'Grimacing Catholicism: Muriel Spark's Macabre Farce', in *Theorizing Muriel Spark*, 205.
6 Muriel Spark, *The Complete Short Stories* (London: Penguin, 2002), 95–103.
7 Muriel Spark, 'The Desegregation of Art', *Proceedings of the American Academy of Arts and Letters* (New York, 1971), 24.
8 Richard Hoggart, 'The Force of Caricature: Aspects of the art of Graham Greene, with particular reference to *The Power and the Glory*', in *Graham Greene: A Collection of*

Critical Essays, ed. Samuel Hynes (Englewood Cliffs, NJ: Prentice-Hall, 1973). See especially 88.

9 Frank Kermode, 'Muriel Spark', in *Modern Essays* (London: Fontana, 1990), 268.

10 Bryan Cheyette, 'Writing Against Conversion: Muriel Spark the Gentile Jewess' in *Theorizing Muriel Spark*, 95.

11 Martin Amis, *London Fields* (London: Penguin, 1990), see, for example, 18, 44, 69, and *Money* (London: Penguin, 1985), see, for example, 28, 217–18, 285, 290.

12 Will Self, *How the Dead Live* (London: Penguin, 2001).

13 Muriel Spark, *The Public Image* (Harmondsworth: Penguin, 1970).

14 Muriel Spark, *Reality and Dreams* (Harmondsworth: Penguin, 1996).

15 Helene Cixous, 'Muriel Spark's Latest Novel: *The Public Image*', in *Theorizing Muriel Spark*, 208, 207.

16 Muriel Spark, *The Prime of Miss Jean Brodie* (Harmondsworth: Penguin, 1965), 26.

17 Muriel Spark, *Memento Mori* (Harmondsworth: Penguin, 1961), 138.

18 Muriel Spark, *Not To Disturb* (Basingstoke: Macmillan, 1971), 83.

19 Muriel Spark, *The Girls of Slender Means* (Harmondsworth: Penguin, 1966), see especially 30.

20 Muriel Spark, *The Abbess of Crewe* (London: Macmillan, 1974), 75.

21 Muriel Spark, *The Hothouse by the East River* (London: Macmillan, 1973), 129.

22 Muriel Spark, *The Driver's Seat* (Harmondsworth: Penguin, 1974), 94.

23 Muriel Spark, *Aiding and Abetting* (Harmondsworth: Penguin, 2001), 95.

24 Bryan Cheyette, *Muriel Spark* (Tavistock: Northcote House in association with the British Council, 2000), 105.

25 Martin McQuillan, ' "The Same Informed Air": An Interview with Muriel Spark', in *Theorizing Muriel Spark*, 225.

6 Magic Realism As Caricature: Angela Carter and Salman Rushdie

1 Angela Carter, *The Bloody Chamber And Other Stories* (London: Penguin, 1979).

2 E. H. Gombrich and Ernst Kris, *Caricature* (Harmondsworth: Penguin, 1940), 26.

3 Gabriel Garcia Marquez, *One Hundred Years Of Solitude* (London: Pan, 1978).

4 Edward Lucie-Smith, *The Art of Caricature* (London: Orbis, 1981), 22.

5 Angela Carter, *The Sadeian Woman* (London: Virago, 1979).

6 Angela Carter, *Nights at the Circus* (London: Picador, 1985).

7 Mary Russo, *The Female Grotesque: Risk, Excess and Modernity* (New York: Routledge, 1994).

8 Sarah Gamble, *Angela Carter: Writing From The Front Line* (Edinburgh: Edinburgh University Press, 1997).

9 Linden Peach, *Angela Carter* (London: Macmillan, 1998).

10 Mary Anne Doane, 'Film and Masquerade: Theorizing the Female Spectator', *Screen* 23, no. 3/4 (September/October 1982), 74–87. The views expressed in this essay are reassessed in 'Masquerade Reconsidered' in *Femmes Fatales: Feminism, Film Theory and Psychoanalysis* (New York: Routledge, 1992).

11 Jonathan Swift, *Poetical Works*, ed. Herbert Davis (London: Oxford University Press, 1967), 519.

12 Draper Hill (ed.), The Satirical Etchings of James Gillray (Mineola, NY: Dover Publications, 1976), plate 22.

13 Salman Rushdie, *The Satanic Verses* (London: Viking, 1988).

14 Salman Rushdie, *The Ground Beneath Her Feet* (London: Jonathan Cape, 1999).

15 Salman Rushdie, *Fury* (London: Jonathan Cape, 2001).

16 'An Interview With Salman Rushdie', *Scripsi* 3, pt. 2/3 (1985), 107–8.

17 Michele Hannoosh's paraphrase of Benjamin in *Baudelaire and Caricature: From the*

Comic to An Art of Modernity (Pennsylvania: Pennsylvania State University Press, 1992), 163.

18 Fredric Jameson, *Postmodernism, Or, The Cultural Logic of Late Capitalism* (London: Verso, 1991).
19 Salman Rushdie, *Haroun and the Sea of Stories* (London: Granta Books, 1990).
20 Catherine Cundy, *Salman Rushdie* (Manchester: Manchester University Press, 1996), 92.
21 Aijaz Ahmad, *In Theory: Classes, Nations, Literatures* (London: Verso, 1992), 141.
22 William Feaver, *Masters of Caricature: From Hogarth and Gillray to Scarfe and Levine* (New York: Alfred A. Knopf, 1981), 70. Henceforth Feaver.
23 Salman Rushdie, *Imaginary Homelands: Essays and Criticism 1981–1991* (London: Granta Books, 1991), 305, 58.
24 Salman Rushdie, *Shame* (London: Picador, 1984).
25 Hans Rothe (ed.), *Daumier on War* (New York: Da Capo Press, 1977), 19, 38, 42, 43, 46, 51.
26 Richard Cronin, *Imagining India* (London: Macmillan, 1989), 46.
27 Salman Rushdie, *Midnight's Children* (London: Vintage, 1995).

7 The Caricaturist As Celebrity: Martin Amis and Will Self

1 Will Self, *Junk Mail* (London: Penguin, 1996), 380–81.
2 John Updike, 'It's A Fair Cop', *Sunday Times Books* (21 September 1997), Section 8, 2.
3 Martin Amis, *Visiting Mrs. Nabokov and Other Excursions* (London: Penguin, 1994).
4 Martin Amis, *Experience* (London: Vintage, 2001), 179.
5 Blake Morrison, 'In the Astronomical Present', *Times Literary Supplement*, 4066 (6 March 1981), 247.
6 Martin Amis, *Time's Arrow* (London: Penguin, 1991), 131.
7 Martin Amis, *Koba the Dread: Laughter and the Twenty Million* (London: Jonathan Cape, 2002), 258.
8 Tom Paulin quoted in Peter Parker (ed.), *The Reader's Companion to Twentieth Century Writers* (London: Fourth Estate, 1995), 21.
9 Martin Amis, *London Fields* (London: Penguin, 1990), 134.
10 See for example Laura L. Doan, ' "Sexy Greedy is the Late Eighties": Power Systems in Amis's *Money* and Churchill's *Serious Money*', *The Minnesota Review: A Journal of Committed Writing*, 34/5 (Spring 1990), 69–79.
11 Raymond Williams, *Culture and Society, 1780–1950* (Harmondsworth: Penguin, 1961), 59.
12 Martin Amis, *Money* (London: Penguin, 1985), 67.
13 Will Self, *Tough Tough Toys For Tough Tough Boys* (London: Penguin, 1998), 151.
14 Will Self, *Cock and Bull* (London: Penguin, 1992), 11.
15 Will Self, *How the Dead Live* (London: Penguin, 2001).
16 Will Self, *My Idea of Fun* (London: Penguin, 1994), 26.
17 Will Self, *Great Apes* (London: Penguin, 1998).

8 Caricature Versus Character: The Self As Cartoon

1 Roy Porter, 'Bodies Politic: Gillray's Graphic Caricature', *tate* 25 (Summer 2001), 25.
2 Salman Rushdie, *Midnight's Children* (London: Vintage, 1995), 231.
3 Cited by Paul D. Herring, 'Dickens' Monthly Number Plans for *Little Dorrit*', *Modern Philology* 64 (1966), 34.
4 Charles Dickens, *Little Dorrit* (Harmondsworth: Penguin, 1967; first published 1857), 297.
5 John Bayley, *The Characters of Love: A Study in the Literature of Personality* (London: Constable, 1960), 7–8.

6 Martin Amis, *London Fields* (London: Penguin, 1989). See especially the prefatory 'Note'.
7 T. S. Eliot, *The Complete Poems and Plays* (London: Faber, 1969), 43.
8 Walter Benjamin, *Charles Baudelaire: A Lyric Poet in the Era of High Capitalism*, trans. from the German by Harry Zohn (London: Verso, 1997), 159.
9 Walter Benjamin, *Illuminations* (London: Pimlico, 1999), 170–74.
10 Hal Foster, 'Pop Eye', *London Review of Books* 24, no. 16 (22 August 2002), 6.
11 Donna J. Haraway, 'Simians, Cyborgs, and Women: A Cyborg Manifesto', in *Simians, Cyborgs and Women: The Reinvention of Nature* (London: Free Association Books, 1991), 174.
12 Richard Hoggart, 'The Force of Caricature: Aspects of the art of Graham Greene, with particular reference to *The Power and the Glory*', in *Graham Greene: A Collection of Critical Essays*, ed. Samuel Hynes (Englewood Cliffs, NJ: Prentice-Hall, 1973), 91.
13 Christine Buci-Glucksmann, *Baroque Reason: The Aesthetics of Modernity* (London: Sage, 1994), 70.
14 Michele Hanoosh, *Baudelaire and Caricature: From the Comic to an Art of Modernity* (Pennsylvania: Pennsylvania State University Press, 1992).
15 Fredric Jameson, *Postmodernism, Or, The Cultural Logic of Late Capitalism* (London: Verso, 1991), 12.
16 Peter Wagner, *Reading Iconotexts: From Swift to the French Revolution* (London: Reaktion Books, 1995).
17 Geoffrey Galt Harpham, *On the Grotesque: Strategies of Contradiction in Art and Literature* (Princeton: Princeton University Press, 1982), 13.
18 Michael Hollington, *Dickens and the Grotesque* (London: Croom Helm, 1984), 15.
19 Ernst Kris, 'The Principles of Caricature' (written in collaboration with E. H. Gombrich) in *Psychoanalytic Explorations in Art* (New York: Schocken Books, 1964), 195.
20 E. H. Gombrich and E. Kris, *Caricature* (Harmondsworth: Penguin, 1940), 26.
21 See John S. Wright's discussion of Bergson's influence on Ellison in his essay 'The Conscious Hero and the Rites of Man: Ellision's War', in *New Essays on Invisible Man*, ed. Robert O'Meally (Cambridge: Cambridge University Press, 1988), 162.
22 Henri Bergson, *Laughter: An Essay on the Meaning of the Comic* (London: Macmillan, 1921), 49.
23 Jonathan Miller, 'Jokes and Joking', in *Laughing Matters: A Serious Look at Humour*, ed. John Durant and Jonathan Miller (New York: Longman, 1988), 10.

Bibliography

Ahmad, A. *In Theory: Classes, Nations, Literatures*. London: Verso, 1992.
Amis, M. *Experience*. London: Vintage, 2001.
Amis, M. *Koba the Dread: Laughter and the Twenty Million*. London: Jonathan Cape, 2002.
Amis, M. *London Fields*. London: Penguin, 1990.
Amis, M. *Money*. London: Penguin, 1985.
Amis, M. *Time's Arrow*. London: Penguin, 1991.
Amis, M. *Visiting Mrs. Nabokov and Other Excursions*. London: Penguin, 1994.
Bayley, J. *The Characters of Love: A Study in the Literature of Personality*. London: Constable, 1960.
Bender, E. T. *Joyce Carol Oates: Artist in Residence*. Bloomington: Indiana University Press, 1987.
Benjamin, W. *Charles Baudelaire: A Lyric Poet in the Era of High Capitalism*, trans. from the German by Harry Zohn. London: Verso, 1997.
Benjamin, W. *Illuminations*. London: Pimlico, 1999.
Bergson, H. *Laughter: An Essay on the Meaning of the Comic*. London: Macmillan, 1921.
Bersani, L. *A Future for Astyana*. London: Marion Boyars, 1978.
Blues, T. 'The Moral Structure of *Catch-22*', in *Critical Essays on Catch-22*, ed. J. Nagel. Encino, CA: Dickenson, 1974.
Buci-Glucksmann, C. *Baroque Reason: The Aesthetics of Modernity*. London: Sage, 1994.
Burton, A. 'Signifyin(g) Abjection: Narrative Strategies in Toni Morrison's *Jazz*', in *Toni Morrison: Contemporary Critical Essays*, ed. L. Peach. Basingstoke: Macmillan, 1998.
Carter, A. *Nights at the Circus*. London: Picador, 1985.
Carter, A. *The Bloody Chamber And Other Stories*. London: Penguin, 1979.
Carter, A. *The Sadeian Woman*. London: Virago, 1979.
Cheyette, B. 'Writing Against Conversion: Muriel Spark the Gentile Jewess', in *Theorizing Muriel Spark: Gender, Race, Deconstruction*, ed. M. McQuillan. Basingstoke: Palgrave, 2002.
Cheyette, B. *Muriel Spark*. Tavistock: Northcote House in association with the British Council, 2000.
Cixous, H. 'Grimacing Catholicism: Muriel Spark's Macabre Farce', in *Theorizing Muriel Spark: Gender, Race, Deconstruction*, ed. M. McQuillan. Basingstoke: Palgrave, 2002.
Cixous, H. 'Muriel Spark's Latest Novel: *The Public Image*', in *Theorizing Muriel Spark: Gender, Race, Deconstruction*, ed. M. McQuillan. Basingstoke: Palgrave, 2002.
Cronin, R. *Imagining India*. London: Macmillan, 1989.
Cundy, C. *Salman Rushdie*. Manchester: Manchester University Press, 1996.
de Man, P. *Blindness and Insight*. London: Methuen, 1983.
Dickens, C. *Little Dorrit*. Harmondsworth: Penguin, 1967; first published 1857.
Doan, L. ' "Sexy Greedy is the Late Eighties": Power Systems in Amis's *Money* and Churchill's *Serious Money*', *The Minnesota Review: A Journal of Committed Writing* 34/5 (Spring 1990), 69–79.
Doane, M. A. 'Film and Masquerade: Theorizing the Female Spectator', *Screen* 23, no. 3/4 (September/October 1982), 74–87.

Doane, M. A. 'Masquerade Reconsidered: Further Thoughts on the Female Spectator', *Discourse* 2 (Fall/Winter 1988–9). Also in Doane (1991) 33–43.
Doane, M. A. *Femmes Fatales: feminism, film, theory, psychoanalysis.* New York and London: Routledge, 1991.
Docherty, T. *Reading (Absent) Character.* Oxford: Oxford University Press, 1983.
Eliot, T. S. *The Complete Poems and Plays.* London: Faber, 1969.
Ellison, R. *Invisible Man.* London: Penguin, 2001.
Ellison, R. *Juneteenth.* London: Penguin, 1999.
Ermarth, E. D. *Realism and Consensus in the English Novel: Time, Space and Narrative.* Edinburgh: Edinburgh University Press, 1998.
Feaver, W. *Masters of Caricature: From Hogarth and Gillray to Scarfe and Levine.* New York: Alfred A. Knopf, 1981.
Foster, H. 'Pop Eye', *London Review of Books* 24, no. 16 (22 August 2002), 6.
Gamble, S. *Angela Carter: Writing From The Front Line.* Edinburgh: Edinburgh University Press, 1997.
Garcia Marquez, G. *One Hundred Years Of Solitude.* London: Pan, 1978.
Gelb, B. '*Catch-22* Plus: A Conversation with Joseph Heller', *The New York Times Book Review*, 28 August 1994, 18.
Gombrich, E. H. and Kris, E. *Caricature.* Harmondsworth: Penguin, 1940.
Hannoosh, M. *Baudelaire and Caricature: From the Comic to an Art of Modernity.* Pennsylvania: Pennsylvania State University Press, 1992.
Haraway, D. J. 'Simians, Cyborgs, and Women: A Cyborg Manifesto', in *Simians, Cyborgs and Women: The Reinvention of Nature.* London: Free Association Books, 1991.
Harpham, G. G. *On the Grotesque: Strategies of Contradiction in Art and Literature.* Princeton: Princeton University Press, 1982.
Heller, J. *Catch-22.* London: Vintage, 1994.
Heller, J. *Closing Time.* London: Pocket Books, 1995.
Heller, J. *God Knows.* London: Jonathan Cape, 1984.
Heller, J. *Good As Gold.* London: Jonathan Cape, 1979.
Heller, J. *Picture This.* London: Macmillan, 1988.
Heller, J. *Something Happened.* London: Vintage, 1995.
Herring, P. D. 'Dickens' Monthly Number Plans for *Little Dorrit*', *Modern Philology* 64 (1966), 34.
Hilfer, T. *American Fiction Since 1940.* London: Longman, 1992.
Hill, D. (ed.) *The Satirical Etchings of James Gillray.* Mineola, NY: Dover Publications, 1976.
Hoggart, R. 'The Force of Caricature: Aspects of the art of Graham Greene, with particular reference to *The Power and the Glory*', in *Graham Greene: A Collection of Critical Essays*, ed. S. Hynes. Englewood Cliffs, NJ: Prentice-Hall, 1973.
Hollington, M. *Dickens and the Grotesque.* London: Croom Helm, 1984.
Howe, I. 'Roth Reconsidered', reprinted in *Philip Roth*, ed. Harold Bloom. New York: Chelsea House, 1986.
Jameson, F. *Postmodernism, Or, The Cultural Logic of Late Capitalism.* London: Verso, 1991.
Kermode, F. 'Muriel Spark', in *Modern Essays.* London: Fontana, 1990.
Krassner, P. 'An Impolite Interview with Joseph Heller', in *The Best of 'The Realist'.* Philadelphia, PA: Running Press, 1984.
Kris, E. 'The Principles of Caricature' (written in collaboration with E. H. Gombrich) in *Psychoanalytic Explorations in Art.* New York: Schocken Books, 1964.
Kristeva, J. *Revolution in Poetic Language*, trans. M. Waller. New York: Columbia University Press, 1984.
Kubitschek, M. D. *Toni Morrison: A Critical Companion.* Westport, CT: Greenwood Press, 1998.
Lucie-Smith, E. *The Art of Caricature.* London: Orbis, 1981.

Matus, J. *Toni Morrison.* Manchester: Manchester University Press, 1998.
McQuillan, M. 'Introduction: "I Don't Know Anything about Freud": Muriel Spark Meets Contemporary Criticism', in *Theorizing Muriel Spark: Gender, Race, Deconstruction,* ed. M. McQuillan. Basingstoke: Palgrave, 2002.
McQuillan, M. ' "The Same Informed Air": An Interview with Muriel Spark', in *Theorizing Muriel Spark: Gender, Race, Deconstruction,* ed. M. McQuillan. Basingstoke: Palgrave, 2002.
Merrill, R. *Joseph Heller.* Boston, MA: Twayne, 1987.
Miller, J. 'Jokes and Joking', in *Laughing Matters: A Serious Look at Humour,* ed. J. Durant and J. Miller. New York: Longman, 1988.
Miller, J. H. *Ariadne's Thread.* New Haven, CT: Yale University Press, 1992.
Morrison, B. 'In the Astronomical Present', *Times Literary Supplement,* 4066 (6 March 1981), 247.
Morrison, T. *Beloved.* London: Pan Books, 1988.
Morrison, T. *Jazz.* London: Picador, 1993.
Morrison, T. *Paradise.* London: Vintage, 1999.
Morrison, T. *Playing in the Dark: Whiteness and the Literary Imagination.* London: Picador, 1993.
Morrison, T. *Tar Baby.* London: Triad/Panther Books, 1984.
Oates, J. C. *Black Water.* New York: Plume, 1993.
Oates, J. C. *Blonde.* London: Fourth Estate, 2000.
Oates, J. C. *Expensive People.* London: Virago, 1998.
Oates, J. C. *Foxfire.* New York: Plume, 1994.
Oates, J. C. *Man Crazy.* London: Virago, 1998.
Oates, J. C. *New Heaven, New Earth: The Visionary Experience in Literature.* New York: Vanguard Press, 1974.
Oates, J. C. *On Boxing.* London: Bloomsbury, 1987.
Oates, J. C. *them.* New York: Fawcett Crest, 1969.
Oates, J. C. *What I Lived For.* London: Picador, 1995.
Oates, J. C. *Wonderland.* New York: Fawcett Crest, 1971.
Ostendorf, B. 'Ralph Waldo Ellison: Anthropology, Modernism and Jazz', in *New Essays on Invisible Man,* ed. Robert O'Meally. Cambridge: Cambridge University Press, 1988.
Parker, P. (ed.) *The Reader's Companion to Twentieth Century Writers.* London: Fourth Estate, 1995.
Peach, L. *Angela Carter.* London: Macmillan, 1998.
Plimpton, G. 'How it Happened', *The New York Times Book Review,* 6 October 1974, 1.
Porter, R. 'Bodies Politic: Gillray's Graphic Caricature', *tate,* 25 (Summer 2001), 25.
Ritter, J. 'What Manner of Men are These', in *Critical Essays on Catch-22,* ed. J. Nagel. Encino, CA: Dickenson, 1974.
Roth, P. 'The Conversion of the Jews', collected in *Goodbye Columbus.* London: Corgi Books, 1964.
Roth, P. *American Pastoral.* London: Vintage, 1998.
Roth, P. *Deception.* London: Jonathan Cape, 1990.
Roth, P. *I Married A Communist.* London: Vintage, 1999.
Roth, P. *Operation Shylock: A Confession.* London: Jonathan Cape, 1993.
Roth, P. *Portnoy's Complaint.* London: Vintage, 1995.
Roth, P. *Reading Myself and Others.* London: Jonathan Cape, 1975.
Roth, P. *Sabbath's Theatre.* London: Vintage, 1995.
Roth, P. *The Anatomy Lesson,* collected in *Zuckerman Bound.* London: Vintage, 1998.
Roth, P. *The Breast.* London: Vintage, 1995; first published in Britain by Jonathan Cape, 1973.
Roth, P. *The Counterlife.* London: Jonathan Cape, 1987.

Roth, P. *The Ghost Writer*, collected in *Zuckerman Bound.* London: Vintage, 1998.
Roth, P. *The Human Stain.* London: Jonathan Cape, 2000.
Roth, P. *The Prague Orgy*, collected in *Zuckerman Bound.* London: Vintage, 1998.
Roth, P. *Zuckerman Unbound*, collected in *Zuckerman Bound.* London: Vintage, 1998.
Rothe, H. (ed.) *Daumier on War.* New York: Da Capo Press, 1977.
Ruderman, J. *Joseph Heller.* New York: Continuum, 1991.
Rushdie, S. 'An Interview With Salman Rushdie', *Scripsi* 3, pt. 2/3 (1985), 107–8.
Rushdie, S. *Fury.* London: Jonathan Cape, 2001.
Rushdie, S. *Haroun and the Sea of Stories.* London: Granta Books, 1990.
Rushdie, S. *Imaginary Homelands: Essays and Criticism 1981–1991.* London: Granta Books, 1991.
Rushdie, S. *Midnight's Children.* London: Vintage, 1995; first published 1981.
Rushdie, S. *Shame.* London: Picador, 1984.
Rushdie, S. *The Ground Beneath Her Feet.* London: Jonathan Cape, 1999.
Rushdie, S. *The Satanic Verses.* London: Viking, 1988.
Russo, M. *The Female Grotesque: Risk, Excess and Modernity.* New York: Routledge, 1994.
Seed, D. *The Fictions of Joseph Heller: Against the Grain.* Basingstoke: Macmillan, 1989.
Self, W. *Cock and Bull.* London: Penguin, 1992.
Self, W. *Great Apes.* London: Penguin, 1998.
Self, W. *How the Dead Live.* London: Penguin, 2001.
Self, W. *Junk Mail.* London: Penguin, 1996.
Self, W. *My Idea of Fun.* London: Penguin, 1994.
Self, W. *Tough Tough Toys For Tough Tough Boys.* London: Penguin, 1998.
Spark, M. 'The Desegregation of Art', *Proceedings of the American Academy of Arts and Letters* (New York, 1971).
Spark, M. *A Far Cry From Kensington.* Harmondsworth: Penguin, 1989.
Spark, M. *Aiding and Abetting.* Harmondsworth: Penguin, 2001.
Spark, M. *Memento Mori.* Harmondsworth: Penguin, 1961.
Spark, M. *Not To Disturb.* Basingstoke: Macmillan, 1971.
Spark, M. *Reality and Dreams.* Harmondsworth: Penguin, 1996.
Spark, M. *The Abbess of Crewe.* London: Macmillan, 1974.
Spark, M. *The Bachelors.* Harmondsworth: Penguin, 1963.
Spark, M. *The Complete Short Stories.* London: Penguin, 2002.
Spark, M. *The Driver's Seat.* Harmondsworth: Penguin, 1974.
Spark, M. *The Finishing School.* London: Viking, 2004.
Spark, M. *The Girls of Slender Means.* Harmondsworth: Penguin, 1966.
Spark, M. *The Hothouse by the East River.* London: Macmillan, 1973.
Spark, M. *The Prime of Miss Jean Brodie.* Harmondsworth: Penguin, 1965.
Spark, M. *The Public Image.* Harmondsworth: Penguin, 1970.
Swift, J. *Poetical Works*, ed. H. Davis. London: Oxford University Press, 1967.
Trimmer, J. (ed.) *A Casebook on Ralph Ellison's* Invisible Man. New York: Thomas Y. Crowell, 1972.
Updike, J. 'It's A Fair Cop', *Sunday Times Books*, 21 September 1997, Section 8, 2.
Vonnegut, K., Jr. 'Something Happened', *The New York Times Book Review*, 6 October 1974, 1.
Wagner, P. *Reading Iconotexts: From Swift to the French Revolution.* London: Reaktion Books, 1995.
Werner, C. H. 'The Briar Patch as Modernist Myth: Morrison, Barthes and Tar Baby As-Is', in *Critical Essays on Toni Morrison*, ed. N. Y. McCay. Boston, MA: G. K. Hall, 1988.
Williams, R. *Culture and Society, 1780–1950.* Harmondsworth: Penguin, 1961.
Wright, J. S. 'The Conscious Hero and the Rites of Man: Ellison's War', in *New Essays on Invisible Man*, ed. Robert O'Meally. Cambridge: Cambridge University Press, 1988.

Index

Printed in the United States
126120LV00002B/68/P

9 781847 062659